THE NEW
CONTRARIAN
INVESTMENT
STRATEGY

Also by David Dreman

Psychology and the Stock Market
Contrarian Investment Strategy: The Psychology of Stock Market
Success

THE NEW CONTRARIAN INVESTMENT STRATEGY

David Dreman

RANDOM HOUSE New York

Library of Congress Cataloging in Publication Data
Dreman, David N.
   The new contrarian investment strategy.
   Includes index.
   1. Speculation. 2. Stocks. 3. Investments.
I. Title.
HG6041.D66   1982   332.6'78   82–40119
ISBN 0–394–52364–4

Manufactured in the United States of America
987

Grateful acknowledgment is made to the following for permission to reprint previously published material:

The American Finance Association: Table adapted from *Journal of Finance,* June 1977, p. 866.

Decision Research: Graph, "Average Changes in Confidence and Accuracy with Increasing Amounts of Information," reprinted by permission of Decision Research, Inc.

Dow Jones & Company, Inc.: Excerpt from "The Outlook: Review of Current Trends in Business Finance," reprinted by permission of the *Wall Street Journal,* copyright © Dow Jones & Company, Inc., 1978; all rights reserved.

Drexel, Burnham, Lambert, Inc.: Table, "Average Price Increase per Year, 1948–1964," reprinted by permission of Drexel, Burnham, Lambert, Inc.

Financial Analysts Journal: Tables, "Annual Earnings Related to Mean Prices" and "Lower P/E Relative to Market and Industry," reprinted by permission of *Financial Analysts Journal.*

Financial Management: Tables adapted from R. Malcolm Richards, James J. Benjamin, and Robert W. Strawser, "An Examination of the Accuracy of Earnings Forecasts," *Financial Management,* Fall 1977, p.82.

Financial World: Excerpts from "The Superstar Analysts," November 1980, copyright 1980 by *Financial World.*

Forbes Magazine: Graph adapted from "A 700-Year Consumer Price Index," reprinted by permission of *Forbes Magazine,* November 15, 1976, issue.

Fortune Magazine: Graph, "Returns on Total Corporate Capital," reprinted by permission of Fortune Art Department/Gabor Kiss, *Fortune,* November 1977.

Harper & Row Publishers, Inc.: Graphs from pp. 208 and 209 in *Social Psychology,* by Muzafer Sherif and Carolyn W. Sherif, copyright © 1969 by Muzafer Sherif and Carolyn W. Sherif;

ACKNOWLEDGMENTS

In the preparation of the manuscript, I have been very fortunate to have had the advice and criticism of a number of talented people. In particular, I'd like to acknowledge the help I received from the following:

On the Street side, I owe a considerable debt to Michael Clowes, Theodore H. Halligan. and Sim Trotter, all of whom combed through the manuscript and recommended constructive changes. Too, I found the interchange of ideas with Jim Michaels, Arthur Gray, Marshall Loeb, Vartanig Vartan, Charles Rolo, and Steve Leuthold stimulating in developing and extending the strategies presented here. I'd also like to thank Susan Osberg, Nan Miller, Margery Adams, Lyn Dominguez, John Bello, and Ed Finalt, who provided excellent research assistance and made many good suggestions.

Professor Edward Connolley, a psychologist at the University of Southern California, and Professor Fred Renwick of the Graduate School of Business Administration at New York University directed my attention to important academic studies revelant to the topic. I'm grateful to Dr. Paul Slovic of Decision Research, Inc., for introducing me to recent work in cognitive psychology, which I think is important to understanding investor behavior.

My relationship with Random House has been a pleasant one. I particularly appreciate the hours that Jason Epstein gave to the manuscript and his major contributions, on both the concept and the editorial levels.

Finally, I'd like to thank the numerous investment organizations and firms— brokerage, advisory, and consulting—that allowed me to use charts, tables, and other materials which I consider important to the text. Needless to say, the caveat that any errors found are the writer's sole responsibility applies here.

PREFACE

In my first book on contrarian strategy, published in January 1980, I wrote at length of both the merits and pitfalls of bonds as investments. Interest rates were then about 6½ percent for tax-free (municipal) issues and 9 percent for long-term government bonds.

By late January 1982, municipal rates had more than doubled, rising to over 14 percent, while government rates had increased to 15 percent. Investors who had purchased these bonds less than three years earlier would have lost more than half of their capital on municipals and 40 percent on their long-term government bonds—a crash worse than any in the stock market since the Great Depression. The bond market has been destroyed by sky-rocketing interest rates—higher, to borrow the words of West German Chancellor Helmut Schmidt, "than at any time since Christ walked the earth."

But it is not only bonds that have gone down sharply. Speculation in commodities, options, and financial futures has also proven a fast track to insolvency. Take commodities, for example. A recent *Forbes* study indicated that over 90 percent of commodity players lose money, with most accounts being liquidated in under four months.

Would you be any better off abandoning financial markets entirely for the "quick fixes" proposed by the bevy of self-proclaimed new prophets the current crisis has dredged up? No, their advice has turned out to be just as disastrous. Buying gold, silver, or collectibles, as most of the new gurus urged in their "gloom and doom" books back in 1979 and 1980, ended in calamity for everyone but the authors themselves. They at least banked fat royalty checks.

Even more disturbing, as the opening chapter will show, the best and the brightest of professional investors—people you would naturally turn to for help in times of turmoil—have proven to be among the least able to cope with developments. The most recent example was their predominantly bearish sentiment last summer, just prior to the sharpest rally in history, which, as we shall see in detail later, may well lead into one of the major bull markets of the century. Unfortunately, such errors are far more the rule than the exception. In fact, the market advice of professionals has been wrong fully 80 percent of the time. If you flipped a coin to select stocks, your chances would at least be increased to fifty-fifty.

The bottom line is an unprecedented level of market confusion and irrationality. Bond prices, near their all-time lows, indicated that investors believed that inflation would continue at or above the recent double digit rates indefinitely. But the crash in the values of commodities, collectibles, and precious metals anticipated just the opposite—investors in these markets believed powerful deflationary forces were at work that must result in much lower prices for an extended period of time. Never before had one set of investment markets collapsed because of the fear of sky-rocketing inflation, while simultaneously another plummeted because of the fear of major deflation.

Such behavior indicates that investors from the rankest beginners to the experienced professional are scared, and indeed they should be, for few of the rules to safeguard capital seem to apply any longer. Because of the complex interactions of powerful new economic, social, and political forces, even the best of the generation's professional economists are baffled. Conventional economic wisdom and the forecasts derived from it rely heavily on predictable outcomes from the past—results that have proved reliable for the major portion of the postwar period. Today what could once have been predicted on the basis of increased taxes, tightened credit, or any of a half-dozen other major economic policy changes often does not bring the results economists were taught to expect. As frequently, diametrically opposite outcomes are derived.

Take tighter money—long believed to be the major solution to dampen inflation, calm an overheated economy, and restore balanced growth. Sky-high interest rates have failed miserably. Instead of balanced and increasing growth, we are currently in the worst recession of the postwar period, with unemployment approaching 10 percent and capacity utilization—already well below optimum levels —continuing to drop. And inflation, albeit moderating, persists. In Margaret Thatcher's England such policies have resulted in higher unemployment than during the Great Depression, substantially lower output, and continued double digit inflation. The remedy, it seems, is worse than the disease itself.

As Eugene Birnbaum, a former member of the Council of Economic Advisers, articulately put it: "[Economists'] response is like a thermostat gone beserk, turning on the air conditioning when temperatures drop to the freezing point and switching on the heat when the mercury climbs."

This book is not a political or economic tract. Still, in order to invest effectively today, one must acknowledge the profound changes that the world economies are going through. Although these have the effect of a financial tidal wave sweeping away many of our preconceived ideas, people would rather not recognize their existence. It's only human to be more comfortable with inertia than with radical change—far easier to think that tomorrow will be like today, and today like yesterday, the year before, or the decade before.

Yet anxiety lingers just below the surface. When Joe Granville said stocks would drop, panic broke through the complacency of thousands, and they sold at any price. His midnight sales recommendation in early January 1981 triggered a $42 billion decline in stock prices the next day—three times the dollar amount lost on Black Tuesday, 1929.

Or in early January 1982, when Salomon Brothers' widely respected interest rate expert, Henry Kaufman, stated that interest rates would move higher, he set off the same kind of reaction. Stock, bond, precious metal, and collectible prices all plummeted lower. Whether market demagogue or market expert, each broke the thin layer of investor complacency.

This economic, political, and social dislocation is more severe than we have seen before, partly because of the far greater interdependence today between financial institutions, companies, and even nations. The repression of Solidarity in Poland, for example, is a major crack in the Communist system. On an economic level, it can lead to massive bankruptcies and financial crisis in the West, because of the billions of dollars Western banks have loaned to Poland and other East European nations.

Yet this is the world in which we must invest. A dour enough message, I know, but my purpose is anything but to write another scenario of financial collapse. Sure, some provide a fast and scary read, but what the prophets of doom forget is that great financial change has always brought major opportunities to those who know how to take advantage of them.

This book will attempt to guide the average investor toward investments that can help protect and enhance his or her capital in today's radically changing world. Because of the lightning pace of financial change in the last few years, such a guide is even more important now than it was when *Contrarian Investment Strategy* was published in early 1980. In fact, many of the better investments under today's conditions were then in an embryonic stage or not even developed.

For this reason I have made fairly extensive additions to the text, adding sections on the advantages and disadvantages of money market funds, NOW accounts, and all-savers certificates; the benefits and pitfalls of a wide variety of new bonds introduced in the last few years; the use of financial futures and stock options; and, probably as important as any of the above, how to both protect yourself and profit from the wildly swinging interest rates of the present time.

Also added are sections that show the advantages and disadvantages of using a discount broker and some guidelines on how to select one, the extended benefits of IRAs under the new tax laws, as well as some ominous implications of these laws for various tax shelters. These sections, I believe, should prove helpful to investors with portfolios of any size.

But new investments are only a part of the equation for success. At least as important is an understanding of the reasons the stock market offers the average investor some of the greatest opportunities in decades if he or she can avoid the pitfalls that have trapped so many. To become aware of these dangers, we will analyze a wide variety of investment markets to see why conventional wisdom so often goes wrong—whether in buying tulip bulbs in the 1630s, Xerox or Polaroid in the early 1970s, gold and silver in 1979–80, or Genentech or Apple Computer in 1981.

Drawing on recent findings in both cognitive psychology and

financial statistics, I have attempted to show how powerful and often destructive the tendency of people, even among experts, to follow current fashions and trends can be. In fact, the investment arena provides almost the perfect atmosphere for these fashions and trends to flourish. The psychological principles at work here apply to any form of investing, from the stock market to real estate to stamp collecting.

The forces one has to contend with are both subtle and complex. The fact that even market professionals succumb to the same mistakes repeatedly, their training and experience notwithstanding, puzzled me for a long time. And to be honest, I became one of the crowd on one or two occasions; the power of group action struck home. Why, I wondered, should so many of us who presumably know better not learn from experience? These events made me begin to study the nature of the systematic errors that time and again crop up for individuals and professionals alike, and the reasons we so often seem to behave like lemmings when common sense and logic dictate we run in precisely the opposite direction.

Today's infatuation with emerging growth stocks and new issues is such an example. Buying precisely these stocks has led individual and institutional investors alike to disaster twice in the 1960s and once again in the early 1970s. Still, in late 1980, major institutional investors of the caliber of Bankers Trust and Citicorp were willing to pay prices bordering on foolishness for just such companies —Genentech, Datapoint, Apple Computer, and Tandem. Take Genentech as an example. If its earnings grew at a 50 percent rate a year for the next decade, or 6,000 percent—an unlikely possibility —it would still be ten times the price relative to its earnings of IBM in 1992. What is indicated is that group consensus can be so powerful that it erases or at least downgrades both crucial past experience and common sense.

Living through a number of these cycles, I became increasingly convinced that the investment methods in which we are all schooled are not sufficient by themselves to make us consistent winners. Without a grasp of systematic ways to protect ourselves against psychological overreactions, chances are we will continue to make the same or similar mistakes time and again.

The book will examine some relatively new methods that provide just such protection. These are based on contrarian principles —principles that normally result in going against the popular opinion of the day. This approach has worked well for my clients and myself over the years—no small inducement to belief. But far more important, the assumptions underlying the method are strongly documented statistically and psychologically. The ideas, although not complicated, require an understanding of investor psychology and the discipline to carry it through. When you understand them you can avoid the mistakes of both the market's pros and the market's patent medicine men.

The bottom line of these methods, of course, is to make money. Using the approach and the new tools I will outline, you should be able to increase your capital, perhaps substantially. Sounds like a pretty bold claim, but it isn't. The contrarian methods we'll study have been gaining increasing recognition from sophisticated investors in recent years because they are down-to-earth, disciplined, and —most important—have proven very successful.

In fact, the methods I proposed in the first book have gained far more attention and acceptance from experienced and knowledgeable investors than I would have thought possible in the short time the work has been out. Contrarian investing (that is, going against popular opinion), as this approach has been named, has become almost a buzz word on Wall Street—so much so that one financial advisor has seriously proposed that we should now become "counter-contrarians."

Through an understanding of just how systematic investor errors are, and the frequency with which they repeat themselves, I hope to show you how they can be avoided. And, far more importantly, how they can be used to take advantage of the major opportunities available in markets today.

Our journey will be wide-ranging through both time and across various fields related to markets, crowd psychology, finance, economics, statistics, and even politics.

Over the course of our travels we will see striking similarities in investor behavior and error although the periods may be separated by decades, sometimes centuries. The first chapters of the book outline the errors made, and the reasons why. The remainder is devoted to showing you how to benefit from these mistakes, as well as exploring the many excellent new investments that are available today. Part of the work will naturally be somber, but it will have its lighter moments as well.

As I wrote in *Psychology and the Stock Market* almost six years ago, the integration of financial and psychological understanding is a new and basically uncharted field. Even today, although a Nobel Prize has been awarded to Herbert Simon for pioneer work in this area, it is a field about as familiar to most market experts as the occult. This helps explain the reason for both the high rate of professional error and the tremendous opportunities still available.

As you shall see, once you understand the principles, there is nothing magical or mysterious about the work. The question I have repeatedly been asked by numerous professionals and other sophisticated investors in lectures and seminars across the country is why, since the documentation is so thorough and the logic convincing, aren't more people following these methods? In fact, one major New York City bank with over ten billion dollars under investment management assigned one of my books to all its money managers as compulsory reading over a weekend to avoid the mistakes I described. Not long thereafter, it went out and bought the gambling stocks favored by just about everybody on the Street—just before they dropped 80 percent in price.

It's easy, then, to understand both the theory and the methods. But you will have to master some tricky psychological pitfalls—traps that make most people, regardless of experience, run with the lemmings. If you read on, you will see why and can decide whether you want to try it.

DAVID DREMAN
September 1982

CONTENTS

LIST OF TABLES AND FIGURES

PART I

CURRENT INVESTMENT PRACTICE

CHAPTER ONE

Investing in a World Turned Upside Down

Sometimes making money has appeared simple. On June 19, 1815, for example, the Rothschilds learned via carrier pigeon that the French had been crushed the previous evening at Waterloo many hours before the news reached London by more customary means. When the market opened that morning, Rothschild agents buzzed the news of a major British defeat, and Nathan Rothschild himself began to sell, which triggered a large break. Near the low point, other inconnu family agents began to buy heavily, not long before the expected arrival of the more conventional couriers. The market that day closed considerably higher than it opened, further adding to the family coffers.

Such exciting coups are the stuff of investor dreams and indeed have occurred in one manner or another for many of the legendary names associated with the world of finance—the Morgans, Rockefellers, Astors, Harrimans, and Kennedys. But for the average investor, making money or even protecting existing capital has never been easy, and in the last decade and a half the task has seemed to become almost impossible.

This book is an attempt to show you why this has happened and what you as an individual trying to survive and even prosper can do in an investment world gone topsy-turvy. . . .

• • •

3

In late 1977 a seat on the New York Stock Exchange traded for $35,000, some $20,000 less than what a taxi medallion cost on the same day. Over the previous eight years, the Big Apple's tough, shrewd, and talkative cabdrivers had seen the worth of their medallions double. During the same period its tough, shrewd, and not so untalkative brokers had watched a seat on the New York Stock Exchange decline by some 94 percent.

So hapless had the market become that several years back an organization called Bull and Bear, Inc., set up two new mutual funds with opposite purposes: a bull fund for people believing the market would go up and a bear fund for investors who believed stocks would go down. Both lost money! That year, the bull fund declined 15 percent and the bear fund 9 percent.

And since then, although seats have again moved ahead of taxi medallions, things have generally seemed to get worse. In August 1982, the market's most widely followed index, the Dow-Jones Industrial Average, was 22 percent below its price of sixteen years earlier, and in constant dollars it had fallen beneath the level it was at in 1951, or for that matter, the end of 1929.

The result is not surprising—individuals have exited en masse from the marketplace. Brokers too have suffered. Scores of member firms, some dating back a century or more, have gone out of business or been forced to merge. Over fifty thousand jobs have disappeared on Wall Street in the last decade. Harvard Business School graduates, those supposed savants of where opportunity lies, now shun the Street like the plague.

Events have proven equally depressing for many people who have avoided the stock market entirely in favor of traditionally safer investments. Investors have never faced the hyperinflation of the present era. The rise in prices in absolute terms in the past four decades is greater than it had been in the previous six hundred years —and the rate was accelerating through the seventies.

This new inflation and its roots seem mystifying even to the experts. Never before have so many interlocking forces kindled inflationary fires—OPEC raising the price of oil sixteenfold since 1972; a cabal of junior OPECs ranging from diamonds to uranium to coffee, all trying to trigger large price hikes and sometimes succeeding; agricultural and industrial prices, stable for almost two decades, more than doubling since 1970, with the probability of rising prices ahead; workers in the free world (and not a few in the Communist bloc) demanding and receiving large wage boosts, which not only offset inflation but often increased their purchasing power in real terms; and businessmen responding to this new environment with "anticipatory price boosts" to offset continually rising prices. All these factors initiate price rises or at least react to those of the others, creating a baffling and seemingly irreversible spiral.*

As the *Wall Street Journal*'s weekly front-page economic review put it in boldface type: "The [government] policy-makers depict themselves as victims of changing economic circumstances that neither they nor their colleagues in academia and industry fully understand. They insist, moreover, that the economic profession hasn't provided them with new tools and the old ones are inadequate."[1]

Economists, like generals fighting a previous war, continue to apply various traditional fiscal and monetary poultices to these problems, remedies that have been working as effectively as bleeding did for the eighteenth-century physician. For a decade we have had repeated "stagflation," and more recently "slumpflation,"† accompanied by an ebbing of confidence at home and abroad. And the situation appears to be getting worse: Margaret Thatcher's British Government, religiously applying the old cures, by late 1980 had brought her country the greatest depression since the 1930s—with even higher unemployment than back then and major riots led by unemployed youths.

True, inflation is down today, but has the problem disappeared? Hardly; well before the decade is over, inflation is likely to rekindle again at sharply higher levels, for the reasons outlined in the final chapter. As an investor you are faced with a tax structure that becomes increasingly punishing as the rate of inflation soars. If inflation reignites at the near 13 percent rate of 1980, as it did briefly in 1981, an investor in a 25 percent tax bracket—the typical bracket of widows and orphans (see table 1, page 6)—would require a 17.3 percent return just to sustain purchasing power, while a businessman in a 50 percent tax bracket would require a 26 percent return. Even if he chose an all-savers certificate‡ yielding 9 percent tax-free, or a

---

*Chapter 13 will look at these problems in greater detail.
†A word coined by Nobel Laureate Milton Friedman.
‡For definition see page 259.

money market fund yielding 12 percent, he would still be losing a part of his purchasing power. As the table shows, if inflation persists at high levels, which is certainly not impossible, the returns required become frightening.

We might have been amused by the 2½ percent interest the English received on their government bonds in the nineteenth century. But 2½ percent was a reasonable rate of return in a period of price stability that by and large lasted close to a hundred years. If inflation goes back to 11 percent, an individual today in the 50 percent tax bracket purchasing a ten-year government 14 percent bond will have only 66 percent of his original capital left (including interest) in constant dollars when the bond matures. It's as if the bonds defaulted and paid 66 cents on the dollar—worse than the performance of most corporate bonds during the Great Depression. In terms of purchasing power, the Englishmen of the last century, even with their low coupons, would have had twice the purchasing power of this modern investor a decade later.

What we have seen in less than a decade, then, is the collapse of most of the time-honored standards for preserving capital—guidelines that have prevailed in Western countries for centuries. The safest investments—bank deposits, bonds, mortgages—may now lead to a rapid meltdown of your money. Conversely, investments that were once considered risky by cautious investors may provide the best solutions today. A Cleveland investment firm, McDonald and Company, summed it up well: "Individuals along virtually the entire income spectrum are forced into a position where the purchas-

Table 1
RETURNS REQUIRED TO MAINTAIN PURCHASING POWER OF CAPITAL

INFLATION RATE	25%	30%	35% TAX BRACKET	40%	45%	50%
8%	10.7	11.4	12.3	13.3	14.5	16.0
9%	12.0	12.9	13.8	15.0	16.4	18.0
10%	13.3	14.3	15.4	16.7	18.2	20.0
11%	14.7	15.7	16.9	18.3	20.0	22.0
12%	16.0	17.1	18.5	20.0	21.8	24.0
13%	17.3	18.5	20.0	21.6	23.6	26.0
14%	18.6	20.0	21.5	23.3	25.5	28.0
15%	20.0	21.4	23.1	25.0	27.2	30.0

ing power of their savings is constantly being eroded if they hold conventional investment vehicles. In these circumstances, a penny saved is a penny lost."

Chinese Ceramics, Postage Stamps, and Doom

Small wonder, given these circumstances, that capital has darted from country to country and from investment to investment. Several years ago, people lined up at housing developments in California, many paying large premiums for second and third homes, not to live in but as speculative vehicles. Prices, the buyers believed, could only go higher. I saw a near tar-paper shack on Malibu Beach with sixty feet of ocean frontage sell for $900,000, up from $750,000 a few years earlier. Illinois farmland was then valued at triple the price of IBM stock relative to the income it would have produced.

Speculative money also flowed into diamonds, jewelry, and artwork. In the past decade, Chinese ceramics have increased at a 23 percent annual rate, U.S. stamps at 23.5 percent, rare books at 21 percent, Art Deco at 19 percent, and old master paintings at 15.4 percent.

Faced with greater economic uncertainties, baffling inflation, and disintegrating confidence in the system, people became more willing to speculate on the past, as represented by precious stones, metals, or artwork, than in the future of our industrial economy.

With the conventional rules for survival disappearing, a group of clever marketers have poured into the void, expertly exploiting the mood of the times. Called gloom-and-doomers by some, survivalists by others, they have built a thriving business on a simple Hollywood principle—fear is big at the box office. With the motto "scare 'em 'n' sell 'em," an endless stream of books with titles such as *The Coming Currency Collapse, Crisis Investing,* and *How to Prosper During the Coming Bad Years* are snapped up by the hundreds of thousands. Each contains images as terrifying as anything in *Jaws, The Exorcist*, or *The Shining*.

Picture a country, if you will, with a depression worse than in the thirties, tens of millions of people in the breadlines, and when the bread runs out, hungry mobs coming to take everything you own.

Can you survive? Sure, if you pay $14.95—or whatever—for the book.

The answers given both in the books or at the expensive conferences where frightened investors shell out from three to five hundred dollars or more a head to attend are simplistic at best. Incisive advice such as moving to small towns to avoid the anarchistic crowds— mountain perches are even better if you can keep the eagles away— storing at least a year's supply of freeze-dried food and water (for the latter, it's wise to own a reliable water bed), and yes, be sure to purchase "ammo" and machine guns to keep away those awful mobs. What else should you own? Naturally, bags of gold or silver—things you can carry away fast—although anyone with $500,000 or so would find it a little difficult to make a quick getaway wtih 83,334 pounds of silver (the current weight of $500,000 invested in the metal).

However, even these images of depression and anarchy have been overworked and are losing their sting. But, as we saw, these people are creative and quick to adapt to the market wants. One recent pitch: the horror of nuclear war and the desperate need for fallout shelters. A well-known gloom-and-doomer in his "1981 Financial Survival Seminar" in Bermuda* featured an Air Vice Marshal, S. W. B. Menual, "who," it claimed, "as Commander of England's troops during World War II survived many nuclear attacks."[2] Since the British, in theory at least, were on our side at the time, and the only atom bombs were ours dropped on Japan, the statement proved somewhat farfetched even for some of the Doomsday Set, and were eventually withdrawn.†

What would have happened if you had followed "the world is ending scenario" since it reached the height of its popularity in the last year or two? You would have lost heavily in gold, been ruined in silver, while watching the very investments you were warned to stay away from push up.

No, the quick fixes won't save you, and in fact, should be labeled dangerous to your investment health. What, then, should you do? Even our institutions seem utterly bewildered. Pension funds, the largest institutional investors, have reduced their equity exposure

---

*People pay to be scared, but since it's tax deductible, why not be frightened to death in a lovely setting. Increasing numbers of these seminars are being held in such places.

†As it turned out, "Air Vice Marshal" Menual held a bureaucratic post in the British Air Force at a much lower rank.

from 74 percent of their assets at the end of 1972 to a little more than 50 percent at year-end 1978, and increased their holdings of bonds sharply. Just in time to witness the utter collapse of bond prices in 1979 and 1980—and a concomitant sharp rise in the price of the stocks they had just sold.

With the failure of most conventional investments and quick fixes to protect the investor in the last decade, many believe this has become a world, as one observer put it, "where gambling or speculation is not a vice but a necessity."[3]

Yet it is in this environment that you must attempt to protect your capital and enhance it if you can. At first, the task may appear overwhelming. True, it is not easy to make money or keep it, but it never has been. Even in far more tranquil and prosperous periods, investors on the whole have not fared well in the marketplace. Although innumerable prophets have appeared with endless theories on how to get rich—indeed, the greater the failure, the more rapidly they seem to sprout—we will see that there are no widely followed methods that can be used with any assurance of success.

In good times and good markets, poor investment results are often masked. While the record of most investors may be lackluster, they generally still make some money or at least break even. In bad times, such as those today, the full extent of the failure is apparent.

Certainly this is a downbeat enough message up to this point, but I'm not out to play muckraker or Chicken Little, or to offer another wrinkle in the how-to-make-a-million genre. Rather, this book attempts to lay out a course for the concerned investor aware of today's problems. By studying the current financial breakdown and its causes in more detail, and the innovative financial instruments to protect you, I believe there is every chance for an upbeat ending, particularly for the individual investor. In fact, some of the greatest opportunities in decades await the average investor. But obviously, after what you've just read, these opportunities will require some explaining.

A Curious State

Even as Art Deco, real estate, jewelry, and Chinese ceramics went through the roof, the largest and strongest companies in corporate

America languished. Never before had they traded for as long a period at a significant discount from the real value of their real estate, plant, and equipment. The stocks of prime companies such as Travelers, Manufacturers Hanover, Mobil Oil, and Texaco are priced to provide 25 to 33 percent returns annually on their after-tax profits —equivalent to 50 to 66 percent before taxes. Such returns are normally reserved for only the riskiest and most unstable of ventures.

And company fundamentals have been improving. Earnings and dividends, considered to be the prime influence on stock prices over time, have been increasing at a faster rate than inflation throughout the decade. Most corporations have been able to offset higher inflation by raising selling prices. And so, in spite of escalating costs, profits and dividends moved up. Throughout the past ten years of accelerating inflation, earnings of S & P's Poor's 500* have increased at an almost 11 percent annual rate, considerably faster than the climb in prices. *In a word, our major corporations have fared far better against inflation than is generally realized.*

Thus, when we measure stocks by a number of the most crucial valuation criteria—book value, P/E ratio, rate of earnings, and dividend increase—we see the popular indices, such as the S&P 500, are at some of the lowest valuations in the postwar period,† a conclusion underscored by the wave of takeovers by both foreign and domestic companies—like Conoco, Santa Fe Drilling, Bache, Shearson Loeb Rhoades—at figures double and sometimes triple the prices they traded at beforehand. And as domestic money flows abroad, foreign investors, attracted by the political stability and strong fundamentals of the American market, invest growing amounts here.

In fact, there is increasing recognition that the American stock market may be one of the last truly undervalued investments left today. Stocks are still trading near their levels of 1949–50, in constant dollars, the point from which the great bull market was launched. From that time, blue chip stocks rose almost 500 percent in the next fifteen years. There are remarkable similarities between that time and today—similarities that should lead to outstanding investment opportunities over the next few years with little risk.

---

*Standard and Poor's 500, the broadest based of the popular indices, accounting for about three quarters of the market value of companies listed on the New York Stock Exchange.

†Again, a more detailed discussion of the fundamentals that I believe make the case for investing in U.S. stocks as strong as it has been in decades will be found on pages 292–299 in chapter 13.

Indeed, the record rally last August and September, for reasons to be outlined in detail in chapter 13, might very well be only the opening salvos of a major bull market, possibly one that will go as far as, or further than, any we have seen in this century to date.

If this is true, why, you might ask, is it so little recognized—particularly by professional investors? And here we come to one of the most important considerations in contemporary markets.

Professional investors—managers of bank trust departments, insurance companies, mutual and pension funds, and others—control vast stores of capital: in all, an estimated 70 percent of the trading and almost 50 percent of the stock ownership on the New York Stock Exchange.

Yet this expert opinion—which investors naturally rely on—is very often wrong and not infrequently dramatically so. In fact, the errors are so great, investors would do better in most instances selecting stocks by throwing darts at the stock pages, or perhaps even having their family dogs choose them by pawing the financial pages —a method tried recently by one frustrated Minneapolis advisor. Indeed, because professionals control so much of the trading and ownership of securities, they may in no small measure have been responsible for the desultory performance of stocks in recent years.

For these reasons I think it is important for us to consider briefly the record of the professionals.

The Professional Record

Let's start with the record of the finest research money can buy. The largest bank trust departments, mutual funds, and pension funds can afford the best investment advice because of the tens of millions of dollars in commissions they command to pay for it. The top analysts in all important industries—computers, pharmaceuticals, aviation, microtechnology, and so on—are chosen each year in a poll conducted by *Institutional Investor* magazine after canvassing hundreds of institutions for their choices.

According to an article in *Financial World*, "At least a hundred of these oracles, and probably more, make six-figure salaries. Income-wise, they are in a class with entertainers or professional athletes. At Merrill Lynch alone more than 30 analysts make $100,000 a year or more." Some make over $200,000 a year and have been offered $50,000 or more to switch firms.[4] The top analysts are often treated on the Street with adulation not dissimilar to that which teenagers reserve for rock stars and film heroes. Naturally, you would think *la crème de la crème* selected from over 15,000 analysts across the country would be sensational stock pickers. True? False.

Financial World, in the aforementioned article, measured the analysts' results. The article stated, "It was not an easy task. Most brokerage houses were reluctant to release the batting averages of their superstars." In many cases, the results were gotten from outside sources such as major clients, and then "only grudgingly." After months of digging, the magazine came up with the recommendations of twenty major superstars. The conclusion: "Heroes were few and far between—during the period in question, the market rose 14.1 percent. If you had purchased or sold 132 stocks they recommended when they told you to, your gain would have been only 9.3 percent," some 34 percent worse than selecting stocks by throwing darts.

The magazine added, "Of the hundred and thirty two stocks the superstars recommended only 42 or just over 1/3 beat the S&P 500." A large institutional buyer of research summed it up. "In hot markets the analysts . . . get brave at just the wrong time and cautious just at the wrong time. It's uncanny, when they say one thing, start doing the opposite. Usually you are right."[5]

But the superstars' shortfall (which we will see repeated in numerous studies in chapter 5) is only one aspect of the overall picture of how the investment pros do. Let's look at another important one, the record of investment advisory services.

Investment advisory services sell their advice to the public on a subscription basis. The function of these services, as most of them readily advertise, is to get you in near the market bottom and out near the top.

Would you have profited by subscribing to such services? In a word, *no*. The accompanying chart (figure 1) was compiled from the recommendations made by approximately seventy-five of the nation's leading advisory services for the 1971–81 period. The chart indicates that there is an almost perfect correlation between the investment advice given and the future course of the market—unfortunately, almost perfectly wrong.

As markets approach their highs, larger and larger numbers of advisors become bullish, and as they move toward their lows, an

Figure 1.

How investment advisory sentiment trails the market.

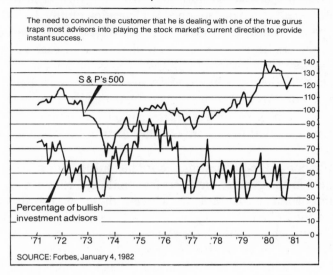

The need to convince the customer that he is dealing with one of the true gurus traps most advisors into playing the stock market's current direction to provide instant success.

S & P's 500

Percentage of bullish investment advisors

'71 '72 '73 '74 '75 '76 '77 '78 '79 '80 '81

SOURCE: Forbes, January 4, 1982

increasingly expanding number stampede for the exits. As you can see, swings in opinion are invariably far wider than the movements of the market. For example, at the market high in late 1972, 65 percent of advisors predicted that stocks were heading skyward. Then, at the bottom of the 1974 market—the worst break in the postwar period—two thirds suspected stocks would continue to free-fall; not long thereafter, we had the beginning of a major bull market.

In fact, for a short time, coinciding almost perfectly with the 1974 bottom, twenty advisors ran bearish ads in a national financial weekly. How many bullish ads did the weekly run in the same period? None.

As you can see, the pattern is repeated again and again. Advisors retreated from being 60 percent bullish in late 1978 to 35 percent in early 1979, when the market declined 8 percent—just in time to miss the strong upward move for the rest of the year. The same thing happened in early 1980, before the even stronger market rally of that year. Predictably, with the sharp break in the second and third quarters of 1981 some 70 percent of advisors were bearish at the end of the September quarter, becoming bullish again as the market turned up in the final three months. Instead of the market's following the advisors, the advisors followed the market!

Moving on to mutual funds: the proper course for them is to be fully invested near market bottoms—with very low cash reserves at such times—after having snapped up bargains dumped on the market by panicky individual investors. Conversely, near market tops, they should be heavy sellers, accumulating large cash reserves by taking advantage of the speculative whims of an excited public. Again, exactly the opposite case prevails. The funds are heavy sellers at market bottoms and heavy buyers near market tops.* The funds also appear to be poor judges of the market's direction.† Additional studies indicate that the record of other institutuional investors is no better.

But poor as the forecasting record has turned out to be, it is only one aspect in the evaluation of professional performance. By far the most important measure is how well these organizations have managed their clients' money over time. Even if they missed the tops and bottoms, they could have done better than the market. How good, then, are their investment records?

A survey of 571 of the largest pension and profit-sharing funds in the country managed primarily by banks and insurance companies for the three-, five-, ten- and fifteen-year periods ended in 1978 indicated that only 22 percent did as well as the market. A more recent study covered 214 pooled equity funds,‡ large banks, and insurance companies that managed over $100 billion. The measurement was for one-, three-, five-, and ten-year periods ending December 31, 1980. The results are presented in table 2. In every holding period the S&P 500 outdistanced banks' pooled funds and half the insurance companies'. Other broad studies of the performance of mutual funds, pension funds, and investment advisors came up with similar results. A. G. Becker, for example, measured the equity record of three thousand of the largest pension funds in the country for 1962–75 and found that 87 percent underperformed the

*Mutual funds were most bearish at the market bottoms of 1966, 1970, and 1974 (cash reserves rose to 9.7, 11.8, and 13.5 percent respectively) and were fully invested near the market tops of 1967 and 1972 (when these reserves dropped to 5.7 and 6.2 percent respectively). (Martin Zweig, *Investor Expectations* [New York: Martin Zweig, n.d.].)

†Ordinarily, common stock mutual funds keep about 7 percent of assets in cash or its equivalent and do not change these reserves markedly. The high and low figures presented are thus quite extreme.

‡The funds of many clients are pooled or commingled. This provides a client with more intensive management and greater portfolio diversity than he would otherwise receive, while allowing the institution economies of scale.

Table 2

AVERAGE ANNUALIZED RETURNS AND ASSETS ENDING 1980

	RETURNS[a]				ASSETS (in billions)
	10 YRS.	5 YRS.	3 YRS.	1 YR.	
Banks	7.0%	13.4%	18.3%	29.8%	
(No. of mgrs.)	(127)	(175)	(179)	(183)	$5.3
Insurance Companies	7.8%	14.3%	19.3%	30.5%	
(No. of mgrs.)	(22)	(23)	(23)	(24)	$13.1
Standard & Poor's 500 Index	8.4%	13.9%	18.7%	32.4%	

SOURCE: Adapted from *Pensions and Investment Age,* May 25, 1981.
a Median results.

S&P 500.* An updated Becker study to the end of 1981 found that the median of 3,500 of the largest profit-sharing, endowment, and other tax-exempt funds with stockholdings totaling over $125 billion did 20 percent worse than the S&P 500 for the last fifteen years and 30 percent worse in the last decade.†

Are commodities any different? Commodities trading requires exceptional knowledge, skill, and discipline. To quote Neil J. Aslan, executive vice-president of Conticommodity Services, Inc., the nation's largest commodities-only broker: "A lot of people shouldn't trade commodities on their own because they don't have the time, knowledge, or money—on the other hand, they can invest in a fund and get the same caliber of management and diversification as a big account." Thousands of new commodity futures players have heeded the advice and entered this marketplace through such funds.[6]

How did Conticommodity funds do? Unfortunately, not well. It lost so heavily in silver futures in the spring of 1980 that the company required its parent, Continental Grain, to come galloping to its rescue and provide it with a capital injection in the tens of millions to save it from bankruptcy. Even so, a $10 million managed commodity fund became insolvent. In November 1980 another managed com-

*When Becker began measuring the performance of institutional investors, it was not exactly greeted with accolades by the money managers. In fact, Becker's parent brokerage firm lost several million dollars in commissions from irate former clients as a result. (A. F. Ehrbar, "Index Funds—An Idea Whose Time Is Coming," *Fortune*, June 1976, pp. 141–148.)
†Steve Myers and Scott Bettin, South Dakota Investment Council; A. G. Becker.

modities fund was liquidated, wiping out over 60 cents on the dollar of its investors' equity.[7]

These findings and a substantial amount of corroborating evidence indicate a widespread failure of modern money management, in spite of the investment professionals' training, intelligence, and experience, as well as the best research money can buy. Rather than fulfilling the hopes of superior performance promised to their clients, the professionals have generally lagged behind the market averages. The most sophisticated generation of financial managers ever has demonstrated an incapacity to manage money effectively.

Some Basic Questions

Our brief tour of the new investment world brings to mind four critical, interrelated questions for which investors must attempt to find answers:

1. Why have professionals, regardless of their training and experience, done so poorly over the years?

2. Why, if stocks in fact do provide excellent value today, has this been so little noted or acted upon?

3. How can the average investor take advantage of both the unsettled environment and professional errors to protect and to increase his personal capital?

4. What other new financial instruments are available to safeguard and enhance one's savings in today's volatile markets?

A Common-Sense Rule

Logic dictates that if one group, such as the experts, seems wrong time and again,* there must be other people who are right. Sometimes, of course, the winners are winners simply by chance—as if they had bet on the jockey's colors at the race track. But others are consistent, and their consistency involves discipline and method. These investors must consciously be doing something quite different from the underperformers.

*We will come back to this topic in chapter 5.

But what is it that causes this success or failure? Much of the answer appears to lie within the realm of investor psychology, one of the most used but least understood phrases on the investment scene today. All of us hear of how investor psychology has turned positive or negative on an industry or company or on the market as a whole. And many an experienced investor has pondered the extreme psychological variations that markets have displayed over time. The problem we face as investors is not that we aren't aware that psychology plays a part, but that we don't really know what this part is or how to invest once we've understood it. Probably there are a few people with brilliant intuitive reactions who can take advantage of market psychology, but most of us are not so gifted.

How, then, do we isolate and identify common investor behavioral patterns in order to use them in a workable investment framework? For a long time, this question could not be answered because the necessary diagnostic tools did not exist. It has only been through work done in recent years that some clear-cut patterns of behavior have been analyzed that show that people in groups often prove wrong, sometimes remarkably so.

As you continue reading, you'll see numerous examples of what happens when people act blindly in groups, ranging from policy making at the higher levels of government to medical diagnostics to crowd stampedes in the stock market. Over and over again, when the degree of consensus was the greatest—in whatever field of activity—the extent of the error was the most pronounced.

I shall try to show that if you want to make money, you must stubbornly cling to contrarian principles. When everyone is rushing in, whether it be to buy Art Deco, Chinese ceramics, or Krugerrands, and systematically deflating another investment, like the stock or bond markets today, history demonstrates that there is a chance and probably a good one to profit by going in the opposite direction. The same rule applies within the stock or bond markets themselves among favored and unfavored companies and industries.

The new findings explain why people in markets often behave like crowds at a theater fire—all running toward the same exit, although many others are available. In one age it was tulip bulbs, in another blue-chip stocks, in others bonds or Art Nouveau—but at any moment most investors rush for the same door at once, and many get trampled.

You might ask if being a contrarian is enough by itself, since it is obvious that crowds and groups can be perfectly right a good part of the time. As an investor, can you really spot when they are wrong and take advantage of such situations?

Fortunately, the answer to both questions is yes. The pressures to which I have alluded lead to predictable patterns of investor behavior, so predictable that it is possible to derive successful investment strategies that will allow you to benefit from other people's mistakes. In fact, numerous statistical studies extending over a period of more than forty years pinpoint investor overreactions in a systematic enough manner so that the investor consistently applying the principles will have a good chance of outdoing the market.

In the stock market, for example, one of the most recent surveys, covering all the stocks on the New York Stock Exchange and the major companies on the American Stock Exchange and over-the-counter markets for a nine-year period, showed certain of these strategies yielding annual returns twice as good as the markets. Our own record through this period showed annual returns of 17 percent or better, about triple those of the market.

The strategies are relatively simple and require little time on your part to learn and use effectively, although the research behind them, as you might well imagine, is complex.

Since no investment strategy should be followed blindly, a good part of this work is devoted to explaining why the methods work. I believe that an understanding of these methods is essential to their effective use. Informed opinion almost always advocates the popular course, so you must steel yourself to stand apart. To be a contrarian is to be an outsider—until you're proven right.

Napoleon once said that "in warfare, the psychological is to the material as three to one." The ratio appears to be at least as high in the stock market. Although no book can teach you how to "get rich," I believe this one can give you a markedly better chance of improving your investment performance. I'm convinced that the individual investor today has an exceptional opportunity to beat both the market and the experts. All that is required is an open mind and the courage of your convictions. If you are a serious investor, I think our journey will prove rewarding.

CHAPTER TWO

Can You Read the Future?

Attempting to foretell the future has been a timeless, if questionable, preoccupation of man, in view of its usual rewards. Still, there are some areas where a knowledge of the future would prove invaluable —a not unimportant one being the accumulation of wealth.

Not surprisingly, then, countless schemes exist to predict the future in financial markets. I was introduced to an intriguing one when I was sixteen. A three-shopping-bag man wandered into my father's local brokerage firm, where I was visiting at the time, and offered me a chance at a financial coup. The shopping bags were large, and each bulged with long, narrow cylinders of tightly wrapped tracing paper. I could see, even at that age, that the man was not your typical brokerage-house type. He could have used a shave, a haircut, and less-worn clothes, but all this was unimportant as he explained to me that he had an unfailing system to make money and that the secret lay right there in his shopping bags.

Over the years, the man said, he had studied the relationship between commodity price movements and the concentric circles found inside tree trunks, from which he had developed a method of predicting future market movements. The shopping bags contained dozens of important tree trunk tracings, all full scale, that he would teach me to read—for only five dollars.

Five dollars was more than I could afford, so I declined. He then offered me an abbreviated version—using tracings of smaller tree trunks—at half price. This method, good as it was, did not provide quite the same results as the use of the larger tracings. Again I declined, possibly forfeiting a chance of becoming a millionaire in my teens.

While we all know intuitively that such advice is valueless, it is anything but easy to judge the quality of the counsel with which the average investor is bombarded—particularly when many of the professional advisors are intelligent, claim outstanding records of success, and display detailed knowledge of their subject. Thus, I think it is important that before examining the methods I will propose, readers unfamiliar with current investment approaches look at them in some detail.

These methods represent the conventional wisdom of the trade, and most expert advice is based upon them. Just as the State Department candidate is required to have some political-science background (if not, as in the past, to have attended the "proper" schools), to pass certain exams, and to have read the prescribed books, so the professional investor must also qualify by studying securities techniques—first at college and later on the job. But as we shall see, when these methods are scrutinized closely, they do not help us very much, if at all.

Some of them remind me a little of the techniques used by the eccentric scientists who inhabited Laputa, the moving island in the sky visited by Gulliver. Initially, the scientists' reasoning seemed sensible, even precise, but a closer investigation proved it otherwise. Thus, measurements for a suit were taken with sextant and compass for greater accuracy, with results leaving much to be desired.

The methods we shall examine, some of which seem to provide valuations with an almost mathematical precision, simply don't work any better than did Laputa's compass and sextant. The simpler tape and pins prove far more effective for a real-world tailor, as should the less complicated investment approaches that will be provided later. But before I get ahead of myself, let's look more closely at conventional investment methods.

The Market's Hatfields and McCoys

Until a decade ago, there were two dominant stock market schools —the technical and the fundamental. And, as is so often the case with economic, political, and religious ideas, each school stood inalterably opposed to the other.

The fundamentalist school, which we will discuss at some length in the next chapter, believes that markets are rational. All stocks have inherent values that can be determined. To ascertain these values, the investor must examine detailed information related to the general economy, the industry, and the individual company, and then apply time-tested evaluative formulas to find the appropriate price. The fundamentalist believes the market is often wrong in its appraisal of a stock's worth. Using his rational criteria, he determines if the current market undervalues, overvalues, or fairly values a given stock, and then makes his decisions to buy or sell accordingly.

The technical school, on the other hand, views such analysis as a colossal waste of time because all fundamental information about the security is already reflected in the price. Supply and demand in the marketplace are the sole factors to study in predicting future price movements. As John Magee, considered the dean of technical analysts, writes, "The market price reflects . . . the hopes and fears and guesses and moods, rational and irrational, of hundreds of potential buyers and sellers, as well as their needs and resources—in total, factors which defy analysis and for which no statistics are obtainable, but which are nevertheless all synthesized, weighed, and finely expressed in one precise figure [the price]."[1]

Joseph Granville, a technical analyst and the leading market personality of the day, says it more sharply: "Technicians look ahead, fundamentalists look backwards. The true language of the market is technical. . . . The majority of those involved in the market are bombarded with mis-timed fundamental data which nine times out of ten haven't a blessed thing to do with where the price of the stock or the market is headed."[2] So speak the McCoys.

Granville, tall, gawky, but not without charisma, usually seen wearing a seersucker suit but on occasion dressed in the flowing robes of an Old Testament prophet, has become the Messiah for many thousands because of four years of good market calls.

Modestly, he tells his followers that by using his methods, he is the first person to have "cracked the secret of markets." Having done so, he can never make a serious market error again and will eventually "win the Nobel Prize in Economics for this feat."

At the hundred or more speeches he gives each year, Granville thunders Old Testament proverbs and dire prophecies: "The market is a jealous God," he shrieks, "it rewards winners and chastises losers. The Holy Bible is a record of winners and losers. The market follows every precept in that Book—if the market does not follow man's ways, what does it follow? God's ways. . . . " Spellbound crowds of "Granville Groupies," as veteran analyst Robert LeFevre calls them, roar their approval.[3]

So large a following has Granville gathered that by January 1981, when he phoned his best subscribers at midnight and later to advise them to sell all they owned (at the same time his lower-paying subscribers were receiving his market letter telling them to buy), the market, as noted, dropped substantially more than in the crash of '29.

To technicians such as Granville, the concept of intrinsic value has no meaning in the marketplace. "How can it?" he would say. Memory would have to be extraordinarily short to forget that General Motors traded at above 80 in 1972 and at 28 in 1974, or that McDonald's dropped from 82 to 13 in the same period, although its fundamentals remained unchanged.

To the pragmatic technician, analysis of price and volume statistics is the key to understanding the direction of future price movements. "[The technician's] central thesis is 'the past is prologue,' " writes Vartanig G. Vartan, financial columnist of the *New York Times.* "They believe that analysis of past price and trading volume patterns—both for individual issues and the market in general—can provide clues to the future. . . . A pure chartist is almost monklike in dedication, believing the essential truth about the market is to be found in squiggles and figures on graph paper. He is unmoved by a plant explosion or a profit explosion."

Technicians think that both individual stocks and the general market move in discernible trends that continue until a clear signal is received of a change in course. Because stocks never proceed in a straight line but invariably retrace a portion of each advance or decline, the analyst must be able to filter the useful information about trends from a vast amount of market static.

A technician will usually favor one method but will use a number of others to confirm or reject his conclusions. In the following pages we will review some of the more common technical theories and methods.

Sunspots and Waves

Unfortunately, any brief overview of a subject as complex as technical analysis can merely outline some of the major landmarks, and then only with broad brushstrokes. The field is replete with interesting concepts applying not only to the stock market but to the analysis of economic activity itself.

A theory was proposed in 1875, naturally by an Englishman, that sunspots have a significant influence on economic activity. Economist William Stanley Jevons observed that sunspots normally occur in eleven-year cycles that correspond to changes in climatic conditions on earth, particularly to magnetic storms and increasing rainfall. Jevons compared the periods of sunspot activity with the fluctuations of commodity prices for a 150-year period beginning in fourteenth-century England. But his paper drew widespread criticism, and he eventually withdrew it, although he never really abandoned his notion.

The concept of powerful waves affecting market and economic behavior has intrigued generations of investors. It also influenced the thinking of a brilliant Russian economist, Nikolai D. Kondratieff. At the age of twenty-five, he already held a high position in the provisional Kerensky government, and under Lenin he founded the Moscow Business Conditions Institute in 1920. Between 1920 and 1928, Kondratieff published a series of major books and papers. Using U.S., English, German, and French statistics, he concluded that the Western world had experienced two and a half long economic cycles since the end of the eighteenth century, each lasting approximately fifty years.

In his work Kondratieff noted that peaks in commodity prices approximated periods of major wars—in November 1814, August 1864, and May 1920—and that sharp drops had occurred thereafter. The third wave, which began in 1890–93, was in progress when he wrote his most important article, in 1925.[4] The Kondratieff wave correctly pretraced the declining business conditions commencing in 1929 and the strong upward path of business in the 1960s and early 1970s in the next cycle, as figure 2 shows.

Ominously, according to figure 2, the current crest has passed, and we are once again approaching the stage of acute crisis and panic. Given the nature of markets, numerous professionals put forward the Kondratieff analysis to justify their wide-scale liquidation of securities during the sharp break of 1973–74. But with the rising market that followed, Kondratieff's theory again fell into neglect on the Street. If the professor's ideas unsettle you as they did me when I first encountered them, you may be somewhat reassured to know that each period of decline and panic was accompanied by massive price deflation, something that hardly seems unlikely today.

Kondratieff was sharply attacked by orthodox Marxists for daring to postulate that the waves were self-correcting rather than indicating the eventual collapse of the capitalist system. In 1930, in one of the earlier Stalinist purges, he was incarcerated, and he died in prison on an unknown date. The influential *Soviet Encyclopedic* dismissed his work with the sentence "This theory is wrong and reactionary."

Another interesting wave theory has been proposed by an American, R. N. Elliot, also a student of cycles. Elliot studied the work of the early-thirteenth-century Italian Leonardo Fibonacci, who had concluded that for the design of the Great Pyramid at Giza the Egyptian architects used the following progression of numbers:

Figure 2.
Twentieth-century business cycles and crisis points projected by the Kondratieff wave.

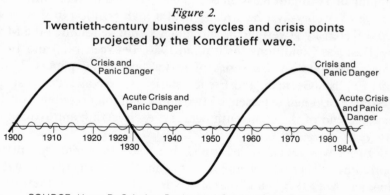

SOURCE: Harry D. Schultz, *Panics and Crashes* (New York: Pinnacle Books, 1975).

2–3–5–8–13–21–34–55–89. In this series, the ratio of successive numbers approximates 1.618, and the reciprocal is .62.

So-called Fibonacci series are frequently found in nature, which may account for how the architects of antiquity derived them. The number of branches on a tree increases each year in a Fibonacci series; the progression is also found in the rings on an elephant's tusks, the diameter of spirals on a seashell, the bumps on a pineapple, the leaves of a tree, and many other such developmental patterns.

Intrigued, Elliot began to apply Fibonacci numbers to the stock market, breaking market movements into waves composed of Fibonacci series. He divided each bearish component of the market cycle into two downswings and an upswing, and each bullish part into three upswings and a downswing. And, as with a snow crystal, the closer Elliot looked, the more intricate the patterns became. Each of the subcomponents could again be divided by the Fibonacci numbers of 3, 5, and 8, and these could in turn be divided by 13, 21, 34, and so on.[5] Not surprisingly, detecting the waves—some of which he named flats, inverted flats, and reverse inverted flats—has proven complex. Although the theory is fairly widely followed, Elliot's students often disagree about the proper interpretation of a given swing, sometimes for years after the fact.

Mr. Dow's Theory

It is ironic that one of the most important technical theories bears the name Dow, after Charles Dow, publisher of the *Wall Street Journal* and cofounder of the Dow-Jones empire, since Dow was at heart a fundamentalist. While he discovered and studied what he considered clear-cut patterns of market activity, Dow thought that stock prices were ultimately determined by earnings—a central tenet of the fundamental creed. Before his untimely death in 1902, he put forward his ideas about stock price movements in a number of editorials in the *Journal,* but he never published a full-fledged theory himself. William P. Hamilton, for several decades after assuming editorship of the *Journal* in 1908, synthesized and broadened Dow's premises to the extent that the current Dow theory is really Hamilton's rendition of the original.

The basis of the theory is that the Dow-Jones averages reflect all the fundamental facts and all the emotions and judgments of millions of market participants. The stock market is thus the best barometer of financial and business activity. Nothing is unknown to it except perhaps acts of God, and even these—as Hamilton wrote of the San Francisco earthquake of 1906—are quickly reflected in market movements. Dow observed that three movements occur within the marketplace at the same time. The most important, the primary trend, is a broad-based upward or downward swing usually lasting from one to several years. For Dow theorists, determining this trend is the master key to successful investing. Figure 3(a) graphs a primary uptrend and figure 3(b) a primary downtrend. In the uptrend, each new peak is above its predecessor, while on the downward leg, each new valley is below the previous one.

The investor, once he discerns that a bull market has actually started, should buy securities and continue to hold them until he receives a clear-cut sell signal. The more aggressive investor may attempt to trade on the intermediate moves, which normally last from one to several months. In figure 3(a), *AB* and *CD* are intermediate downtrends in a bull market, while *FG* and *HI* in figure 3(b) are intermediate upward reactions in a bear market. Normally, intermediate swings retrace one third to two thirds of the previous advance or decline. Finally, there are minor trends lasting from only hours to as long as several weeks.

Since the beginning, Dow theorists have discussed the phases of the market using the symbolism of tides, waves, and ripples. (In fact, there is some speculation that Dow conceived the basic elements of his theory because of his interest in the sea.) As long as the cap of each wave is higher than the previous cap and the trough is above

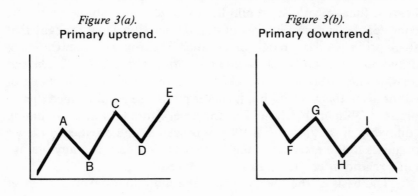

Figure 3(a).
Primary uptrend.

Figure 3(b).
Primary downtrend.

the previous trough, it is safe to assume that the market tide is rising. With a falling tide, the order is reversed. While the theory's followers acknowledge that market behavior is not nearly as predictable as the tides, the principles remain the same.

Another important rule developed by Hamilton is that a primary trend in either industrials or rails has to be confirmed by the other average. If, for example, the industrial average signals the start of a new bull market by moving above the previous peak, this signal can't be considered reliable unless the rails give it too. Acting in tandem, the two averages filter out many of the false breakout signals one or the other may temporarily reflect.

Although the concepts are simple in principle, it has been difficult in practice to pinpoint the signals. Even expert Dow theorists have widely differing opinions of the primary trend at critical market junctures. Hamilton correctly predicted the market break in a famous editorial, "A Turn of the Tide," on October 25, 1929. Had his advice been followed, investors would have saved 260 points (86 percent) of the drop to the 1932 low. However, he first called the bear market turn in 1926, after which the industrial average almost tripled.

The World of Charting

The technician's single most important tool is the chart. Through the recognition of dozens of different chart patterns, he believes he can pinpoint the all-important trends. The most common form of chart is the bar chart or vertical line chart, illustrated in figure 4, on page 28. These are normally plotted on a daily basis, though weekly or monthly movements are tracked for longer-term perspective. The thin vertical lines in the upper part of the figure indicate the daily trading range, with the small horizontal tick across the line showing the closing price. The series of vertical lines at the bottom of the chart represent daily volume.

Trend lines are as important to the chartist as to the Dow theorist because of the paramount principle that a trend once started does not easily change course. The chartist can thus follow an established market direction until he receives some sign of a reversal. He draws trend lines to connect a series of reactions to a primary move. Figure 5(a) is an uptrend; the trend line connects the reaction lows

Figure 4.
Vertical line chart.

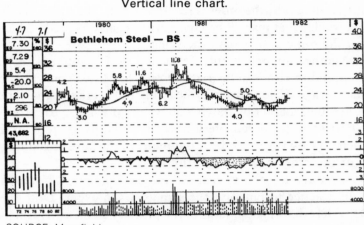

SOURCE: Mansfield.

at the bottom of the channel. Conversely, in figure 5(b), the trend line connects the reaction highs at the top of the channel, with the primary trend being down. Trend lines can also be curved to fit intermediate bottoms, as in figure 5(c), or intermediate tops, as in figure 5(d).

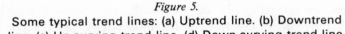

Reversal Formations

A key task of the technician is to recognize a change in trend. Spotting one quickly allows him both to protect his current position and to benefit from the new market course. Technicians have iden-

Figure 5.
Some typical trend lines: (a) Uptrend line. (b) Downtrend
line. (c) Up-curving trend line. (d) Down-curving trend line.

(a)   (b)   (c)   (d)

SOURCE: Harvey A. Krow, *Stock Market Behavior: A Technical Approach to Understanding Wall Street* (New York: Random House, 1969).

tified a large number of patterns that they believe clearly indicate a reversal of direction either for the averages or for individual stocks.

One of the most important reversal patterns is the head and shoulders, shown in figure 6. This shape normally emerges after a spirited advance by a stock for a period of weeks, perhaps even months. In the classic pattern, the first peak (the left shoulder) is formed with rising volume on the way up and declining volume on the fallback. Shortly thereafter, a second advance begins on slightly less volume and forms the middle peak (the head). Usually, the nadir of the head is above that of the left shoulder. The pattern is completed by the formation of the right shoulder on low volume. If the right shoulder breaks through the neckline on the decline, the chartist reads a strong sell signal. By contrast, he considers a reverse head and shoulders pattern, such as that shown in figure 7, to be bullish.

There are numerous siblings in this family of formations, some

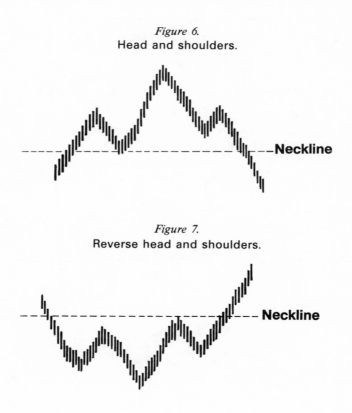

Figure 6.
Head and shoulders.

—Neckline

Figure 7.
Reverse head and shoulders.

— Neckline

of them with names sounding like sideshow attractions—aborted head and shoulders, deformed heads, multiple heads and shoulders, and two heads with one shoulder, to cite but a few.

Double tops and bottoms are other common patterns. In a double top, illustrated in figure 8, the left peak is ordinarily somewhat taller than the right. Volume usually runs fairly high on the first peak, but drops significantly in the formation of the second—the last charge of the dying bull. The pattern is completed when, after the second top, the price falls below the level of the valley between the peaks. The bull is now officially dead and can be dragged out of the arena, as the braver bears begin to sell short.

The double bottom in figure 9 is the reverse of the double top and flags a lucrative buying opportunity. There are also such things as triple tops and bottoms. But few actually exist; according to experienced technicians, most sightings of these, like those of UFOs, turn out to be false.

There are many other reversal patterns, as is shown in figure 10. The nomenclature of the chartist is filled with such terms as "dia-

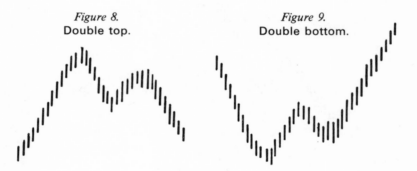

Figure 8.
Double top.

Figure 9.
Double bottom.

Figure 10.
Other reversal patterns: (a) Saucer bottom. (b) Coil bottom.
(c) Spike top.

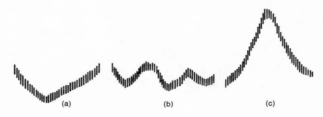

(a)   (b)   (c)

mond wedges," "exhaustion gaps," "fan movements," and "flags flying at half mast." Though one author pointed out that the labels on the formations are unimportant except to improve an investor's status as a name dropper, it is essential for the technician to be able to recognize the numerous possible patterns. Since each can give false signals, the technician's judgment and experience play powerful roles in shaping his decisions.

Other Technical Measures

It is not surprising, then, given the complexity of properly reading trends, that sophisticated technicians rely on numerous backup indicators to confirm favorite yardsticks. Support levels and resistance zones have long served this purpose. A support level indicates a valley a stock has climbed out of; a resistance zone is usually a previous peak. At a support level, sufficient demand is available to halt a further decline in price, at least for a time. A resistance zone, on the other hand, prevents further upward movement; enough stock is placed on the market at that price to halt temporarily and perhaps to stop a stock's climb altogether.

The reasoning behind both concepts is primarily psychological.

A buyer has purchased stock at a previous top—say, 20—made on high volume, and unhappily watched it decline to 16. If the stock again approaches 20, he and many others who bought it at that price will try to sell. Their supply of stock will provide resistance against further upward movement.

On the other hand, a support level forms under a stock when it approaches a previous area of heavy trading. People shrewd enough to sell at 20 in the last instance may want to repurchase the stock when it drops back to 16, particularly if this was an area of large turnover earlier. Other buyers who missed the rise to 20 might also go in at this point, helping put a floor under the stock.

Relative strength is another tool popular among contemporary technicians. Stocks are bought that are performing better than the market, while those that are performing worse are weeded out. Alternatively, price-volume systems are used with relative strength or as independent indicators. Stocks moving up on high volume are considered to be in a strong uptrend, with the converse also applying.

Finally, filter techniques are used when a stock appears to be reversing a trend. If other indicators show that an advance is ending and a stock declines a further 10 percent, it may be sold; or if the indicators show that an advance is beginning and the stock rises 10 percent, it may be purchased. The amount of the movement—the filter—will be determined by the technician in conjunction with his other tools.

Although the technician's information has multiplied almost exponentially with the advent of the computer, the basic problem remains. To quote Joseph Granville again, while the "indicators may be crystal clear in definition and theory, they often break down and render false signals."[6] In practice, perfectly symmetrical formations are extremely rare. Frequently, as I have indicated, patterns are so complex that even leading chartists may disagree about their interpretation. And the level of static surrounding the actual market movements is often so intense that the numerous indicators can flash red, yellow, and green all at the same time.

"There is nothing wrong with the charts, only the chartists"— so an old Wall Street saying goes. Maybe so, but as we can see, there is little doubt that an extremely high degree of interpretive capability is required of anybody willing to undertake the task.

To compound the problem, many wolves disguised in technician's clothing await the tyro. A friend of mine, an office manager with one of the brokerage giants, recalls how the firm's own commodity technicians would have dozens of managed accounts buy wheat or soybeans once they believed they had spotted definite breakouts. Because the firm followed the prudent principle of "cutting your losses and letting profits ride," a stop-loss order* was placed for each account 3 or 4 cents under the market in the commodity, protecting that customer. Wheat would be bought at $3.08, for example, with a stop-loss placed at $3.04. Accordingly, if the new trend proved false, the client would sell at only a small loss.

This was fine in theory. In practice, the wolves were also astute technicians and could determine the levels of the stop-loss orders set by the firms. By selling short, they forced the price down to this point (in our case, $3.04), triggering a rash of sell orders, all at market.† The resultant unloading invariably dropped the price enough for the wolves to buy back at a profit. After being ravaged by this pack a

---

*The stock is sold automatically when it falls to a predetermined price.

†To be sold at whatever price can be received; if there are few buyers, the decline can be significant.

number of times, the firm's technicians adopted more circumspect stop-loss procedures.

The Technician's Moment of Truth

Technical analysis is widespread on Wall Street, and the daily market commentaries in most newspapers are liberally sprinkled with its jargon. While fundamental research has a greater overall following, many a fundamentalist sneaks "a peek at the charts" before making a final buy or sell decision. Thus, there was considerable consternation among the many believers in the technical school when, in the past two decades, academic research began to demonstrate that no trends, tides, or waves could be shown to actually exist. Technical analysis, the academic findings strongly intimated, had no basis in fact.

To the technician, indeed to most financial readers, such findings seemed implausible. We can all see at a glance that stock charts show clearly discernible patterns. The professors, however, provided some extremely convincing evidence that seeing does not always warrant believing.

The first findings that price movements were random—that they displayed no predictable pattern of movement—emerged at the turn of the century. Louis Bachelier, a brilliant French mathematics student, presented such evidence in his doctoral dissertation, written under the supervision of the internationally famous mathematician Jules Henri Poincaré.[7] Bachelier's work, which dealt with commodity prices and government bonds, concluded that past price movements could not be used to predict future changes. This work lay dormant for sixty years, until financial researchers rediscovered it in 1960.

About the same time other academicians had embarked on the same course. One early study showed that randomly chosen series of numbers, when plotted on a chart, closely resembled actual patterns of stock price action.[8] Another found that stock price fluctuations were remarkably similar to Brownian motion, the random movements of microscopic particles suspended in fluids.[9]

A good many researchers tested the proposition that stocks move in discernible trends. Important work was conducted by Arnold Moore in 1964,[10] Clive Granger and Oskar Morgenstern in 1963,[11] and Eugene Fama in 1965.[12] Granger and Morgenstern used the advanced new statistical technique of spectral analysis. Their data base included seven hundred weeks of price information for various industries in the 1939–61 period as well as the Standard & Poor's and Dow-Jones indices between 1915 and 1961. Eugene Fama analyzed the price movements of thirty stocks in the Dow-Jones averages for intervals of one to fourteen days over a five-year period.

All the studies demonstrated that future price movements cannot be predicted from past changes. Without exception, the findings indicated randomness in price—day to day, week to week, even month to month. A new hypothesis, called random walk by its proponents, grew out of the work.

The random walk hypothesis states that past price and volume statistics do not contain any information by themselves that will allow the investor to obtain results superior to those he would achieve by simply buying and holding securities. The theory thus maintains that technical analysis is valueless as a forecasting method. No matter how convinced the technician is about the market's or the stock's next move, he has no more chance of being right than he would have by tossing a coin. Statisticians tell us that when a true coin is tossed, even if it comes up heads a dozen times in a row, there is still a fifty-fifty chance that it will come up tails on the next throw. Or, in market terms, if a stock closes higher for a dozen days in a row, the next day the stock has a fifty-fifty chance of closing down. An overwhelming body of statistical research has now been developed refuting the central thesis of the technical school: that markets display major trends that can be readily identified.*

The Computer Dreadnought

If you have met technicians, you know that most are tough and grizzled veterans who have been through many a market campaign. They are not about to be told by a bunch of computer-worshiping Ph.D.'s, some barely approaching thirty, that they are obsolete.

The technicians could fall back on a second line of defense, and

---

*This is only the first stage of the random walk hypothesis. A more comprehensive form with far broader implications to the investor will be presented in the next chapter.

they did. Although the new research indicated overall randomness, they said, there could be useful directions in price changes within a given period, such as week to week or month to month, which would appear clear only when selected data, such as reversal patterns, were used.

The technicians challenged the academics to test their systems directly rather than by merely studying overall price movements. This proved to be a mistake. By the beginning of the 1970s, computerized research had become very stylish in academe. The technicians were met by a wave of peach-fuzzed youths armed with spanking-new computers. The trustworthy technical tools were systematically dissected by the academics and just as systematically relegated to the scrap heap.

A number of earlier tests were conducted on various filter systems, ranging in size from 1 to 50 percent.[13] After commissions were deducted, none of the systems worked successfully.

Spurred on by their success, the academics approached the untouchable itself—the formidable Dow theory. Under merciless computer examination, peaks, valleys, support, and resistance levels all melted away. Price action proved random after both buy and sell signals. Even the double and triple peaks and valleys—the Maginot Line of the theory—gave no clearer signals.

Price-volume systems held up no better.[14] The size of neither price nor volume changes appeared to influence the direction of future price movements. Stocks moving up on high volume were just as likely to decline in the next trading period, and stocks going down in heavy trading might as likely reverse course. Relative strength met the same fate. All in all, the findings were enough to make many a chartist want to slink into the East River.

Nothing remained. One ambitious project analyzed 540 stocks trading on the New York Stock Exchange over a five-year period. In a most unsportsmanlike gesture, the academics programmed their computer to recognize thirty-two of the most commonly used patterns—including head and shoulders formations, and double and triple tops and bottoms—and to act on the information as a chartist would. The computer would sell, for example, if the right shoulder broke through the neckline of a head and shoulders formation, or buy if the market pushed higher through a triple top. When the results were measured, no correlation was found between the buy and sell signals and subsequent price movements.[15]

The computer *Wunderkind* had won again. Tests had shown conclusively that the technician's charting techniques did not result in superior returns.

The evidence supporting the random walk hypothesis is voluminous and still expanding. Although some research has indicated that a number of marginally profitable trading rules do work, they all involve substantial brokerage charges. Once these are deducted, the trader will have lost all his expected profits, sometimes more.

Every technician I know claims that his particular system works, of course. And he will say that in the end, it is his judgment that is important in determining which of the dozens of available tools to use and what emphasis to put on each. To examine this assertion, an infinite number of tests would have to be devised. But in the previous chapter, we saw the caliber of practitioners' judgments at crucial market turning points, as well as the overall record of professional performance—not particularly supportive of their claims. To the best of my knowledge, nothing has been forthcoming from the technicians, either in theory or in practice, that disputes the academic evidence.

To me, the case made for random walk is convincing to this point. Still, it was strange how, near the bottom of the 1974 market, as prices cascaded four or five points a day, I was jolted momentarily when a leading technician said the Dow would drop another two hundred points—though I was convinced that a sharp recovery was imminent. Perhaps there is a part in all of us reserved for the faith healer, the Ouija board, or the technician. It was also interesting to see how, when the market had rallied three hundred points, this prominent oracle managed to retain his aura with the financial press. (He was looking for another three-hundred-point advance this time.)

Curiously, in spite of the fact that the major tenets of technical analysis had been continuously refuted for a period of almost two decades, chartists continue to flourish, boasting of their successes and forgetting their equally numerous bad calls as though their doctrines had never been challenged. In fact, their importance and status has been increasing on Wall Street in recent years, which brings us back to Joe Granville again.

Despite his recent string of first-rate calls, is he really a Messiah who has discovered techniques that will stand up in markets permanently? Hardly. When I asked him about his record in the early 1970's, when we were both guests on the "David Susskind Show" in

June 1980, he admitted good-naturedly that it was bad—so bad that he had left the stock market entirely, turning instead to writing a book entitled *How to Win at Bingo* (to his credit, it sold 500,000 copies). More recently, even with his string of good market calls, his individual stock selections have fared worse than the market. Though Joe has a fine sense of humor and is a marvelously entertaining speaker (accompanied by his ventriloquist's dummy and a pet chimpanzee, and with a gaggle of vaudeville routines), chances are he'll cost a lot of people large amounts of money before he bows out from the market stage.

And this gives us the first key to a pattern we will find repeated in the chapters ahead. Theories in the end rest far less squarely on facts than on the willingness of their followers to believe that they work. Facts that seem to support the theory are pressed forward, while other, damaging evidence often slips by.

Einstein said it all succinctly decades ago: "The theory shapes the observations."

CHAPTER THREE

Fundamental Analysis— The Slippery Rock

In the last chapter we looked at the case made by the technical analyst and found it wanting. Neither his charts nor his numerous other indicators prove to have any value when subjected to statistical measurement. Some academic researchers have cheerfully suggested that the technician broaden his indicators to include the signs of the zodiac or tea-leaf reading, which, the professors say, are at least as scientific.

Now let's examine fundamental analysis, the method practiced by the great preponderance of bank trust departments, pension funds, mutual funds, and investment advisors, as well as by most brokers. As we have already seen, this school states that the value of a company can be determined through a rigorous analysis of its sales, earnings, dividend prospects, financial strength, competitive position, and other related measures. To arrive at the proper worth of a stock, the analyst synthesizes and weighs all relevant information, often supporting his work with actual visits to senior company management.

The fundamentalist believes that stock prices will often diverge sharply from intrinsic value. His methods allow him to search out worth, buying solid companies that are underpriced and selling those overvalued. The market, he thinks, must eventually recognize the error of its ways and correct them.

To use a simple but appropriate analogy: value for the fundamentalist is like an anchor to which a boat is moored by a long line. Like the boat, price moves respond to the prevailing market winds. Often it is blown far in one direction, only shortly thereafter to be tossed as far in the opposite. Knowing where the anchor lies allows the investor to profit from the various gusts.

The fundamentalist does not claim to know exactly where the anchor rests; even the best analysis can only find its approximate location. But the anchor nevertheless is there, and because it is, the skillful practitioner can benefit from the prevailing market winds time and again.

Fundamental theory is considered to be far more sophisticated than its technical sibling because the former draws on the advanced techniques of accounting, business, and economics. Not unexpectedly, then, it has always been the currency of the investment establishment. All the same, as we shall see, it is a currency that has depreciated steadily in recent years.

The Intrinsic Value Theory

Research has demonstrated that earnings and dividends are the most important determinants of stock prices over time. The core of fundamental analysis is thus the development of techniques that will estimate these factors accurately. One of the most exacting methods of establishing a stock's value, called the intrinsic value theory, was introduced in the late 1930s by John Burr Williams.[1] According to the rational economic school that Williams represents, the investor values a stock in terms of what he expects to receive from it over time. Williams holds that the price of a stock is worth the present value of its anticipated dividends. He believes that if earnings could be projected and from them the dividends, one could derive a precise estimate of worth.

To do this, he used a method known as discounting. A payment received a year from now is worth less than one received today, since you could invest the current payment and have it with interest twelve months hence. Likewise, a payment two years from now is worth less by the interest for this time span, and so on. Discounting the stream of dividends by the appropriate rate of return, the analyst arrives at the current value of a stock.* All very neat and precise, but not very representative of how investors value stock—at least on this planet.

Williams's work was extended by Nicholas Molodovsky, the late editor of the *Financial Analysts Journal.* Molodovsky recognized that security analysts are more comfortable estimating earnings and then projecting the proportion paid out in dividends. The Molodovsky formula is found below.†

Lest you think that this is the last word on the subject, more complex equations have been developed to adjust for changes in the rate of earnings growth during different time periods. One formula solves for four separate growth rates for the company and a final rate of residual growth once the company matures.‡

---

*Williams's calculations begin with the following formula, which requires only some knowledge of high school algebra to understand:

$$\frac{D_1}{1 + R}$$

In this formula, D_1 is the dividend in the first year, and R is the rate of return the investor wants in order to buy the stock. This return includes not only interest, normally the going rate on good long-term bonds, but also an added sum to compensate for the greater riskiness of the equity investment. The formula to derive the present value (V) of all dividends is written as follows, with $D_2/(1+R)^2$ the current value of the second year's dividends, and so on to the last dividend, n years out:

$$V = \frac{D_1}{1+R} + \frac{D_2}{(1+R)^2} + \frac{D_3}{(1+R)^3} + \cdots + \frac{D_n}{(1+R)^n}$$

In this example, if D is $2.00, R is 10 percent, and dividends increase 11 percent a year for the first three years, the present value of these dividends would be calculated as follows:

$$\frac{\$2.00}{1+.10} + \frac{\$2.22}{(1+.10)^2} + \frac{\$2.46}{(1+.10)^3} = \$1.82 + \$1.83 + \$1.85 = \$5.50$$

To get the current worth of the stock, one would discount this stream over the company's expected life.

†The Molodovsky formula is:

$$V = \frac{E_1P}{1 + R} + \frac{E_2P}{(1 + R)^2} + \frac{E_3P}{(1 + R)^3} + \cdots + \frac{E_nP}{(1 + R)^n}$$

Where E is the earnings, P is the percentage paid out in dividends, and R is the rate of return in each year.

‡Intrinsic value $= \dfrac{e_0(1 + g_1)p}{1 + r} + \dfrac{e_0(1 + g_1)^2p}{(1 + r)^2} + \cdots + \dfrac{e_0(1 + g_1)^{n_1}p}{(1 + r)^{n_1}} +$

$\dfrac{e_0(1 + g_1)^{n_1}(1 + g_2)p}{(1 + r)^{n_1+1}} + \cdots + \dfrac{e_0(1 + g_1)^{n_1}(1 + g_2)^{n_2}p}{(1 + r)^{n_1+n_2}} +$

$\dfrac{e_0(1 + g_1)^{n_1}(1 + g_2)^{n_2}(1 + g_3)p}{(1 + r)^{n_1+n_2+1}} + \cdots + \dfrac{e_0(1 + g_1)^{n_1}(1 + g_2)^{n_2}(1 + g_3)^{n_3}p}{(1 + r)^{n_1+n_2+n_3}} +$

$\dfrac{e_0(1 + g_1)^{n_1}(1 + g_2)^{n_2}(1 + g_3)^{n_3}(1 + g_4)p}{(1 + r)^{n_1+n_2+n_3+1}} + \cdots$

Before you close this book, deciding it's not for you, let me say that I am demonstrating the formulas only to show what hasn't worked, *not* what has. As we shall see, this dose of castor oil not only won't help you, but may prove positively harmful to your investment health.

There is nothing wrong with the formulas themselves. In fact, if we could see into the future with perfect clarity, they would be very useful. And for those of us who find algebra distasteful, I am sure that given our current nurturing of graduate students, we could find any number willing to do the calculations for us at the going minimum wage.

No, the real problem is that forecasting the future has always proved perilous. Just how perilous even one year ahead will be seen later. Yet the models call for projections ten to twenty years out or more, not only for earnings but also for the growth rate of dividends and the discount rate. These estimates, as chapters 5 and 7 will detail, are implanted in quicksand. While the formulas appear "scientific," thanks to their mathematical complexity, a dangerous false precision is built into them, which the theorists, concentrating on the elegance of the equations, often seem to forget.

In his book *Investments: New Analytic Techniques,* [2] Professor J. Peter Williamson clearly demonstrates the problem in his valuation procedure for IBM. Using a formula similar to the last of the three just given, he initially forecast an earnings increase of 16 percent for ten years and 2 percent thereafter, and applied a 7 percent discount rate and a 40 percent dividend payout ratio. These figures gave him a value of $173, about half the then-current market price (1968). Extending the 16 percent growth rate to twenty years, he got a value of $433, well above the market price. When he changed the discount rate to 10 percent, the value dropped to $206, again well under the market. Modifications resulted in other major price variations.

As intricate and impressive as a valuation formula may appear, it is only the frame housing the forecasting engine. If you do not have an engine that can reliably and continuously predict the complex variables of earnings, dividend payout, and rate of return, the frame

$$+ \frac{e_0(1 + g_1)^{n_1}(1 + g_2)^{n_2}(1 + g_3)^{n_3}(1 + g_4)^{n_4}p}{(1 + r)^{n_1 + n_2 + n_3 + n_4}} +$$

$$\frac{e_0(1 + g_1)^{n_1}(1 + g_2)^{n_2}(1 + g_3)^{n_3}(1 + g_4)^{n_4}(1 + g_5)p}{(r - g_5)(1 + r)^{n_1 + n_2 + n_3 + n_4}} .$$

is of no practical use. More likely it is dangerous. As Williamson's example illustrated, investors can crank any numbers into the equation that their current mood dictates and wind up with the price they want.

Sketches have been found in a notebook of Leonardo da Vinci's for an aircraft that aeronautical engineers believe might well have been airworthy. Not having a workable engine, Leonardo did not proceed further—an example perhaps lost on some of the present-day model builders.

The Bible of Wall Street

Although fundamental analysis has had its share of abstract theoreticians, it also has had some eminently practical ones. Next, we'll look briefly at some of the major tenets of security analysis, first to become more familiar with its principles and then to explore various problems that may preclude their successful implementation. The background here is important to the investment strategy that will be evolved in Part III.

The most systematic work in the field is the 778-page epic *Security Analysis,* by Benjamin Graham and David Dodd, first published in 1934 and revised three times subsequently.[3] This book has been called the bible of fundamental practitioners, and for decades Graham has been regarded as the leading prophet.

In the 1920s, relying on his own valuation techniques, Graham became a highly successful portfolio manager—so much so that he attracted the eye of Bernard Baruch, who offered him the chance to become his junior partner. Graham declined, having made $600,000 the previous year on his own. However, the year was 1929, and Graham's clients suffered in the Crash like everybody else. But he managed to keep them solvent, and over the next several decades he consistently compiled a creditable investment record.

Benjamin Graham was a classical scholar, fluent in Greek, Latin, German, and Spanish. But his first love was investment theory, and he devoted more than forty years to teaching it, first at Columbia and later at UCLA. One of his early students was a young academic, David Dodd, who eventually became his coauthor.[4]

Graham's investment techniques stress the preservation of capital. Investors are advised to keep between 25 and 75 percent of their capital (depending on their personal circumstances) in high-grade bonds, bank accounts, and other assets that were riskless in his time. The remainder can be invested in well-diversified portfolios of ten to thirty stocks. Each company selected has to be large, prominent, and conservatively financed, with a long record of continuous dividend payments. Stocks should always be bought by applying stringent valuation formulas, which normally eliminate new issues, concept stocks,* and growth stocks. In *Security Analysis* rigorous investment procedures are laid out to determine intrinsic value. Because of the difficulty of pinpointing real worth precisely, Graham always insisted on an "adequate" margin of safety as a protective cushion in his calculations. His rules were so stern that some fund managers only half-jokingly spoke of him as the reincarnation of an eighteenth-century Yankee businessman—there wasn't an ounce of speculation in him.

Assessing Earning Power

The principal method of appraising stocks according to Graham and Dodd is through the determination of earning power. The investor should measure the record of a company over an extensive period, usually seven to ten years, to gauge its basic profitability. Using its financial record and supporting data, he should meticulously analyze its earnings and dividend trends, financial strength, debt structure, depreciation reserves, bank lines of credit, backlogs, capital spending plans, and other relevant information. Qualitative factors such as the growth prospects of the company, the strength of its management, its position in its industry, and product development should also be assessed. After thorough analysis, he will be in a position to work out conservative projections of future earning power.

Graham and Dodd devote a full section to accounting, some 175 pages in all. It is essential that the analyst understand numerous accounting conventions that can significantly overstate or understate earnings. To get as accurate a picture as possible of the actual operat-

*Stocks in a company that may or may not have a financial record but definitely has a "good story to tell" that promises an outstanding future.

ing profit, adjustments must be made for each accounting item that will distort earnings.*

The authors' preoccupation with accounting principles is not simply an obsession. "Creative" accounting has always been an exceptional tool in the hands of the adroit corporate manipulator. In the go-go market of 1967–68, two computer leasing firms, Data Processing & Financial General and Levin-Townsend, both traded at 40 times earnings, almost triple the average ratio of the S&P 500, thanks to their rapidly growing earnings, produced solely by clever accounting. When more conservative reporting policies were adopted, their earnings disappeared entirely, and both dropped 90 percent from their highs. And University Computing, a Dallas-based computer service company of the era, topped even this, trading as high as 118 times accounting-manufactured earnings before plummeting 98 percent.

Graham and Dodd recommended that security analysts use a fairly extensive list of financial ratios to measure a company's performance. One of the more important ones is the return on equity —the aftertax profit divided by net worth.† Another is pretax return on sales.‡ While there are, of course, variations from industry to industry, the higher and more stable these ratios, the better regarded the firm. The two ratios will range from 10 or 12 percent for the average company to as high as 20 or even 30 percent for the more spectacular growth stocks.

A number of important ratios deal with financial strength. The current ratio§ is one of the most commonly followed. For most companies, a current ratio of 2 to 1 or better is considered sound, although this too will vary from industry to industry.

Other ratios will be used to determine how capable a company is of meeting its debts, since in bad times a high debt structure can lead to default and possible bankruptcy. A commonly used rule of thumb for industrial concerns is that common shares should represent at least 50 percent of the capital structure, which is the combined value of its common stock, preferred stock, and bonds.

---

*For example, a one-time gain from the sale of a plant or land must be excluded from that year's operating income.

†The value of all common stock and retained earnings. This ratio calculates the owners' (common stock holders) capital in the business.

‡Income before taxes as a percentage of sales.

§The ratio of current assets to current liabilities. This ratio determines how able the company is to pay its near-term debts—those due in a year or less.

After satisfying himself as to the accounting, financial strength, and profitability of a business, the analyst, Graham and Dodd advise, should project trends ahead for seven to ten years. To do so, averages should be taken of past sales and earnings figures, with conservative projections into the future made from these. The emphasis is placed on the past record of earnings and whether it can continue rather than on whether the company can expand rapidly.

Security Analysis lays out four essential components of common stock evaluation, repeatedly cautioning the practitioner to tie the first three firmly into the record of the past:

1. Expected future earnings
2. Expected future dividends
3. A method for valuing expected earnings
4. The asset value

Once average future earnings are estimated, an evaluative measure is used to establish what the price should be. The price/earnings (or P/E) ratio is the yardstick investors most commonly use to determine price. It is simply the current price divided by earnings per share. If a stock is trading at 10, earned $1.00 last year, and is expected to earn $1.25 this year, it is said to be trading at a price/earnings ratio of 10 on the latest full year's earnings and at 8 on the anticipated earnings for the current year. The higher the P/E ratio, the more favorable the company's prospects are believed to be, while the lower the multiple the more lackluster its anticipated future.

A cardinal conviction of Graham and Dodd's is that investors tend to overreact to near-term prospects—to overprice companies for which these are favorable and underprice those for which they are poorer. The formulas establish multipliers that are designed to keep the disparity between P/E's for companies with differing outlooks on a tight leash, as all too often the forecasts have proven wrong. For example, in the 1955 edition of *The Intelligent Investor,* a book written by Benjamin Graham for individual investors,[5] the spread between stocks with better and poorer outlooks was 8 to 20. Companies with average prospects were given a multiplier of 12. Although the P/E ratios have changed with changing market conditions over the years, the same principle has always been maintained.

Other Valuation Techniques

Security Analysis provides a second method of evaluating stocks—
that of ferreting out companies trading at a significant discount to
their book or net asset value.* Again, to adopt this approach, the
student must be steeped in the intricacies of accounting. Graham and
Dodd were fascinated by the fact that the net asset or book value is
often the most important factor in determining the worth of a private
company, but that once the firm becomes public, the market shifts
its focus dramatically, concentrating almost exclusively on earnings
instead. Various formulas are provided for the investor to take advantage of companies selling under book.

In recent years, the basic methods of security analysis have been
extended by other theorists to include computer techniques and
various forms of economic forecasting. One approach relying on the
computer is called probabilistic forecasting. The analyst's uncertainties about variables in his estimates can be quantified into probabilities. For example, if the price of lead is essential in calculating a
mining company's earnings, the practitioner can make a number of
calculations of demand under varying sets of industry conditions for
this commodity, and assign probabilities that each price will occur.
From these data, both a range of earnings estimates and the likelihood that each will occur can be projected.

Conditional forecasts allow the analyst to tie his estimates into
those of the economist. Taking the economist's model of GNP,
capital spending, disposable income, level of interest rates, and other
inputs, the analyst forecasts sales and earnings at different levels of
economic activity. Using the computer, projections are made of how
a company should fare at various stages of the industry and general
economic cycles. Such advanced techniques allow the analyst to
delineate his individual company projections more sharply.[6]

Although all fundamental analysis is derived from the same
tree, one branch, the growth school, has dominated it for considerable periods. This branch perplexed Graham and Dodd. As they write
in *Security Analysis,* "We are haunted as it were by the spectre of

---

*The value of the common stock after deducting all liabilities and preferred shares.
Usually this is calculated per common share by dividing the total by the number of shares
outstanding.

growth stocks—by the question of how best to deal with them in the
context of our own basic principles." Let's face this specter next.

An American Dream

Had someone put $10,000 into Haloid-Xerox in 1960, the year the
first plain paper copier, the 914, was introduced, the investment
would have been worth $16.5 million a decade later. McDonald's
earnings increased several thousand times in the 1961–66 period, and
then, more demurely, quadrupled again by 1971, the year of its eight
billionth hamburger. Anyone astute enough to buy McDonald's
stock in 1965, when it went public, would have made fortyfold his
money in the next seven years. An investor who plunked $2,750 into
Thomas J. Watson's Computing and Tabulating Company in 1914
would have had over $20 million in IBM stock by the beginning of
the 1970s. It is hardly surprising, then, with our industry based as
it is in science and invention and their by-products of rapid expansion and sudden change, that the growth school has so often ruled
fundamental analysis.

American history is full of stories of investors who seized dynamic new opportunities and made fortunes. In 1910 a leading
banker, unable to control his laughter, walked out of a meeting after
an auto manufacturer told him that the industry would someday
produce half a million cars. By 1929 almost six million were streaming
off the assembly lines. At the turn of the century, someone believing
in the growth of mass merchandising and buying Sears would have
made eleven thousand times his money by 1950. And so it goes.

The tradition of Xerox, McDonald's, General Motors, and
Sears is deeply rooted American. Participating in new, potentially
vast enterprises produces an exciting sense of communion with the
Edisons, Watsons, Carnegies, and Fords, and more important, a
chance to reap spectacular gains by our foresight. In an age when the
opportunities for the individual entrepreneurs are progressively diminished by the large, impersonal corporations, it is a vision hard not
to follow.

The growth analyst sharply hones his analytical tools to attempt
to pinpoint those companies that can expect rapid and stable expansion. Like his more conservative Graham and Dodd counterparts, he

takes the past record as his starting point, but his emphasis lies on the future. Companies are sought out that he believes will continue to have superior profit margins and earn above-average returns on equity. A growth company should be far less affected by economic uncertainties and should produce rising earnings through both inflationary and recessionary conditions, when many firms falter.

Growth stock analysis must accurately spotlight future trends: how well a new line of computers will do for Digital Equipment, how many SX-70 cameras Polaroid will sell, how big a market exists for a new drug of Upjohn's. Extensive analysis goes into determining product growth, market share, development of competition, maintenance of profit margins, and dozens of other important factors affecting growth rates. Growth stocks have traditionally traded at lofty multiples—often two, three, four, or even more times the P/E ratios of their more pedestrian compeers—which makes an error in projections fatal.

A growth company is believed to have a remarkable degree of control over its destiny. It normally has a solidly entrenched position in a large and rapidly expanding market. Sometimes its muscle comes from patent protection, as with the large ethical drug companies (or in the recent past with Xerox and Polaroid); sometimes from a superb and hard-to-duplicate marketing force, as in the case of Avon ("which never had a *product,*" as one money manager remarked with grudging admiration, "that couldn't be duplicated in a garage"); and sometimes from an imaginative adaptation of production and marketing techniques long standard in manufacturing to a service industry, as is true of McDonald's.

Growth companies have excellent managements, some with the vision to create entirely new markets. Xerox's management foresaw the importance of dry copying and correctly predicted that its revenues would grow from $30 million in 1960 to $1 billion ten years later. On the other hand, Sperry Rand, the original developer of the computer, estimated a total market of less than half a dozen or so data processors and was left in the dust by IBM.

The growth stock analyst must thoroughly analyze the factors contributing to growth. Can the company continue to control both its costs and its sales prices? What prohibits destructive competition from entering the marketplace? How labor-intensive is it? (Normally, a growth company is not.) Are its raw materials abundant and a small part of the overall selling price? (A change in the price of steel will affect Chrysler much more than a higher transistor price will affect IBM.)

Growth stocks are often self-financing—that is, their profitability is high and stable enough to pay for a good part if not all of the plant and equipment required for rapid expansion. A fast-growing company that can generate the bulk of the funds it needs internally is of course far more desirable than one that must rely heavily on outside borrowing or on the sale of common stock, which would dilute the present shareholders' equity. The higher the return on capital, the more likely the firm will finance its own growth.

As in the case of more basic fundamental analysis, the tenets of growth stock investing are varied and extensive. But once again, unfortunately, a system that appears eminently sensible in theory has proved exceptionally refractory in practice.

Why Don't They Work?

To judge from the record presented in chapter 1, fundamental research has had no greater success than technical analysis. However, the whys are considerably more bewildering because the fundamental school seems to build on much more solid underpinnings.

Graham and Dodd, always skeptical of growth techniques, have given some good reasons why this branch of analysis may not work. The first lies in the nature of the analysis itself. While conceding value analysis is always difficult, they believe that a forecast based on the clearly measurable earnings power of the past is more secure than one built on growth trends extrapolated into the future. Such projections, they repeatedly warn, are fraught with danger. Earnings forecasts even for prime growth companies can be very chancy. Then, too, for every real growth stock there are many that appear to be but are not.*

The second problem with growth investing is that even if the analysis proves accurate, there is still the question of what multiple should be used to evaluate earnings. The record of the Kidder, Peabody Top 50 in figure 11 illustrates as much. The Top 50 are the fifty favorite stocks on the New York Stock Exchange as determined by their P/E ratios.† A comparison of this index with the Standard

*For details, see chapter 8.
†In computing the table, Kidder excludes companies with nominal earnings.

& Poor's 500 from 1973 to the end of 1980 is enlightening: the P/E's of the Top 50 dropped 50 percent—from ratios averaging more than 3 times the S&P to 1.5 times before moving up again.* Investors had simply changed their minds about what to pay for the prime growth stocks. The evaluation problem, then, appears to be just as difficult as the forecasting problem. High P/E's can be subject to drastic revisions as market moods change.

Figure 11.
Relative price/earnings ratios of the Kidder Peabody Top 50.

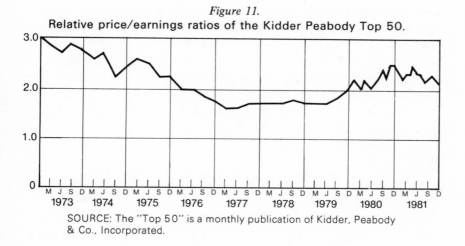

SOURCE: The "Top 50" is a monthly publication of Kidder, Peabody & Co., Incorporated.

Now let's turn to a more troublesome question: If the scenario described in the first chapter is accurate, why have the proponents of even the more basic Graham and Dodd model not fared better? First, despite Graham's admonitions, one of his most important rules has been downgraded or disregarded entirely in practice. Standard security analysis has increasingly emphasized correctly estimating near-term company conditions, such as sales and earnings, while continually downplaying other important fundamental factors.† Thus, forecasting, with the same inherent dangers indicated previously, also plays an overly important role in more basic fundamental analysis as it is practiced today. Perhaps this is the reason Graham once said he might be one of the most read and most forgotten men on Wall Street.

*The stocks in the Top 50 change every month; the original Top 50 from 1972 have now declined even more.

†Among such other criteria, price/earnings ratios, book value, yield, and financial strength.

Second, although certain issues may appear to be substantially undervalued, there is no guarantee that the market will recognize this to be so. If it doesn't see this as the case, the stocks may continue to trade at low prices for many years to come.

A third reason was given by one of Graham's most successful followers, Warren Buffett, who accumulated some $75 million in the 1960s and then proved canny enough to get out near the market top and stay out. Buffett said that his success came from a consistent application of fundamentals that "others cavalierly disregarded."[7]

But were many of these fundamentals in fact "cavalierly disregarded"? Or were there instead very important problems with the methods that led to their abandonment, most often involuntarily, by their adherents? Part II will examine this important question—central to the poor professional record—in some detail.

Meanwhile, let's look at another device born of mixed fundamental and technical lineage—market timing.

Market Timing—Myth or Reality?

A fascinating aspect of markets is how ideas that have fallen into wide disrepute can be periodically recycled, repackaged, and reintroduced as entirely new products. A good example is the current resurrection of market timing. The essence of the theory, as the name implies, is to time purchases and sales according to the phase of the market.

If this could actually be done, the rewards would be high. In the past decade, catching the major swings would have more than tripled the results of simply buying and holding the S&P 500 over the period.

One professional, defending the resurgence of the theory, wrote that "1973 was a bad year for those who doubted the value of market timing." He then goes on to give the following incisive advice: "In general, the strategy should be to buy and hold good long-term stocks when they are going up, and let someone else hold them when they are going down." More simply stated, buy low and sell high—a principle not unknown to Mesopotamian merchants some five millennia earlier. Investment placebo or not, the advice is currently well heeded.

Market timing has become extremely popular among professional money managers and their clients. A study by Leuthold Associates, the Minneapolis-based publisher of a respected advisory service, found that 168 firms managing $88 billion (42 percent of all pension fund assets) claimed to "make some use of market timing."[8] And a number of the nation's major banks, including Morgan Guaranty, Manufacturers Hanover, Chase Manhattan, Irving Trust, and Crocker National, have indicated that they have used the procedure.

Their consistent underperformance of the market averages in recent years has led some institutions to the path after a great deal of soul-searching. Others have set their feet on the road less hesitantly. In the words of one candid money manager: "Sure, we're telling our clients we're prepared to use market timing. What the hell else can we tell them after 1973–74?"[9]

As noted, market timing is, in practice, a hybrid of fundamental and technical ingredients, blending business analysis and technical projections. Market timers watch such economic conditions as the trend and level of interest rates, the degree and direction of business activity, corporate profits, and industrial production. If, for example, inflation is decelerating, interest rates have peaked and are edging down, and employment is beginning to pick up after a decline, economic factors are considered very favorable. And if simultaneously technical patterns are encouraging, a buy signal has been given—one with pennants flying and bands marching, at that. On the other hand, if interest rates are ominously moving higher, business is declining, and corporate profitability and employment are beginning to slip, while technical patterns look menacing, we know it is time to sell. What could be simpler?

Unfortunately, in the real world, market movements give dozens of signals, all madly flashing buy, sell, and hold at once. To further complicate the situation, institutions as a group watch the same leading technicians (Joe Granville, Robert Farrell, Edson Gould, Eliot Janeway, and a handful of others) and the same indicators as well as each other. Thus, the major money managers are all likely to react to the same information at about the same time. Since they currently control a large percentage of all stock trading, market timing, if it is widely practiced, may create a self-fulfilling prophecy serving to accentuate market swings.

Various academic and institutional studies of market timing

have indicated the failure of the method. William Sharpe, a leading academic researcher, found that a money manager who wishes to market-time profitably must be right three times out of four after commissions and advisory costs,[10] something our chart in chapter 1 shows has not happened. Another major study, by Merrill Lynch, found that "the great majority of funds lose money as a result of their timing efforts, and when the effects of commission costs are included, virtually everyone loses money."

Once again, as we saw in the last chapter, the evolution and acceptance of widely popular investment theory seems to have little to do with the underlying realities.

A Purposeful Random Walk

If fundamentalists are perplexed about why results aren't better, the academics certainly are not. Starting in the past decade, they progressively began to shift their research firepower from the technical to the fundamental front. Extensive studies were made of the performance of large groups of mutual funds, the great majority of which subscribe to security analysis. Evidence began to mount that the funds did no better than the market. Michael Jensen, for example, measured the record of 155 mutual funds between 1945 and 1964, adjusting for the fact that some were more and others less risky than the market as a whole,* and found that only 43 of 115 funds outperformed it after commissions.[11]

In 1970 Friend, Blume, and Crockett of the Wharton School completed the most comprehensive study of mutual funds yet

---

*Techniques have been developed by financial academics to measure the volatility of a single stock or a portfolio against the market (normally an index like the S&P 500) over a period of time. From these correlations, predictions of future movements relative to the market can be made. Such past correlations are claimed to have useful predictive value. Beta is a commonly used measure of volatility. The market is considered to have a Beta coefficient of 1. Stocks or portfolios with a higher coefficient are more volatile than the market, while those with a lower one are less so. Thus, a portfolio with a Beta coefficient of 2 should move, on the average, about twice as far as the market in either direction, while one with a coefficient of 0.5 should show about half the movement of the market. While some adjustment for the relative riskiness of different portfolios of stocks is necessary in order to measure them against either the market averages or one another over a period of time, the problem is that none of the risk adjustments introduced to date has any predictive value, which unfortunately makes them of no use for practical measurements. Too, the assumptions of investor behavior that these risk adjustments are based upon are far-fetched, as the evidence we shall view shortly will indicate.

made.[12] They measured 136 funds between January 1, 1960, and June 30, 1968, and found that the funds showed an average return of 10.7 percent annually. During the same time span, shares on the New York Stock Exchange averaged 12.4 percent annually.* The study was then extended to cover the year ending July 1969. For this period, the average fund decreased 3.8 percent, compared with a decrease of 3.3 percent for the value-weighted average of the Big Board stocks. Hardly comforting to those fund managers who present the picture of superior performance.

Academic analysis proved to be as unsparing of the fundamental practitioner's sensibilities as it had been of the technician's. Friend, Blume, and Crockett also established that if the degree of risk remains unchanged, there is no correlation between a fund's performance record in one period and its performance in another, dispatching the myth of the hot money manager. Funds in the top 10 percent in one period might be in the bottom 10 percent the next, or vice versa.

Other widely prevailing beliefs were treated as harshly. No link was found between portfolio turnover and subsequent performance. Rapid turnover does not improve results, but in fact seems to damage them slightly. And the idea that high sales charges are justified cannot be sustained. Any relationship between performance and commission charges (front-end loads,† as they are commonly called) appears to be mildly negative. No-load funds and funds with low sales charges perform marginally better. Finally, if the risk factor is held constant, there is little difference in the results of funds of various sizes. In sum, the report firmly concluded that no evidence exists that mutual funds can outperform the market.

To explain discoveries such as these, academic investigators proposed a revolutionary new hypothesis. Called at first the stronger form of the random walk theory, it has come to be known as the efficient-market hypothesis. It holds basically that competition between sophisticated and knowledgeable investors keeps stock prices about where they should be. This happens because all facts determining stock prices are analyzed by thousands of interested investors. Incoming information, such as a change in a company's earnings

---

*Value-weighting for the number of shares of each company outstanding (which gave far more emphasis to the changes of the larger companies), the increase was 9.9 percent.

†Those funds charging a commission ranging as high as 8¾ percent of principal on purchase. No-loads do not charge a front-end commission.

outlook or a dividend cut, is quickly digested and immediately reflected in the stock price. Like it or not, competition by so many investors, all seeking hidden values, makes stock prices reflect the best estimates of their real worth. Prices may not always be right, but they are unbiased, so if they are wrong, they are just as likely to be too high as too low.

Because the market is efficient, the theorists continue, investors should expect to receive only a fair return commensurate with the risk of purchasing a particular stock. Securities or portfolios with greater risk should normally provide larger rewards over time.

Since meaningful new information affecting the overall market and individual companies enters the marketplace unpredictably, prices react in a random manner. This is the real reason that charting and technical analysis do not work. Nobody knows what new inputs will enter the marketplace, whether they will be positive or negative or whether they will have a general impact or affect only a single company or industry.

According to the efficient-market hypothesis, it is most unlikely that any investor or his advisor will outrun the pack over time, regardless of method. The competition is just too keen. In fact, money managers who trade a good deal, trying to stay in front, will probably perform worse because of the high cost of commissions. As we have seen, the track record of professionals appears to confirm as much. Because the market is highly efficient, the theory goes on, the investor's best strategy is to buy and hold a portfolio bearing the degree of risk he desires.

The efficient-market hypothesis has much wider implications than the original random walk theory, which said only that investors would not benefit from technical analysis. The new argument effectively tears the very heart out of fundamental research—the detection of overvalued and undervalued issues. For if enough buyers and sellers have correctly evaluated and acted upon new information, such stocks will be very rare indeed.*

The theorists also admit that markets may not always be efficient for the stocks of smaller companies or for obscure convertibles or warrant issues, and that some extremely gifted individuals may

---

*Here the efficient-market theorists acknowledge a paradox. Since it is fundamental analysis that is largely responsible for keeping markets efficient, if enough practitioners believed the efficient-market hypothesis and stopped their analytic efforts, markets might well become inefficient.

divine major developments from public information. But these possibilities are considered extremely rare—financial albinos. For most publicly traded companies, the markets are believed to be highly efficient. Which means we cannot outsmart them.

Although they might wish to shoot one another on sight, the efficient-market adherents and the chartists share the same essential premise. James Lorie and Richard Brealey, stating the academic view, have written, "A startling idea—current prices reflect what is knowable."[13] Actually, what is startling is the similarity to Charles Dow's statement: "The market as a whole represents a serious, well-considered effort on the part of far-sighted and informed men to adjust prices to values such as exist or which are expected to exist in the not too remote future."[14] Or William Peter Hamilton's remark: "It cannot too often be said that the stock market reflects all everybody knows about the business of the country."[15] Once again the same basic thought leads to widely divergent market paths.

And Still More Tests!

The extensive measurements of the performance of mutual funds and other classes of money managed professionally provided support for the efficient-market hypothesis. Another line of testing has been formulated to determine how quickly the market adjusts to new information, since a major proposition of the theory is that it does so almost instantaneously, so investors normally cannot benefit.

One important study explored the market's understanding of stock splits. In effect, when a stock is split, there is no free lunch— the shareholder still has the same proportionate ownership as before. If markets are efficient, enough knowing investors would sell the stock that has split if prices were run up by more naive traders. This proved to be the case. Tests confirmed that stock prices after a split maintain about the same long-term relationship to market movements as before.[16]

Another study, measuring the earnings of 261 large corporations between 1946 and 1966, concluded that only 10 to 15 percent of the data in the earnings reports had not been anticipated by the reporting month, indicating the market's wide awareness of information.[17] Other tests came up with similar results, all demonstrating that the market quickly adjusts to new inputs.

The strongest form of the efficient-market hypothesis claims that no information, including that known by corporate insiders or by specialists trading the company's stock (who have confidential material about unexecuted orders on their "books"), could outperform the market. In the few studies done to date, some evidence has surfaced that both insiders[18] and specialists[19] display an ability to beat the market. However, these exceptions to the concept of perfectly efficient markets are considered inconsequential.

In the space of the last few dozen pages, we have seen the academic dismantlement of the two most important market theories of our day and their replacement, at least intellectually, by a third. The new theory has swept like a brush fire, first through the universities and then progressively through the SEC, legislators, the financial press, individual and corporate investors, and finally among professionals themselves. On the assumption that it is impossible to outdo the market, index funds have been formed that attempt only to mirror the results of the averages—a fitting tribute to the power of an idea conceived less than two decades earlier. At the same time, sad, for in accepting the new way, the money manager acknowledges that his prime raison d'être—to earn superior returns for his client —is beyond reach.

But it's not time to throw in the towel yet. Although the efficient-market hypothesis seems to unravel some of the investment knots we have seen, it fails to untie many others. How, for instance, could professional investors not merely equal the market in recent years, but in fact do worse? How could the bulk of professional opinion prove so consistently and dramatically wrong at crucial market turning points? Or how, if investors are so unfailingly rational, could periods of euphoria and panic occur so often through market history?

None of these phenomena are possible, according to the theory. One nonacademic observer noted that Disney fell 86 percent between 1972 and 1974, with its P/E ratio declining from 64 to 21, though earnings and profit margins improved throughout this period. "When was the market efficient?" he asked. "When it took Disney up to 119⅛, or when it put it back to 16⅝?" Obviously, perfectly efficient markets should not exhibit such behavior.

Thus, before accepting the academic theory that ours is the best of all possible financial worlds—that our advanced analytical methods result in highly efficient markets—let's move back to the questions posed a few pages earlier. Are there flaws, and perhaps very serious ones, in the analytical methods themselves that lead to consistent investment error? We will find the answers in the next section.

PART II

UNDERSTANDING YOUR PSYCHOLOGICAL ODDS

CHAPTER FOUR

The Strange World
of Reality

London during the first days of 1524 was a city awaiting its doom. Crowds of anxious people of every social stratum gathered to listen to the numerous astrologers and fortune-tellers along bustling thoroughfares. All said the same thing: on February 1 the Thames would suddenly rise from its banks, engulf the entire city, and sweep away ten thousand homes. The vision was described in terrifying detail to increasingly larger throngs.

It had started the preceding June, when a few soothsayers began to bandy about the prophecy, which quickly permeated their ranks. Month after month the warnings were repeated with total assurance, and as time passed, they became accepted by most of the population, even though the Thames had always been the most docile of rivers.

At first, only a handful of families began to leave the city, but as the time grew near, people left in ever-increasing numbers. Long streams of laborers on foot, trailed by their wives and children, tramped the muddy roads to higher ground, fifteen or twenty miles away. They were joined by their more prosperous neighbors, whose horse-drawn carts were piled high with possessions. Nobles and clergy followed suit, fleeing to safe country estates. By the middle of January over twenty thousand people had departed. London was rapidly becoming a ghost town.

Electing to stay, the prior of Saint Bartholomew's built a tower-like structure on Harrow-on-the-Hill and provisioned it for two months. He also acquired several boats manned by expert rowers—just in case.

When the ill-fated day arrived, some braver souls stayed behind to watch. The soothsayers had predicted that the river would rise slowly, allowing those fleet enough to escape. The hour finally came and, to the consternation of the watchers, nothing happened. The tide quietly ebbed and flowed, and ebbed and flowed as it always had. An awareness slowly spread over the good people that they had been had. Still, to be safe, most stayed up that night and continued their watch.

The next morning, with the Thames continuing to flow peacefully within its banks, the crowd, joined by the returning evacuees, was boiling with fury. Many shouted to throw the pack of soothsayers into the river.

Fortunately, the prophets were prepared. In a clever maneuver —seemingly not lost on present-day chartists—they said they had scrupulously rechecked their calculations the previous night and found a minute error. London was most certainly doomed; the stars were, as always, undeniably right. But, because of the minor oversight, the great flood would occur in 1624, not 1524. The good townspeople could go home—at least for a while.[1]

This story, whose many variations have been replayed through history, has a great deal more to do with financial markets than you might at first think. In the last two chapters, we examined the most popular tools of present-day investors and found them wanting. Some might be dismissed almost on sight. Others, particularly thorough fundamental methods, such as those outlined by Graham and Dodd, seem far more logical. But although the tools appear to be practical, they rest on a bed of psychological quicksand. Without understanding how investors form opinions and the psychology that affects their decision making, people's odds are considerably reduced in the marketplace.

A good place to start examining what goes wrong with established investment methods is to observe how groups or crowds affect our ability to exercise independent judgment, even in areas where we think we can be totally objective. In this chapter, we will look at crowd behavior and how it can influence us as investors.

It is important to recognize that people in groups tend to be continually swept by one idea or trend after another. Sometimes, as

in the London of 1524, they have no supporting facts and still participate in crowd action that to an impartial observer borders on the
insane. On each occasion most people justify and often enthusiasti-
cally back the new thinking. While we can always look back and
shake our heads at group folly in the past, it is far harder to remain
unaffected by these influences in our own time.

The American Civil Liberties Union considered itself very brave
indeed to defend the right to demonstrate of a handful of Nazis in
1978, a group who—though thoroughly repugnant—represented no
real threat at the time. But at the height of McCarthyism during the
early 1950s, the ACLU was swept along like most people and refused
to defend suspected Communists. And while we may laugh at the
absurd carryings-on of the seventeenth-century Dutchmen who frantically sold their gold, jewelry, crops, and houses to buy tulip bulbs,
investors made remarkably similar decisions in the 1960s and 1970s
—only this time in stock rather than tulip markets.

To survive in the marketplace, it is essential to avoid being
carried away by the current mood of the crowd. The investor must
find some means of being able to withstand the tide—a task anything
but simple. It is necessary first to understand exactly how these
crowd influences affect investment decisions and why they are so
powerful. Armed with this knowledge, you can develop strategies
that should allow you not only to resist the pull of current opinion
but to take advantage of it.

Dr. LeBon's Crowd

The potent force of massed human beings is a phenomenon recognized since antiquity, one often discussed by the philosopher or
portrayed by the dramatist. Still, a more scientific analysis of crowd
behavior, like many other such philosophical curiosities, was not
undertaken until the latter part of the nineteenth century. Only then
did rigorous investigation begin.

In 1895 a Frenchman, Gustave LeBon, wrote what continues to
rank as one of the most incisive works on mass psychology, *The
Crowd*. According to LeBon, "The sentiments and ideas of all per-
sons in a gathering take one and the same direction, and their con-
scious personality vanishes. A collective mind is formed, doubtless

transitory, but presenting very clearly defined characteristics. The gathering has then become . . . a psychological crowd."[2] In such situations, the actions of individuals may be quite different from those the same individuals would consider when alone.

One of the most striking features of the crowd to LeBon was its great difficulty in separating the imagined from the real. "A crowd thinks in images, and the image itself calls up a series of other images, having no logical connection with the first . . . a crowd scarcely distinguishes between the subjective and the objective. It accepts as real the images invoked in its mind, though they most often have only a very distant relation with the observed facts. . . . Crowds being only capable of thinking in images are only to be impressed by images."[3]

At times, as LeBon saw, the image evokes cruel behavior; the belief in witches and sorcerers sent tens of thousands to the stake in the sixteenth and seventeenth centuries, and the "isms" of this century have taken tens of millions of lives. At other times, the image can inspire heroism, as in the crowd that swept the Bastille or the Republican crowd that with bare hands stormed the fascist barracks in Madrid in 1936. With the benefit of hindsight, the image may become droll, as when London was abandoned to the Thames. But, to capture the crowd, the image must always be extremely simple. LeBon believed the individual regresses in a crowd and "descends several rungs in the ladder of civilization. Isolated, he may be a cultivated individual; in a crowd he is a barbarian. He possesses the spontaneity, the violence, the ferocity, and also the enthusiasm and heroism of primitive beings."[4]

LeBon was an astute, if not particularly sympathetic, observer of crowds, and his description of crowd behavior is strikingly applicable to what we can readily discover taking place in financial markets. Certainly all the elements are present: numbers of people, intense excitement, and that essential simple image. Indeed, few images are more simple and yet as beguiling as *instant wealth.* Each such image carries the crowd far into the realm of fantasy, and sometimes beyond the boundaries of sanity. Despite the assumption of the rationality and omniscience of investors claimed by our academic friends, the last word on the subject often seems to be the roar of the crowd.

Each time, as LeBon foresaw, the image was not only simple and enticing, but seemingly infallible. And, as he predicted, people lost their individuality. Crowd contagion swept intellectuals, artists, nobles, and businessmen in every period as easily as it did the common people. Actually, those who should have known best often led the way. And so, to see just how strong its pull can be, we might look a little more closely at the behavior of crowds in the marketplace.

The Mississippi Scheme

The French, usually pacesetters in fashion, launched one of the first of the gigantic speculative manias, beginning in 1716. The Mississippi Company, as the venture was dubbed, resembled in many ways the classic "South Sea Bubble," which was soon to develop on the other side of the Channel.

The central character in the Mississippi Company was John Law, the son of a Scottish banker. A tall, dashing figure, Law had fled to the Continent with a death sentence on his head, the result of his having killed a rival in a duel over a love affair. Having studied banking in Amsterdam, Hamburg, Vienna, and Genoa, Law had a fairly sophisticated understanding of the use of credit. He was able to convince the French Regent of the merits of using paper money to lower interest rates, increase employment, and expand business. A national bank was established, which issued paper money up to twice the value of the country's gold and silver. The beginnings proved sound enough, and the bank prospered.

Law's vision, however, was much grander. Two years later, in 1718, he secured the right to the development of the vast Mississippi basin, then a territory of France.

Under Law's orchestration, a gigantic speculative bubble began to take shape. The stock in the new venture was first sold to the public on very attractive terms. Three quarters of the payment could be made in Louis XIV *billets des états* at face value, although this particular currency then traded at an almost 80 percent discount.

To eliminate any doubt as to the prosperity of the scheme, Law promised a dividend of 40 percent of the face value of the stock in the initial year. Using the discounted Louis XIV notes to subscribe, a shareholder would receive 120 percent of his investment in dividends alone in the first twelve months! This, and the lure of the Indies, proved too much. Few were bothered by the fact that the company was just starting and had no assets. Enthusiasm easily checkmated logic; three hundred thousand applications were made for the first fifty thousand shares. Dukes and marquises and comtes, with their duchesses, marchionesses, and comtesses, jostled in the streets with prostitutes and peddlers, seeking to subscribe. Some of the nobility took apartments while waiting their turn in order to avoid rubbing shoulders with the "great unwashed" around them.

The demand for the stock seemed inexhaustible. Law issued a steady stream of new shares at progressively higher prices. Only months after the original stock sale, a new issue was offered and was oversubscribed at 5,000 livres—ten times the initial price.

Law was an expert at painting the canvas of concept. To make the potential even more dazzling, he acquired the tobacco monopolies, as well as the East China, India, and Africa companies, and merged them all into the Mississippi Company. Indians were paraded through the streets of Paris, bedecked with gold and silver, to demonstrate the wealth of the territories. Engravings showing Louisianan mountains bursting with gold, silver, and precious stones were widely distributed.

The price rise of the Mississippi Company was breathtaking and in itself became almost hypnotic. "The tendency to look beyond the simple fact of increasing value to the reasons on which it depends greatly diminishes," wrote John Kenneth Galbraith of investor behavior in 1929.[5]

Professor Galbraith's wry observation is as apt for the rue de Quincampoix, where the stock was traded. Large crowds became acclimated to prices working constantly higher—day after day, week after week, and month after month. Previous and now "old-fashioned" standards of value were left far behind.

It was difficult for anyone to escape the the scheme's almost irresistible appeal, and few did. At the height of the frenzy in 1720, the Mississippi Company had appreciated forty times from the initial offering price of 500 livres in 1716. The market price of the shares was now worth eighty times all the gold and silver in France.*

---

*Madness, perhaps, in retrospect, but only a few years ago the experienced senior investment officers of America's largest and most powerful financial institutions did almost exactly the same thing. They decided that there were only fifty or so stocks to buy out of a total of twelve thousand public companies, and they bid them up to astronomical prices. Avon Products, for example, was valued for more than the entire U.S. steel industry, although it was dwarfed in size and profitability. At the time, the heads of these institutions, including Morgan Guaranty, Banker's Trust, and Citibank, vigorously defended the course they were following

The rue de Quincampoix was packed with speculators of all classes. Every available space was used for trading. A cobbler rented his stall to traders for ten times his normal wages. The rents for houses on the street rose twelve- to sixteenfold from previous levels. Fortunes, naturally, were made—a banker was said to have made 100 million livres, a waiter 30 million. The word *millionaire* came into use for the first time.

The wild speculation took on many of the aspects of a carnival. Tents were erected to trade stock, to sell refreshments, and even to gamble. One man set up a roulette wheel in the midst of the packed throng and did a thriving business. The major roads leading to Paris were made almost impassable because of the masses trying to reach the city. Over three hundred thousand people came from the provinces to participate in the trading!

Law was idolized by the crowd. So great were the surrounding throngs anywhere he went that the Prince Regent provided him with a troop of lancers to clear the way. Enormous bribes were paid to his servants to get an interview with him, and even members of the aristocracy had to wait for weeks for an appointment. One lady drove around Paris for three days looking for Law, instructing her coachman to upset the carriage when he was sighted. When at last they tracked him down, the coach was driven into a post. It turned over, and the lady screamed shrilly to attract Law's attention. As Law came to her aid, she confessed the ruse and asked to subscribe to the next stock issue, to which he smilingly obliged.

Although Law exaggerated the opportunities, he did make a genuine effort to develop Louisiana and was successful in increasing French shipping, establishing new industries, and sharply raising French commercial activity. Nevertheless, the soaring prices of the Mississippi Company stock had little to do with the situation. When this awareness began to spread, a panic followed, in both the paper currency and the Mississippi shares.

LeBon was well aware of how swiftly the image guiding the crowd could change. "These image-like ideas," he wrote, "are not connected by any logical bond or analogy or successor, and may take each other's place like the slides of a Magic Lantern."[6] And so they

---

before Congress as "most prudent." As in the case of the Mississippi Company, both expert and average opinion was convinced that they had found the new Golconda. The subsequent performance of some of the more popular stocks is found in table 4, page 93.

did. The Mississippi shares, which previously represented spectacular riches, now meant doom.

Law attempted to stem the tide. Anticipating Cecil B. De Mille
by several centuries, he staged a spectacular in the streets of Paris.
Six thousand of the city's poorest inhabitants were pressed into
service, given new clothes, picks, and shovels, and marched through
the streets, presumably on the way to mine Louisiana gold. However,
even this major production stopped the panic for only a few days.

When the Mississippi bubble burst, the aftermath was devastating. First a few investors, then gradually more, and within weeks
almost all realized that the speculative frenzy was insane. A desperate rush to sell began, but few buyers could be found. People now
focused on the emptiness of the scheme. Rumor again spread
through the rue de Quincampoix, this time that the company had few
assets and would be forced to omit its dividend entirely.

The image had changed for good. By late 1720 the stock had
fallen to 200 livres, some 99 percent below its peak only months
before. Law left the country in disgrace and died in obscurity nine
years later in Venice. To the end, he loved risk. No longer gambling
the economic stakes of one of the two most powerful nations on
earth, he was content to wager his few available shillings with pass-
ersby on whatever local action moved him.

What Is Social Reality?

The vision of the jeweled and powdered French dukes, comtes, and
marquises frantically scurrying about the rue de Quincampoix,
breathlessly followed by their duchesses, comtesses, and marchionesses, décolletage aheaving, may be amusing, but are there
lessons to be learned that also apply to modern markets?

History has shown that group madness need not last for only
brief periods. The fear of the flooding of the Thames occurred over
many months, the Mississippi bubble was in full bloom for four or
five years, and the persecution of witches and sorcerers went on for
centuries. In each of these cases, the image created its own reality,
reshaping the perceptions, actions, and attitudes of the crowd. How
were such strange realities brought into being and nurtured, and why
should supposedly rational people succumb so easily to them?

Social psychologists tell us that our beliefs, values, and attitudes can be thought to lie along a continuum. At one extreme are those based on indisputable physical evidence—if I throw a crystal goblet against a wall, it will shatter; or if I point my skis straight down a long, steep slope, it's pretty unlikely I'll reach the bottom intact. Such outcomes, termed physical reality, are abundantly clear and don't require other people's confirmation.

At the other end of the continuum are beliefs and attitudes that, although important to us, lack firm support. What facts are available are sparse and difficult to evaluate. In this category are such questions as the existence of God, whether there is a "best" political system, or, of primary interest here, what a stock or the market is really worth at a point in time.

Psychologists have demonstrated that the vaguer and more complex a situation, the more we rely on other people whose intelligence we respect, both for clarification and as standards against which to judge the correctness of our own views. This helps us reduce the uncertainty we have toward our own beliefs. Most investors, for example, attempting to assimilate many contradictory facts in order to put a value on the Mississippi Company shares, undoubtedly sought the opinions of other intelligent investors to form their own assessments. When people use others as yardsticks against which to determine the correctness of their own views, they are utilizing what psychologists call social comparison processes.

We can do this in very commonplace ways, rarely giving it a second thought. I was once in a Middle Eastern restaurant in New York where the men's and ladies' rooms were marked with what to me were unintelligible symbols. I was momentarily puzzled, until a man who obviously knew where he was going strolled confidently through one of the doors, solving my problem. Or consider the case of the *Wall Street Journal* reporter who wrote of a recent dinner he and his wife had with a desert sheik. After the meal, two other distinguished Western guests sat back and belched heartily. The reporter and his wife, guessing that this was the proper sign of approval for the hearty fare, followed suit with gusto.

Similarly, a speaker may gauge the worth of his talk from the audience's reaction. After one of his speeches, Lincoln, judging from what he thought was the indifferent response of the crowd, turned to a friend and said, "It's a flat failure and the people are disappointed." The speech was the Gettysburg Address.[7]

The greater the anxiety is and the more indeterminate the situation appears to be, the more readily we rely on the behavior of others to gauge the proper course, treating much of the information we receive from them as being no less real than if we had directly observed it from physical reality. We thus forget its personal and tentative nature.

The term *social reality* refers to how a group of people perceive reality. As Leon Festinger, who first proposed the theory, described it: "When the dependence upon physical reality is low, the dependence on social reality is correspondingly high. An opinion, attitude, or belief is 'correct, valid, and proper' to the extent that it is anchored in the group of people with similar beliefs, opinions, and attitudes."[8] The ensuing social reality can then be a strange amalgam of objective criteria and crowd fancy. Facts, such as are available, can be twisted or distorted entirely to conform with prevailing opinions.

And this brings us back to the strange aberrations of people in crowds that we have seen in this chapter. In each instance, the information was vague, sometimes complex, and anxiety producing to the people of the time. Few standards existed to help them. Fortune-tellers may have been right in some of their earlier prophecies, establishing their credibility for the new auguries. During the Mississippi Scheme, one could see the substantial gains made by those who bought early, and that noblemen, confidants of the Regent, and shrewd businessmen were buying the stock—most said the price rise was only beginning.

People then as now were uncertain, sometimes anxious, and as a result wanted to compare their opinions with those of other individuals whom they respected. Great numbers were drawn by the need to verify their individual views into conformity with the group's beliefs; the larger the nucleus of the group, the greater the attraction of its beliefs to those who had initially resisted them.

Just how easily people's behavior can be influenced by others in uncertain and even mildly anxiety-producing circumstances can be seen from the following laboratory experiment of S. Schacter's.[9] Subjects were injected with a drug called epinephrine, which temporarily causes heart palpitations and hand shaking. The subjects were told that the drug was a vitamin supplement called "Suproxin." In each case, the subject was placed in a room with a stooge, planted there by the experimenters, who allegedly had also been injected with "Suproxin." With no forewarning, the subject searched for an explanation as his heart beat faster and his hands began to tremble. He started to watch the stooge, who, as you can guess, was not inactive. In one case, he behaved lightheartedly, singing, dancing, constructing and flying paper planes, in general acting in a high-spirited, zany way. Other subjects were each put in a room with a stooge who was gloomy and morose, made angry remarks, complained about a questionnaire both were filling out, and in a sudden fit of pique, ripped his up.

How did the subjects react? Feeling the effects of the drug, and watching the behavior of the stooges, the great majority adapted behavior patterns to match.

The record outside of the laboratory is not much different. Because there are so few objective guidelines, social reality has always had a merry time in the fashion world, for males and females alike. At the turn of the century, the dictate was for women's hemlines to drag along the ground; in other periods, they were well above the knee. In the late nineteenth century, to be *au courant* demanded an exceptionally narrow waist (seventeen or eighteen inches), and many a poor woman had her floating rib removed to conform to the dictate. In 1943 so many women tried to imitate the hairdo covering one eye of then-reigning film queen Veronica Lake that, according to United Press International, "the Federal Government branded her a menace to the war effort; it claimed too many lady airplane workers imitating her peek-a-boo bob had scalped themselves in the machinery."[10]

Crowd fashions and fads are no different today. Take jogging, for example. It may be healthy—the jury still seems out here—but it has certainly become contagious. It has mainly taken over from the previous physical fitness exercises, such as jumping rope (very "in" several years ago, but now advised against by some doctors because it may cause shin splints), yoga, and the RCAF-X4 plan.

Whether it's on a quiet Vermont byway or early morning in Riverside Park, there is a strong likelihood of meeting someone jogging these days. Many a poor middle-aged businessman or matron goes through the motions, panting heavily, tongue hanging out and eyes bulging, all supposedly in the name of physical fitness. Fashionable jogging outfits costing $300 or more are sold at Bergdorf Goodman and Saks Fifth Avenue. And the elegant ladies of the East Side now lunch at expensive restaurants while sporting their faultlessly tailored jogging wear, never for a moment meant to be sweated in.

Perhaps this isn't a fad—but already numbers of books on walking have been released.*

Does the same hold true of past fashions in the marketplace? Uncertainty, anxiety, lack of objective reality, and sudden and violent shifts in the image of the group were certainly integral to crowd behavior here too. Each interpretation of what was realistic was established and maintained by the consensus of the group. In every mania the group was injected (in a manner not unlike the epinephrine experiment) with an image of spectacular wealth, which changed its behavior. This new social reality was fabricated of the dreams, hopes, and greed of many thousands of investors. Many watching a particular bubble saw as much clearly. Yet most could still believe that things really would be different this time. . . .

The Reality of 1962

Let's next stop briefly at the Wall Street of 1962 to examine the workings of social reality on modern investment crowds. Are they any different from those of years past?

After the 1929 crash speculative fervor burned out for a generation. In fact, the Dow didn't break its 1929 high of 381 until November of 1954, at which time the nation was prosperous, industrial activity was increasing, and consumer income was rising, as were corporate earnings and dividends. The market, with only a few minor setbacks, continued to work solidly higher through the balance of the decade. "Time," Disraeli wrote, "is the Great Physician." And so it was. A new generation of investors, untutored in the lessons of disaster that their parents had learned, was now firmly at the helm. Confident of the future, they were intrigued with the tremendous investment opportunities that were present in the dynamic—pre-Arthur Burns—economy.

Just as the eighteenth-century investors were propelled by the unlimited wealth of the New World, so modern investors now saw the possibility of unlimited profits through modern science. Because of these expectations, the major technology companies of the time—IBM, Xerox, Polaroid, and Texas Instruments—commanded towering prices.

*One title: Walk, Don't Run.

Even more striking, when viewed with the hindsight of twenty years, was the 1961–62 period's enormous similarity to the English South Sea Bubble of the early eighteenth century—in the willingness of people to buy almost any new venture. In 1720, companies that made wheels of perpetual motion or converted gold from lead were in demand. In 1961–62, esoteric technological companies exerted enormous appeal. Whether it was alchemy in the first place or science in the second didn't matter much, as investors understood the prospects of each equally well. The crowd on the cobblestones in Exchange Alley, where the bubble companies traded, or watching the action on luminous electronic tapes in the boardrooms of space-age America behaved the same.

The beginnings, as usual, were sound enough. Many small technological companies sold to the public in the 1950s showed spectacular appreciation. An investment of $1,000 in Control Data when it was first offered in 1958 was worth $121,000 by 1961. The same $1,000 put into Litton Industries in the mid-1950s moved up fiftyfold during that period. Seeing these profits and believing in the unlimited wealth to be gained in anything scientific, investors scrambled to buy the shares of any small company that was being offered to the public for the first time. A frenzied new-issues boom took place in 1960 and 1961. All that was required was that the company be in electronics, computers, medical technology, or pharmaceuticals. Any company ending in "ics" or "tron" was enthusiastically bid up. Nytronics, Bristol Dynamics, and Supronics shot to immediate premiums. Some of the gains were spectacular: Dynatronics was issued at 7 and rose to 25 instantly; Risitron Laboratories went from 1 to 3⅞. Simulmatics, a company incorporated only two years earlier and with a negative net worth of $21,000, was offered at 2 and immediately quoted at 9.

The public appetite for such stocks was almost insatiable. One elderly woman called her broker to buy shares in "Hebrew National Electronics." The broker explained that the company was not in electronics at all, but was a kosher meat packer and processor. She accepted the news with disappointment and a tinge of anger. Several months later, when the stock had also moved up, she again phoned the broker. "They are too in the electronics business!" she said indignantly. "They sell electronic salami slicers."[11]

As the fever spread, new issues were underwritten in many industries outside technology. The boardrooms were filled to overflowing, and the talk on commuter trains and in theater lobbies was of hot new issues and the best little underwriting houses.

Promoters, not really very different animals in 1962 from what they had been in 1718, understood the appetites of the crowd and scoured the countryside for acceptable merchandise. "Why go broke? Go public," the prospective underwriting client was told. Shopworn goods were rechristened with sparkling new space-age names. Many of the hottest underwriting firms were one- or two-man companies.

The mania was intensified by the underwriters' advertising of the success of their merchandise. One firm, Michael Lomasney and Company, ran an ad that stated that had an investor purchased $1,000 of each of the sixteen issues it had underwritten in the past eighteen months, he or she would have had $36,800 by September of 1961. This was topped by another small underwriting firm, Globus, Inc., with offices, appropriately enough, on Madison Avenue. "If you bought each of Globus' issues," their ad rang, "you would have tripled your money by late 1961." The froth danced higher and higher.

This was, of course, a house of cards, but nobody seemed to notice—or care. With money being made at every turn, a stream of how-to literature came off the printing presses. Nicolas Darvas, a gypsy dancer, wrote a book entitled *How I Made Two Million Dollars in the Stock Market.* Another writer published a book modestly promising *How to Make a Killing on Wall Street.* *

The realization came, as always, that this was a fool's paradise. By the latter part of 1961, speculative ardor had cooled noticeably. In the sharp break of April–May 1962, a panic enveloped the new bubble companies. While the market recovered in short order and went on to new highs, most of the underwritings traded at pittances of the former values. An SEC study of five hundred randomly selected issues offered in the 1950s and early 1960s showed that 12 percent had simply vanished, 43 percent had gone bankrupt, 25 percent were operating at a loss, while only 20 percent displayed any

---

*Even the art world was unable to avoid the get-rich-quick craze. One service—the Art Market Guide and Forecaster—put together an average of five hundred artists and called it the AMG index, after its own initials. One ad read: "With the art market for paintings up 97 percent since the war—and 65 percent in the last year alone—you can lose immense profits by failing to keep informed of the monetary value of art, present and future."(Robert Sobel, *The Big Board* [New York: Free Press, 1965].)

earnings whatever. Of the latter, there were only twelve which had any real promise. And, as an unpublished study made by the New York Stock Exchange indicated, of 300 underwritings by its member firms (these firms in theory at least have higher standards than the less-regulated nonmembers), the median price in 1962 had declined a remarkable 97 percent! Social reality had led the crowd down the same strange path in 1962 as it had in 1720.

The Compellingness of Crowd Opinion

Why do social comparison processes produce an investor consensus that is often so far off the mark? Part of the answer seems to lie in how easily people's opinions are drawn together under conditions of uncertainty.

An excellent experiment to show this was devised by psychologist Muzafer Sherif.[12] Sherif took advantage of the little-known autokinetic light phenomenon. A tiny pinpoint of light beamed for a few seconds in a darkened room appears to move, although in fact it is stationary. Sherif asked his subjects to calculate the extent of the movement as carefully as possible. (Since the light appeared to be moving, the subjects believed it actually did.) With no reference points upon which to anchor judgment in the blackened room, individuals gave answers ranging from a few inches to eighty feet—the latter subject believed he was in a gymnasium rather than a small room.

After one hundred trial sets, the median guess of each subject was recorded. Figure 12 on page 78 shows that it ranged from one to over eight inches (as the line on the extreme left of both charts indicates). However, when subjects were brought together, the judgments converged. Figure 12(a) indicates the amount of convergence there was in each succeeding one-hundred-test figure with two people present; figure 12(b) with three. In the latter case, from individual medians varying from under an inch to almost eight inches, the group's convergence by the third one-hundred-set test moved to slightly over two inches.

Sherif added another variable by including a confederate. If the subject estimated the light moved twenty inches, the confederate might estimate two. His influence was enormous. By the end of the trials, most subjects' estimates came very close to those of the confederates, which remained stable throughout.

Writing of these experiments, psychologist William Samuels noted: "The majority of subjects in such studies indicate little awareness that their perceptions have been manipulated by the estimates of others, for they maintain that they had previously made their own estimates *before the others spoke.* The influence process then may be a rather subtle phenomenon. Partners who are well liked, who have high status, who are reputed to be competent on the judgmental task, or who merely exude self-confidence when announcing their estimates are all especially effective in influencing a subject's personal norm of movements."[13]

It is also interesting to see how much a naive subject's judgment could be shifted under subtle manipulation—as much as 80 percent or more without pressure of any sort. Because one of the prime features of the stock market is uncertainty, opinions frequently move toward a consensus and, not unlike the autokinetic light experiment, toward the most authoritative-sounding or outspoken points of view available at the time—usually those of the experts, whose record we already know. Then throw in anxiety, another very powerful force

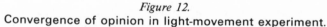

Figure 12.
Convergence of opinion in light-movement experiment.

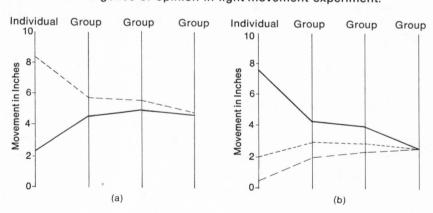

SOURCE: Figures from pages 208 and 209 in *Social Psychology* by Muzafer Sherif and Carolyn W. Sherif. Copyright © 1969 by Muzafer Sherif and Carolyn W. Sherif.

leading toward consensus. During the best of times the stock market is uncertain and difficult, and in its worst moments can induce first-rate terror. People find it natural under such circumstances to take comfort and security in the opinions of savvy, smart money. Small wonder that the consensus of the many appears to be a refuge, not a trap.

Earlier, we saw just how elusive the anchor of objective reality and the concept of value on which it is based actually are. It is not surprising, then, given the nature of the psychological forces at work, that we too can often find ourselves dashing frantically down a rue de Quincampoix, an Exchange Alley, or a Wall Street . . . which brings me to the next wild adventure: the "go-go" market of 1967–68.

God Has Been Good to Solitron Devices

The fascinating yet disturbing aspect of financial manias, knowing what we know about social comparison processes, is that few lessons can be learned from the past. The same mistakes made in almost the same fashion inevitably crop up again and again.

Looking back at the bizarre speculative period of a decade ago, one might feel almost as though the clock had stopped at the height of the 1961 enthusiasm and only started ticking again in 1967. Investors resumed the previous speculation at an increasingly intensified pitch, with all memory of the previous crash seemingly erased. Remarkably an even larger new-issues boom commenced, and interest again focused on many of the now familiar technology stocks of 1962 —Xerox, Polaroid, Texas Instruments, and IBM.

This was the time when youth took over Wall Street. With youth came changes in the investment game: value was no longer to be found in the stodgy blue chips favored by their elders. The action now was with new issues, growth stocks, and concept stocks. A group of sideburned, flamboyantly dressed young men in their twenties and thirties came to the helm. They were the freewheeling, high-spirited embodiments of the times who were determined to clear out the dogma, error, and cobwebs of the past. Called "gunslingers," the new breed was out to change the world with the sureness of their instincts and the quickness of their reactions. They believed that rapid moves in and out of stocks led to exceptional results. Often entire portfolios would be turned over two or three times a year. This new style of buying or selling was called "go-go" investing. The sole objective was "performance," which meant achieving higher returns than the market averages and competing gunslingers.

In the deadly competition that soon developed, all bench marks of fiduciary responsibility were forgotten. Criticism that the new methods were highly speculative was tossed aside, in the words of one gunslinger, "as coming from the cultural alienation of an out-dated generation."

On Wall Street a new tide of folk heroes moved in—Gerald Tsai, Fred Carr, Fred Mates, Fred Alger, and John Hartwell, to name a few. They were often treated with awe by the financial press and the public—at the time, it seemed, with good reason. Gerald Tsai, the initial go-go star, used rapid-fire trading to increase the Fidelity Growth Fund, which he managed, by 65 percent in 1965. Starting his own Manhattan Fund in 1967, he doubled the 20 percent rise in the averages. But Tsai's performance was dull when compared with many of the others. Fred Carr's Enterprise Fund rose 118 percent in that same year as he moved stocks in and out of his portfolio at a breathtaking rate. In one quarter Enterprise traded two hundred companies, more than some staid mutual funds turned over in a decade. In late 1968 the Mates Fund of Fred Mates was up a stunning 158 percent for the year.

Many of the new breed assiduously avoided the major industrial giants, "buggywhip companies," as they were sometimes contemptu-ously called. At the height of the go-go market in 1968, when num-bers of concept companies had gone up twenty-five- or even fiftyfold, giant AT&T made an eight-year low. One money manager summed it up in *Forbes:* "Excitement, not solidity, is what makes stocks move now." Again social reality took hold and investors frolicked away, unfettered by the time-tested standards of the past.

The gunslingers bristled with confidence. John Hartwell, who in 1968 managed $425 million, ignored the prudent policy of wide diversification, stating: "If you have more than half a dozen positions in an account of, say, $500,000, it only means you are not sharp enough to pick winners."[14]

All eyes were focused on relative performance. The winners of the go-go derby would receive large flows of funds from the enthusi-astic public, while the losers would have the money quickly taken away. In spite of its excellent record, Gerald Tsai's Manhattan Fund had net redemptions in 1968 as the public moved into better-performing vehicles, such as those of Fred Carr and Fred Mates. As one manager phrased it: "In this market, the crowd is betting on the jockeys, not the horses."

Outstanding fund managers could make a million dollars or more a year, and they lived high—gold faucets in bathrooms, fifteen-room penthouses on Park Avenue or in The Dakota, and summer homes on the Adriatic. Because of the public's obsession with them, performance rankings became the go-go manager's lifeblood. Fred Alger once flew to Europe to protest to Bernie Cornfeld, then running the vast International Overseas Fund network, that one month he was ranked number two rather than number one because of a typographical error. The mistake was immediately corrected.

Performance was achieved mainly by financial sleight of hand. Substantial gains were made by buying large blocks of thinly traded companies, pushing them higher. Legions of admirers usually followed in the wake of the go-go stars, making the price rise: a self-fulfilling prophecy for a while. Because of their tremendous ability to generate commissions, the major go-go managers would get large blocks of hot new stocks at the issue price, which immediately went to substantial premiums, generating instant profits on their books. The gunslingers would also buy letter stock—stock not authorized to be traded in public markets—at a substantial discount. The discount would often be two thirds or more of the going market price. The fund would immediately revalue the stock at a one-third discount from the market, and—*voilà!*—a 100 percent profit.

It is a tribute to the power of a speculative frenzy that though these and many other practices were widely known and sometimes criticized at the time, very few people seemed to care how questionable the gains really were. Only the "bottom line" mattered—that the funds were performing well.

The rapid trading of huge blocks of stock made this the golden age of the brokerage firm. Many an institutional salesman who could scarcely distinguish an asset from a liability made six figures a year from his gunslinger clients, and most fully believed they deserved it. One fellow became a brief legend by leaving a hundred-dollar tip after a single round of drinks.

The gunslinger's mode of operation was simplicity itself. One merely had to have an exciting story and a record of rapid sales and earnings growth to substantiate it. Almost no attention was paid to how real the earnings actually were. And it was, again, the day of the black-box operation. Companies in technology were bid up to astronomical prices as investors envisioned futures of limitless growth. The chairman of one small technology company that had multipled tenfold in price told his annual meeting in 1968: "God has been good to Solitron Devices."

Money managers and clients alike became intoxicated by the gains. One investor, dazzled by the sensational promises of the go-go managers, went to his investment advisor, David Babson, a crusty old New Englander, and told him his objective was no less than 40 to 60 percent a year. For the previous ten years, Babson had increased his client's money at a not unimpressive 10 percent rate to $126,000. To illustrate the absurdity of his client's request, Babson showed him that a 40 percent rate of growth would have resulted in this sum becoming $100 million in twenty years, while a 60 percent rate of growth would have made it $1.5 billion!

For those of us playing at the time (I had come to Wall Street a year or so earlier), it was indeed the golden age. Everywhere the atmosphere was giddy with success. Almost any investment we tried, be it computer service, uranium exploration, or flight safety instruments, worked out, and many did spectacularly. With our stocks quadrupling, several going up tenfold, and one over fiftyfold, it was hard not to attribute the gains to our intelligence and surefootedness.

The longer the odds, the more sensational the payout. The favorites went up even more than the Mississippi Company over a similar period of time. With so much money being made so quickly, it was almost impossible not to be sucked into the speculative whirlpool, and not many resisted.

All around us, thousands of professionals wrote research reports condoning the current price movements and recommending a plethora of exciting new opportunities. As experiments have shown, the expert's support of a concept more firmly locks it into place. Very often people are persuaded by a message, not because of its compelling logic but because they consider the communicator an expert.* (Thus the old adage of the singer, not the song.) Not only were the

*Those interested might see, for example, S. E. Asch, "The Doctrines of Suggestion, Prestige, and Social Psychology,' *Psychological Review* (No. 55, 1948): 150–177; and C. I. Hovland, I. L. Janis, and H. H. Kelley, *Communication and Persuasion* (New Haven, Conn.: Yale University Press, 1953).

experts bullish, but their record of success in the immediate past was good, further enhancing their credibility.

Once again, as in the 1920s, everybody talked stocks. One of my friends (let's call him Peter) was at the time in group therapy —he said to straighten himself out, but from our talks it seemed more likely to meet new, interesting women. Whatever the case, the red-hot market permeated the group. Peter, both intelligent and articulate and not in the least reluctant to express his views, quickly became the center of attention. The sessions, under the encouragement of the analyst, an avid investor himself, turned more and more into stock-picking seminars. One diffident middle-aged businessman had joined the group because he believed himself a financial failure. He bought one of my friend's suggestions, University Computing, and saw it rise fortyfold. Buying more and more on margin as the price shot up, he became the ultimate business success, a multimillionaire. The transformation in his self-confidence was amazing, so much so that Peter now had trouble maintaining his position as group guru. But the business-man's fantasy was most temporal—the stock eventually led him to bankruptcy, whereupon Peter was made to return the Piaget watch he had been given in appreciation. At this point, my friend wisely turned to computer dating, which he hoped would better provide self-realization.

Some authorities became alarmed at the level of speculation. The American Stock Exchange, on which many of the smaller and more speculative companies traded, published a list in February 1969 of 109 speculative companies in which it forbade members to trade for their own accounts.[15] Former SEC chairman Manuel Cohen said at the time: "Frankly, I would have liked the AMEX to have applied the ban to all of its securities." However, most defended the reality of the moment. As one market expert wrote in a major financial magazine:

New Environment

I would therefore like to propose the thesis that as the result of all that has been happening in the economy, the world, and the market during the last decade, we are at least in a different—if not a new—era and traditional thinking, the standard approach to the market, is no longer in synchroniza-tion with the real world.

Possibly the market ought to be considered as having gone into a sort of orbit in outer space, in the sense that while we can see how we got where we are, we really have never been here before, and therefore cannot be certain of what happens next.[16]

This seems to most clearly summarize the thinking of all investors in all manias. When the 1968 bubble finally burst, it was the most severe crash since 1929. Forty-seven billion dollars, or three times the amount lost on Black Tuesday, 1929, vanished in thirty highfliers alone. Most of the speculative favorites fared even more poorly. National Student Marketing dropped from 140 to 3½, Solitron Devices (whom the Lord apparently no longer favored) from 286 to 10¼, Parvan Dohrman from 142 to 14, and Four Seasons Nursing Homes from 110 to zero!

Gone were the performance stocks, along with most of the high-living performance managers. Many of my own friends lost not only their profits, which were sometimes thirty to forty times their original investments, but their initial stakes as well. I was luckier, but it did take some stomach-wrenching weeks of large losses to set off the warning bells of the imminent danger. Like everyone else, in spite of all I had read about crowd manias, I found it hard to believe that this wonderful orbit in outer space was over.

The Gambling Mania

Finally, for those of you who might think that bubbles, even those of a decade earlier, are now ancient history, we might briefly look at one that has taken place recently. The mania is, appropriately enough, in gambling stocks, and investors played it with as much gusto as any in the past.

With the legalization of gambling in Atlantic City, and the opening of the first casino there by Resorts International in late May 1978, speculative money poured into the gambling stocks. It didn't matter that the record of many was lackluster at best, and that some were operating deep in the red. People saw only large profits ahead. Again, all past standards of value were forgotten as the gambling stocks skyrocketed. Just how much some of them soared is shown in table 3.

Resorts International's A stock went up over nine times, and its

Table 3
GAMBLING STOCK COMPARISONS

	PRICE 12/30/77	SEPTEMBER 1978 HIGH	PERCENTAGE INCREASED FROM BEGINNING OF 1978	PERCENTAGE DECLINED FROM HIGH TO 1981 LOW
Resorts International B	7½	108¼	1,428	85
Resorts International A	7½	70	933	82
Caesar's World	4½	22⅝	989	72
Golden Nugget	5¾	44⅝	776	63
Playboy	7½	32¾	436	83
Bally	11¾	47¾	412	64

thinly traded B stock rose fourteenfold.* As a bench mark, back in 1720 the English South Sea Company (considered by many to be one of the classic speculative outbursts) appreciated 813 percent in roughly the same period of time.

It didn't matter how many new casinos were to be built in Atlantic City—threatening Resorts International's highly profitable temporary monopoly. Speculators believed the more casinos, the better—a greater number would attract larger throngs, and each would coin gold. The players happily bid up any company that had any intention of building in Atlantic City, and many that did not.

It also didn't matter that stocks that had tripled, quadrupled, quintupled, or risen even more had only the remotest connection to gambling, if any at all. As *Barron's* editor Alan Abelson pointed out on September 4, 1978, Allied Leisure, whose stock had risen from 1½ on July 31, 1978, to 6⅝ one month later, was actually in Chapter 11 (bankruptcy proceedings) the previous year. Speculators were betting that the company, which made "some form of coin-operated amusement devices," would benefit if gambling was legalized in Florida. The price action showed few considered that even if gambling was sanctioned, Florida companies would have no monopoly on such devices and this one couldn't even earn a profit.

Even a maker of tombstones got into the act by announcing it was considering investing in a casino in Atlantic City. From a low

---

*In no small measure due to a short squeeze: people who had sold the stock short could find no stock to borrow with the small amount of B stock outstanding, and were forced to buy it at much higher prices.

of 2¼ in late December 1977, the stock moved as high as 25 before entombing numbers of investors as it again dropped well under 10 by November of 1978.[17] Despite numerous warnings, speculation continued to roll merrily along.

Once again, although valuations bordered on the insane, the speculation had a momentum all its own. Men who clearly saw the absurdity of current prices and moved too soon were stung as in manias past. One of the Street's ablest money managers, who reputedly ran up a personal fortune once approaching $40 million from six figures a decade earlier, quickly grasped the unsoundness and tried to profit from it by selling short. He lost an estimated $10 to $15 million.[18]

While the full story has not been played out to the time of this writing, it's likely that the current bubble will end like all of the others, with the image of instant wealth suddenly and violently disappearing.

The above section was written three years ago during the first flush of the gambling mania; it didn't take genius then to see how similar it was to bubbles past. And once again reality turned out to be far different from the wildly optimistic image projected at the time.

Rather than unlimited numbers of eager players packed like sardines in every conceivable cranny, business has been slow. As *New York Times* financial reporter Steve Lohr recently wrote about Atlantic City, "Midnight should be a time of bustling activity at casinos —but even some of the popular Black Jack tables are vacant except for dealers idly fingering cards. Rows of slot machines fail to attract a single customer—a Las Vegas style rock group plays to an audience of mostly empty seats."[19]

By August 1981, with six casinos operating, the average take per house had dropped sharply. Sure, there were 37 million people or one-sixth of the nation's population within 300 miles of Atlantic City, as the original enthusiasts noted. But, unfortunately, most were "day-trippers," people who took the virtually free transportation from New York or Philadelphia not to gamble heavily but primarily to enjoy an outing. They spent most of their time at the quarter slot machines or two-dollar Black Jack tables. The New Jersey Casino Commission also made the owners place an inordinately large number of their tables and slot machines at the disposal of the nickel and dime players at the expense of the higher rollers. Atlantic City—to date, at least—has turned into a very costly but not very profitable version of Disneyland.

The Commission also imposed a host of staffing and security regulations on the casinos that result in employment costs substantially higher than those in Vegas. Finally, Atlantic City lacks the first-rate hotel rooms necessary to attract the lucrative convention traffic, and of the rooms currently available about half are described as "small and seedy." Estimates indicate more than double the number of first-class rooms would be necessary to bring in large-scale conventions.[20]

The bottom line has been chilling to profits. The Atlantic City casinos posted a $7.3 million loss in the first quarter of 1981 and several companies that seemed eager to build have now deferred or canceled their plans entirely. The effect on the stock prices of the casinos, as the final column of table 3 indicates, is even more telling. Resorts A and B stock and Playboy are down over 80 percent from their highs of three years ago; the others, approximately two-thirds.

Fortune in markets, as in gambling, changes quickly. The gaming stocks, the most sought-after companies in 1977 and 1978, are now among the groups most shunned by investors.

Last Year's Bubble

After the disaster of the new issue/high technology markets of 1961–62 and 1967–68, one would think it almost inconceivable that investors could repeat the identical mistakes once more. At least I did. In spite of my study of the subject, I underestimated the power of group consensus.

As I wrote this section, investors were once again possessed by one of these manias. As the prices of new issues and high technology stocks doubled, tripled, and moved up even tenfold, we heard the same rationalizations that abounded in 1961 and 1968.

In the words of one expert, "The new money pouring into little stocks should boost prices and support shares with high P/E's. *The market collapse of the late 1960s and early 1970s has faded into such distant memories that investors no longer flinch at the mention of a company with an unfamiliar name.*" (Italics mine.) Moreover, he continued, "The institutional interest has picked up with rising prices and by mid-1981 had become sensational. The influx of institutional money seems likely to continue for years."

Once again, reality gave way under the impact of gains to be made in the exciting concept companies. Take Apple Computer. A manufacturer of small-scale computers for home and small business use, it went public at 100 times earnings with a market value of $2 billion—greater than that of such giant companies as Warner-Lambert ($1.8 billion), Gillette ($1.1 billion), and St. Regis Paper ($1.16 billion), although these companies dwarf Apple in size and profitability. Even so, the demand for Apple shares was almost a hundredfold the available supply.

But topping even Apple was Genentech, which we looked at briefly earlier. The company is in the glamorous business of gene-splitting and making modified life forms, both of which are in the experimental stage. Still, it was initially sold to the public at 800 times current earnings with a market value of $750 million. As *Forbes* editor Jim Michaels wryly noted: "Price/earnings ratios? Forget it. That's old-fashioned. Try Genentech at 120 times sales."[21]

Although exotic, Genentech's technology is in its infancy, with absolutely no assurance of profitable commercial products. Nevertheless, the demand for the stock was estimated to be anywhere from 500 to 1,000 times the available supply. Shades of investors in eighteenth-century England merrily paying huge sums for companies that promised to extract gold from sea water or sulphur from hellfire!

As the speculative cauldron boiled cheerfully along, the public once more was in the mood to buy anything—even Broadway shows. Among the gaggle of fast-buck issues put out by New York underwriter John Muir & Co., before its demise in 1981, was a 750,000-share offering for a Broadway show, *The Little Prince,* at $2.00 per share. By April 1982 it was down some 99 percent, to 2 cents a share.*

As one underwriter candidly put it, "We're basically selling hope, and hope's been real good to us."[22] Again, as in the 1960s and early 1970s, three people with a smattering of a background in

---

*The underwriting markups together with other expenses for this issue were an incredibly high 17 percent as against 2–4 percent for larger, more established firms. In other words, only 83 cents of each dollar invested went into *The Little Prince* production itself—a relatively high tariff to pay for instant failure.

technology could get together, sell stock, and become instant millionaires. One classic case was Western Oil Shale Corporation. According to *Business Week*, [23] the company went public and for a time had a market value of almost $50 million. The reason: "Faith in a multi-million Federal boondoggle to bankroll alternative energy sources." As of that time (and as a matter of fact, to the present) Congress has made no funds available for such companies. Western Oil Shale had no revenues, and actually reported losses in the previous two years, its sole resources being its three employees. The prospectus further noted "no commercially feasible method of extracting petroleum from oil shale has been developed to date," and also indicated that there was no assurance one could be found. It concluded with the following statement: "Many companies are more financially able to fund research projects of studying various methods of extraction of petroleum from oil shale and to finance the development of such methods." But these are only facts. Enthusiastic investors bid the stock up from its original offering price of 2 to 14½ before it dropped back some 80 percent to under 3.

The advisory services as usual got a piece of the action. One, *New Issues,* based in Florida, had the following message emblazoned on its direct mail advertising: THE CLOSEST THING TO A SURE THING THAT WALL STREET HAS TO OFFER. Indeed, the company boasted that had you followed all its recommendations in the past year and a half, you would have made 100 percent on your money. (Remember the identical claims made by similar services eighteen years earlier.) What *New Issues* failed to note was that it was impossible to get the red-hot issues because the demand for them was a hundredfold or more the available supply. In short, the service's record was best suited for those who liked to dream of riches. But if fantasy is what the customers were willing to pay for, fantasy was what the dream merchants provided.

The giant speculative cauldron boiled higher and higher. Many of the same gurus who had led investors to the slaughter a generation earlier and prudently kept a low profile subsequently once more demanded front, stage center, with their claims of gains of 20 or 30 percent annually or even more in recent years. None of these experts of course offered to display their previous records. If one was unkind enough to examine them, most lost 70 to 80 percent of their clients' money in 1969–70 and again in 1973–74. Even gains of 30 percent annually from 1975 to the end of 1980 would still leave clients underwater at the end of the latter year. But again, these were merely facts.

One of the best-known of the emerging growth wizards, in an interview with the *New York Times*, [24] justified the high P/E's investors were paying at the time with the following logic. Some of the new technology stocks were able to sell additional shares to the public at very high prices and invest the proceeds in money market funds earning returns of as much as 16 or 17 percent. The substantial interest income received resulted in much larger profits for the companies, which in turn would make enthusiastic investors pay even higher multiples for the stock.

In other words, say you had $1,000 and could earn $170 a year directly in a risk-free money market fund. But you buy a risky technology company sporting a multiple of, say, 60. This way (if we assume for illustration that all income comes from the money market fund), your $1,000 gets $17 of earnings—or one-tenth as much—and with almost no dividends. Is this a good reason for trading an absolutely riskless investment for a highly risky one? If you don't think so, we're both missing something that makes perfect sense to the guru. But then again, similar situations made sense to him in 1962 and 1968.

Finally, it would not seem fitting to leave the recent fantasy without at least a brief look at the latest flock of "bucket shops." Many are located in Denver and service the wild market for penny shares of oil and gas stocks. In 1979 and 1980 alone, well over 200 of these issues were sold to the public for an estimated $500 to $700 million. [25]

As in the past, the great majority of the new underwriting firms had been set up recently to feed on the public's speculative appetite. Most shares were offered for pennies, usually under a dime. Still, they were anything but a bargain. Some companies own secondary wells that produce as little oil as 50 or 100 barrels a day. Most hold promises or worthless leases. Almost all such companies sold to the public posted deficits, and few had any revenues whatsoever. [26] According to one observer, "The majority of these companies will not be here five years from now."

So great had the demand to buy these penny stocks become that salesmen flocked to Denver from all over the country to get a piece of the action. Typical of the sophisticated financial background of the new brokers were previous experience selling used cars in upstate

New York or managing coin-operated Laundromats in central Ohio. But with markups of 10 percent or more, the treks were well worth it. Many new arrivals became "Denver Night Brokers," who stay on the phone all night to answer calls or return calls from enthusiastic customers.

"On a given night," according to the *New York Times*, [27] "six brokers will handle phone calls, as many as 200 of them. A slow night is 100 calls." First Financial, one of the fastest growing underwriters, employed sixty-five such brokers, and had "15,000 accounts, more than half from outside Colorado." Reports in the *Times* indicate that the alertness, if not the enthusiasm, of brokers in many of those firms, was helped not a little by liberal use of cocaine.

In many respects, this frenzy was even worse than than of the 1960s because the general market was much lower than at the time of the previous bubbles. Thus, relatively speaking, new-issue high-tech prices were actually almost double those the previous time around.

One underwriter, viewing the recent cycle, expressed the opinion countless others have had before him: "It's early in the game; hopefully, we'll be smarter this time." Another undoubtedly put it more accurately: "I see the danger signs. I'm afraid a whole generation of people who haven't owned stocks will be dragged in and go bankrupt."[28] Probably the best summation was made by B. L. Davenport of the SEC: "There is no question that the big money is being made in the market by the brokers. The question that bothers me most is who will be the last buyer."[29]

Not Very Different

All manias, though separated by centuries, have had surprisingly similar characteristics. They started in prosperous economies, where people were looking for new investment opportunities and wanted to believe they existed. Each mania had sound beginnings and was based on a simple but intriguing concept. The rise in prices, in every case, became a self-fulfilling prophecy, attracting more and more people into the speculative vortex. Rumor always played a major role, at first of fortunes made and of good things to come, and later in prophecies of doom. In almost every case, the experts were caught up in the speculation, condoning the price rises and predicting much higher levels in the future. At the height of both the 1961 and the 1967–68 markets, money managers stated that the valuation standards of the past no longer applied—things really were different this time. And on both occasions, the statements were uttered shortly before the end.

Another point common to all speculative manias is the greater fool theory. Some of the more independent or cynical thinkers were not in fact overwhelmed by the consensus thinking of the time. They believed stocks should never have reached the preposterous levels that they had, that the crowd really was mad. But they thought it would get madder still (if a portfolio had gone up sixfold, why not eightfold or even tenfold?). There would thus be a chance to profit from the folly, which would only become more outrageous. Thus wrote British Member of Parliament James Milner in 1720 after being bankrupted by the South Sea Bubble: "I said indeed that ruin must soon come upon us but I owe it came two months earlier than I expected."[30] Not very different from the *Dun's Review* article at the height of the 1968 market, 248 years later: "The overriding question at the moment is: how long can a speculative boom go on? How many months, investors and dealers ask, before we see a repeat of 1962?"[31] Even knowing this, most found it impossible to stop.

As speculation grew more widespread, it became the major topic of the day. In almost every period, credit was abundant and cheap. Near the end, prices rose sharply and turnover increased markedly. Finally, there was a sudden shift in the social reality, resulting in a panic that carried prices far below those initially prevailing. It's also interesting to see the similarity in the declines in each of the speculative manias. As table 4 shows, all are on the order of 90 percent.

Four general principles seem to emerge from a study of financial speculations. First, an irresistible image of instant wealth is always presented that draws a financial crowd into existence. Second, a social reality is created that blinds most people to the dangers of the mania. Opinions converge and become "facts." Experts become leaders approving events and strongly exhorting the crowd on. Overconfidence becomes dominant, and standards of conduct and the experience of many years are quickly forgotten. Third, the LeBon image of the magic lantern suddenly changes and anxiety replaces overconfidence. The distended bubble breaks with an ensuing panic.

Table 4
MARKET FAVORITES FROM DIFFERENT ERAS

	HIGH PRICE	LOW PRICE	PRICE DECLINE FROM HIGH (IN PERCENT)
Holland, 1637			
Semper Augustus (tulip bulb)	5,500[a]	50[a]	99
England, 1720			
South Sea Company	1,050[b]	129[b]	88
France, 1720			
Mississippi Company	18,000[c]	200[c]	99
1929–32			
Air Reduction	233	31	86
Burroughs	97	6¼	94
Case	467	17	96
General Electric	201	8½	96
General Motors	115	7⅝	94
Montgomery Ward	158	3½	98
1961–62			
AMF	66⅜	10	84
Automatic Canteen	45⅝	9¾	79
Brunswick	74⅞	13⅛	82
Lionel	37⅞	4½	88
Texas Instruments	207	49	76
Transition	42⅜	6¼	85
1967–70			
ITEK	172	17	90
Leasco Data Processing	57	7	88
Ling-Temco-Vought	135	7	95
Litton Industries	104	15	86
National Student Marketing	143	3½	98
University Computing	186	13	93
1971–72			
Avon	140	18⅝	87
Clorox	53	5½	90
Disney	119⅛	16⅝	86
Levitz Furniture	40¼	3⅞	90
MGIC	97⅞	6⅛	94
Polaroid	149½	14⅛	91

[a]Florins.
[b]Pounds sterling.
[c]Livres.

And fourth, we do not, as investors, learn from past mistakes—things really do seem very different each time, although in fact each set of circumstances was remarkably similar to the last.

As we have seen, even though the investors of the 1960s and 1970s were armed with exacting fundamental tools, these did not save them from behaving in a fashion almost identical to the frenzied English and French of centuries earlier.

Is there some way to resist the crowd? That was the question that led to the search for a new investment method on my part, a method based on psychological as well as financial principles, for the former are at least as important in handling the problems raised. As we'll see next, the trouble lies in the methods used by sophisticated investors. Rather than making them experts in handling speculative excesses, the techniques very often result in their leading the stampede.

CHAPTER FIVE

The Not-So-Expert Expert

We have just seen how easy it is under conditions of uncertainty to follow the prevailing uppers and downers of the crowd. But it is still unclear what launches these lemminglike drives and why experts, in spite of their training, prove as susceptible as (if not more so than) the average investor in leaping into the torrent. Warren Buffett, the highly successful money manager we met earlier, posed precisely this question in 1966 and concluded: "Curiously enough, there is practically nothing in the literature of Wall Street attacking the problem, and discussion of it is virtually absent at Security Analysts Society meetings, conventions, seminars, etc."[1] More than a decade and a half later, there are still no good answers. We shall shortly see why.

Buffett's question had a much more universal ring than he may have perhaps thought at the time. Almost all of us have learned in our school days of classic miscalculations experts have sometimes made. Lord Cardigan hardly demonstrated the benefit of an extensive military background when he led the Light Brigade, well bedecked with blue ribbons for beautiful horseflesh, steeplechasing, and musical riding, into the barrels of three hundred Russian cannon at Balaklava. Nor was Yale economist Irving Fischer's comment "Stocks are now at what looks like a permanently high plateau," uttered a few days before Black Tuesday, 1929, the brightest financial statement of the century. The same might be said for the political judgment of Neville Chamberlain, standing at Croydon Airport upon his return from Munich, waving a document, and shouting, "I bring you peace in our time."

The illusion of expert invincibility is one that most of us put behind us long ago. What had not been known until recently is that under certain conditions, *experts err predictably and often.* There is a consistency to the mistakes made by professionals in fields as diverse as psychology, engineering, and publishing. And, as we shall see in this chapter and the next, the conditions for such errors are as fertile in the stock market as anywhere.

The problem of expert failure can be traced to man's capabilities as an information processor. Just how much information he can handle effectively under varying circumstances has come under intense scrutiny in recent decades, and some of the results are striking. We will see that the vast storehouses of data about companies, industries, and the economy that current methods require the investor to comprehend may not always give him or her an extra "edge." In fact, ingesting large amounts of investment information can lead to making worse rather than better decisions. Impossible? At the end of the chapter, you'll see that the favorite stocks and industries of large groups of professional investors, chosen by exactly the methods we are questioning, fared far more poorly than the averages over an almost fifty-year period.

To outdo the market, then, we must first have a good idea of the forces that time and again victimize even the pros. Once these forces are understood, the investor can build defenses and find routes that skirt the pitfalls.

The Not-So-Expert Expert

Just how good is man as a processor of information, and where does he run into trouble? Nobel Laureate Herbert Simon, one of the pioneers and leaders in the field, has studied both questions intensely over more than four decades. According to Simon, "Every human organism lives in an environment which generates millions of new bits of information every second, but the bottleneck of the perceptual apparatus certainly does not admit more than 1,000 bits per second, and possibly much less."[2] We react consciously to only a minute portion of the information that is thrown at us. But Simon states that even the filtering process is not a passive activity which provides a pretty reasonable representation of the real world, but "an active process involving attention to a very small part of the whole and the exclusion from the outset of all that is not within the scope of our attention."[3]

Simon notes: "The capacity of the human mind for formulating and solving complex problems is very small compared with the size of the problems whose solution is required."[4]

Researchers in many fields began to ponder whether such cognitive limitations actually existed, and if they did, how they might affect the decision-making process in their own disciplines. Could they, as Simon may suggest, result in a serious curtailment of the professional to carry out his responsibilities effectively in a complex field?

Some of the first experiments in cognitive limitation were conducted in the field of clinical psychology, which, like psychiatry, requires the practitioner to make complex diagnostic decisions if proper treatment is to be administered. One of the pioneer investigators was Paul Meehl. In the late 1940s and early 1950s, Meehl made twenty separate surveys of groups of clinical psychologists who, after thorough examinations, recommended treatment for psychotic and schizophrenic patients.[5] In each case the groups of psychologists made predictions of how they believed the patients would respond to the particular treatment they prescribed. These predictions were then compared with the average recovery rates based simply on the standard treatments in the past. Meehl expected the psychologists' diagnoses would undoubtedly improve the prescribed treatment and result in higher recovery rates. The past averages based on standard treatment would be the floor from which the effectiveness of the diagnoses could be gauged. But, in the words of one researcher, "This floor turned out to be the ceiling." The predictions of the groups of clinicians were inferior to the simple averages in eighteen out of twenty studies and as good only twice!

Further studies showed that there is no correlation between the amount of training and experience a clinical psychologist may have and his or her accuracy. One indicated rather surprisingly that psychologists were no better at interpersonal judgments than individuals with no training, and sometimes worse.[6]

Do such findings extend beyond the couch? Apparently so. A

group of radiologists reading X-ray films failed to diagnose lung disease 30 percent of the time, although the symptoms were clearly evident.[7]

And, in a classic study of tonsillectomies in the mid-1930s (a fashionable operation at the time), a sample of one thousand school-children from the New York City school system were examined by a group of doctors. A total of 61 percent were found to have had their tonsils removed. The remaining children were examined by a second group of physicians, who stated that 45 percent needed tonsillecto-mies. Another set examining the diminishing group recommended removing 46 percent of the rapidly depleting stock of tonsils. A final examination was carried out on the survivors and, sure enough, the diagnosis indicated 45 percent of these children should have the operation. At this point, only sixty-five children remained. Fortu-nately, the doctors decided to call off further testing before tonsils became extinct in the New York City school system.[8]

Configural Who?

Dozens of such studies have made it clear that expert failure extends far beyond the investment scene. And the problems very often reside in man's information-processing capabilities. Current work indicates he is a serial or sequential processor of data who can handle informa-tion reliably in a linear manner—that is, he can move from one point to the next in a logical sequence. In building a model ship or a space station, there is a defined sequence of procedures. Each step, no matter how complex the particular technology, is linked to the preceding step and will be linked to the succeeding stage until com-pletion.

However, the type of problem that proved so difficult to the professionals we just examined was quite different; here configural, or interactive, rather than linear reasoning was required for the solution. In a configural problem, the decision maker's interpretation of any single piece of information changes depending on how he evaluates many other inputs. Take the case of the security analyst: where two companies have the same trend of earnings, the emphasis placed on growth rates will be weighed quite differently depending on their respective industries and their financial strength. In addition, the assessment will be tempered by the dividend trend, the current payout ratio, profit margins, returns on capital, and the host of analytical criteria we looked at previously. The evaluation will also vary with changes in the state of the economy, in the level of interest rates, and in the companies' competitive environment. Thus, a successful investor must be adept at configural processing, integrating many diverse factors, since changes in any may require a revision of the total assessment.

Not unlike juggling, each factor weighed is another ball in the air, increasing the difficulty of the process. How good, then, are professionals, both within and outside of the investment field, at conducting this type of reasoning? Are they always as good as their methods demand?

A special technique using a statistical test called ANOVA (Analysis of Variance) has been designed that evaluates the configural capabilities of the experts. In one such study, nine radiologists were given a highly configural problem, that of deciding whether a gastric ulcer was benign or not.[9] To make a proper diagnosis, the radiologist must work from seven major cues either present or absent in an X-ray. These can combine to form fifty-seven possible new combinations. Experienced gastroenterologists indicated that a completely accurate diagnosis could only be made by configurally examining the combinations formed from the seven original cues.*

Although the diagnosis requires a high level of configural processing, the researchers found that in actual practice, it accounted for only a very small part of all decisions—some 3 percent. Over 90 percent came from serially adding the original individual symptoms.

A similar problem requiring a high degree of configural reasoning is found in deciding whether or not a psychiatric patient is to be allowed to leave the hospital for short periods. Here there were six primary cues that could be present or absent (for example, does the patient have a drinking problem?) and sixty-four possible interactions. The hospital staff included nurses, social workers, and psychologists. Again, the use of configural thinking was little in evidence, although it was essential for optimum solutions.[10] In another test thirteen clinical psychologists and sixteen advanced graduate students attempted to determine whether the symptoms of 861 pa-

*For those of a technical bent, these can combine into patterns ranging from fifteen possible two-way interactions, twenty possible three-way interactions, fifteen possible four-way interactions, six possible five-way interactions, to one six-way interaction.

tients were neurotic or psychotic, a highly configural task. The findings were in line with the first two examples.[11]

Curious about what results would be found in the stock market, Paul Slovic, a respected researcher in this area, devised a test to see how important configural (or interactive) reasoning actually was in the decisions of market professionals themselves. In one study thirteen stockbrokers and five graduate students in finance were given eight important financial inputs (trend of earnings per share, profit margins, outlook for near-term profits, etc.) that they considered most significant in analyzing companies. The optimum solution could only be found in a configural manner. As it turned out, configural reasoning, on average, accounted for only about 4 percent of the decisions made—results roughly equivalent to those of the radiologists and psychologists.

Moreover, the emphasis the brokers initially said they put on various inputs varied significantly from what they actually used in the experiment.[12] For example, someone considering the trend of earnings per share over time most important might actually place greater emphasis on near-term prospects. Finally, the more experienced the brokers, the less accurate the assessment of their own scales of weighting appeared to be. All in all, the evidence rather clearly indicates that most people are low-level configural processors, in or out of the marketplace.

Security Analysis—A System Designed for Anatol Karpov?

In light of what we have just seen, we might ask how dependable current investment methods actually are. To answer this question, let's look more thoroughly at the manner in which a company is evaluated by fundamental analysis. Suppose, for example, an analyst decides to examine Aetna Life and Casualty. How will he go about it?

Examining the company's financial statements, one sees it is a gigantic operation. In 1980 it had revenues of $13.3 billion, $508 million in net income after taxes, 39,100 home office employees, and 25,000 agents. It writes group insurance for one out of ten workers in the country, automobile insurance for 4.8 million drivers, as well as homeowner's insurance for 1.4 million dwellings. But these are only openers: it also writes twenty-seven other major property and casualty insurance lines, many dozens of different policies in life, health, and pension areas, and it is engaged in several other, non-related ventures as well.

Since chapter 3 indicated that the most important determinant of value is an assessment of the company's earnings power, the analyst will probably start here. To do his job properly, he'll have to look at many dozens and possibly hundreds of inputs.

In the case of Aetna, he normally will review in some detail the recent history and prospects of each of its major lines. He may, for example, begin with the property-casualty business, which accounts for about 50 percent of Aetna's income. The company has twenty-eight important lines in this area, with the largest—automobile insurance—accounting for 40 percent of overall divisional revenues. Since the results of these lines can have a significant bearing on the overall outlook, the analyst will probably try to get as thorough a picture of each operation as he can. He may take the auto insurance segment, for example, and subdivide it into commercial and private passenger; these in turn can be split between bodily injury and property damage.

But if he is the thorough type—and most of the dying species of institutional analysts are—he will go further, possibly getting breakdowns from management on how each of these lines is faring in important states.

But we're not finished with our friend yet. In fact, his most difficult innings lie ahead. Multiplying this information by the large number of other businesses Aetna writes extends the length and perhaps tediousness of the analysis manifold. However, if tediousness were his only concern, the analyst might happily accept it. A far more serious problem is that much of the information he is able to ferret out has a high degree of uncertainty attached to it.

Facts provided to him by management as the basis for his various estimates are partial or incomplete at best and sometimes prove to be entirely incorrect. Varying amounts of information are normally available about individual lines. Obviously, no company will relate all the necessary profit and loss and claim experience data to an outsider.

The analyst may be told that the automotive property line is "up nicely" or that automobile liability is "so-so" in the year to date. If he asks how one should translate a "so-so" or an "up nicely" into a reasonable earnings estimate, more times than not he'll be met with a shrug and told it's corporate policy not to divulge the information, and once in a while he'll be told, "That's your problem."

In any case, the analyst is left on his own. He must rely on personal judgment, deciding whether "nicely" means up 10 percent or 30 percent, or "so-so" means flat or down sharply. Checks can be made with trade sources and the competition, but the information provided will also be qualitative and sometimes misleading. Thus the analyst's judgment is extremely important at every stage of the assessment.

In analyzing an insurance company, it is also important to evaluate the appropriateness of the current rate structure. Because of competition and rising inflation, there is a large element of doubt about how good rates actually are. Even company officers, who spend years in a particular division, can often be wrong in their assessments. In the 1973–74 period, for example, the insurance industry badly misjudged the consequences of rising inflation in its property-casualty business and did not increase rates sufficiently, taking enormous losses as a consequence. Yet, at the time most managements believed their rate structures were sound.

Forecasting the earnings of a large industrial company is not much easier. Often operating in hundreds of different markets, many of which produce intermediate products,* sometimes in up to one hundred separate countries, the analyst is bombarded with vast amounts of difficult-to-quantify information on competitive conditions, capacity utilization rates, and pricing. What will be the effect on Ford of a new compact introduced by GM, or a sports car by Volkswagen? How badly will Du Pont polyester operations be hurt if Celanese cuts prices on one or two grades of polyester tire cord? All pertinent information must somehow be synthesized and evaluated in order to arrive at the earnings estimate.

Earnings forecasting, then, depends on large numbers of underlying assumptions, many of which are rapidly changing and very hard to quantify, which means their accuracy is always in doubt.

In addition to the forecasting problems, the harried analyst must also assess the quality of management, the company's expan-

---

*These are the raw materials for another manufacturing process. Many plastic resins, for example, go into a thousand or more end products (ranging from carpets to tires). Estimating the outlook for the myriad of intermediate markets is an extremely difficult task.

sion plans, its finances, the probable dividend rate, the quality of its accounting, and dozens of other vital factors. And all estimates are contingent on general economic conditions, which means correctly gauging the level of interest rates, unemployment, inflation, industrial production, capital spending, and other important variables. Economists themselves are as often wrong as they are right in these estimates. (For details on the record of forecasting, please see chapter 8.)

Finally, even if the analyst could surmount all of the obstacles so far listed, he would still need to know as much about many other companies in order to determine whether the company he chose represented the best value.

The theory appears anything but undemanding on its poor adherents. The amount of information they are expected to process is staggering. And since a good part of it is qualitative and difficult to pin down, the money manager or analyst is required to use his judgment scores of times along the way. Ideally, the professional needs to have information-processing capabilities not dissimilar to those of a fairly large-scale computer. He must have a central storage file for the massive amounts of information of a political, economic, industry, market, and company nature he needs, and he must be able to update and cross-reference it as numerous new and sometimes contradictory developments occur. The Bionic Man might be capable of as much, but work in the behavioral sciences pretty clearly indicates that most human beings are not.

But the requirements of the theory do not end here. One also needs a very high level of configural, or interactive, reasoning ability in order to apply different weights to the scores of factors upon which the analysis is contingent. And we've already seen that man is simply not a good configural processor of information. The reach of conventional investment theory may very well exceed the grasp of many of us to use it properly. The method brings us well into the range of information overload. One of the things that can happen follows.

How Much Knowledge Do We Need?

Under conditions of complexity and uncertainty, experts demand as much information as possible to assist them in their decision making. Seems logical. And naturally, there is a tremendous desire for such incremental information on the Street, because investors believe the increased dosage gives them a shot at extraordinary profits.

But as I've indicated earlier, that extra "edge" may not help you. A large number of studies have shown pretty conclusively that increasing the amount of information available to an expert decision maker doesn't do much to improve his judgment.[13]

In a study of what appears to be a favored class of guinea pigs, the clinical psychologists,* the subjects read the background information on a large number of cases. As the level of information increased, the diagnostician's confidence rose dramatically, but his accuracy continued to be low. In the test, the psychologists were given background information on a case and asked what they thought their chances were of being right. Thirty-three percent estimated they were correct; 26 percent actually were. When the amount of information was increased fourfold, 53 percent thought they would be correct; 28 percent proved to be.

Interestingly enough, the above findings seem fairly universal— no improvement with more information. The same results were obtained, this time using track handicappers. Eight experienced veterans of the racing forms were progressively given five to forty pieces of information they considered most important in picking winners. As figure 13 shows, the degree of confidence rose directly with the level of information, but the number of winners, alas, did not.[14]

The parallel between these examples and the investment scene is striking. Wall Streeters place immense faith in the detailed analysis of its experts. In-depth research houses turn out thousands upon thousands of reports, sometimes running up to a hundred pages or more and sprinkled with dozens of tables and charts. Washington listening posts have been set up to catch the slightest indications of impending changes in government policies affecting companies or industries,† and scores of conferences are called to provide the money manager with penetrating understanding in dozens of important areas.

*Eight were clinical psychologists, eighteen were graduate students in psychology, and eighteen were advanced undergraduates.

†Sounds impressive, but, I think, a waste of the client's money. Many times it seems the primary source of the listening post is the *New York Times*, the *Washington Post*, the *Wall Street Journal, Business Week, Time*, or *Newsweek*.

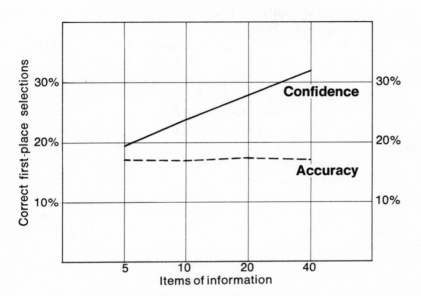

Figure 13.
Average changes in confidence and accuracy with increasing amounts of information.

The more detailed his level of knowledge, the more effective the expert is considered. A few years back, for example, a leading investment magazine related the story of an analyst so knowledgeable about Clorox that "he could recite bleach share by brand in every small town in the Southwest and tell you the production levels of Clorox's line number 2, plant number 3. But somehow, when the company began to develop massive problems, he missed the signs." As in the case of the psychologists and the experts of the racing sheets, the amount of information available had little to do with the outcome. The stock fell from a high of 53 to 11.[15]

This outcome is, unfortunately, no exception. The inferior investment results noted in chapter 1, as well as those that we will view next, were based on just such detailed research. To quote a disillusioned money manager several years back: "You pick the top [research] house on the Street and the second top house on the Street —they all built tremendous reputation, research-in-depth, but they killed their clients."[16] Perhaps a good point to note now is that *in-depth information does not mean in-depth profits.*

Drowning in Facts

I hope it is becoming apparent that these configural relationships are extremely complex. In the marketplace investors are dealing not with twenty-four or fifty-seven relevant interactions, but with an exponential number. We have already seen how experts working with far fewer inputs have proven remarkably inadequate at interactive judgments. Because these psychological findings are largely unknown on Wall Street, as elsewhere, investment experts continue to be convinced that their major problems could have been handled if only those extra few necessary facts had been available. They thus tend to overload themselves with information, which usually does not improve their decisions but only makes them more confident and more vulnerable to serious errors.

A famous market theorist of another era, Garfield Drew, saw the end result of this problem clearly. In 1941 he wrote: "In fact, simplicity or singleness of approach is a greatly underestimated factor of market success. As soon as the attempt is made to watch a multiplicity of factors even though each has some element to justify it, one is only too likely to become lost in a maze of contradictory implications . . . the various factors involved may be so conflicting that the conclusion finally drawn is no better than a snap judgment would have been."[17]

Under conditions of anxiety and uncertainty with a vast interacting information grid, the market can become a giant Rorschach test, allowing the investor to see any pattern he wishes. In fact, recent research in configural processing has shown that experts can not only analyze information incorrectly, they can also find relationships that aren't there—a phenomenon called illusionary correlation.

Trained psychologists, for example, were given background information on psychotics, and were also given drawings allegedly made by them. (These, in reality, were very carefully prepared by the experimenters.) With remarkable consistency, the psychologists saw cues in the drawings that they expected to see —muscular figures "drawn" by men worried about their masculinity, or big eyes by suspicious people. Not only were these characteristics not stressed in the drawings, in many cases they were in fact less pronounced than usual.* Because the psychologists focused on the anticipated aberrations, they missed important correlations actually present.[18]

The complexity of the marketplace naturally leads to an attempt to simplify and rationalize what seems at times to be unfathomable reality. Often investors notice things that are simply coincidental, and then come to believe that correlations exist when none are actually present. And if they are rewarded by the stock going up, the practice is further ingrained. The market thus provides an excellent field for illusionary correlation. The head and shoulders formation on the chart cuts through thousands of disparate facts that the chartist believes no man can analyze. Buying growth stocks simplifies an otherwise bewildering range of investment alternatives, just as the Kondratieff wave occurring every fifty years clarifies economic activity which to many might otherwise appear to defy analysis. Such patterns, which seemed to have worked in the past, are pervasive in the marketplace. The problem is that some of the correlations are illusionary and others are chance. Trusting in them begets a high risk of error. A chartist may have summed it up appropriately: "If I hadn't made money some of the time, I would have acquired market wisdom quicker."

Now, unquestionably there are people with outstanding gifts for abstract reasoning that permit them to cut through enormously complex situations. Every field will have its Bernard Baruchs or Warren Buffetts, its Bobby Fischers or Anatol Karpovs. But these people are decidedly few. In chess, for example, there is only one grand master for every few hundred thousand or so players. And even masters or experts, while more plentiful, still represent only a small fraction of those who pursue the game regularly. It seems, then, that as in chess, the information-processing capabilities and the standards of abstract reasoning required by current investment methods are probably too complicated for the majority of us, professional and amateur alike, to use to beat the market regularly.

---

*The belief that all paranoid patients accentuate certain characteristics in their drawings belongs in the category of psychologists' old wives' tales.

The Loser's Game

At this point, some of you might ask whether the problems in decision making, particularly in the stock market, are being exaggerated. The answer, I think, can be found by looking at the favorite investments of market professionals over time.

We've already looked at the record of the "all-star analysts" in chapter 1. Let's move on to a large international conference of institutional investors held at the New York Hilton in February 1970. Over two thousand strong, the delegates were polled for the stock they thought would show outstanding appreciation that year. The favorite choice was National Student Marketing—the highest-octane performer of the day. From a price of 120 in February, it dropped 95 percent by July of that same year. At the same conference in 1972, the airlines were selected as the industry expected to perform best for the balance of the year. Within 1 percent of their highs, the carrier stocks fell 50 percent that year in the face of a sharply rising market. The conference the following year voted them a group to avoid.

Are these simply chance results? In my earlier book, *Psychology and the Stock Market,* I included seven surveys of how the favorite stocks of groups of large numbers of professional investors had subsequently fared. In all the surveys, the choices of the professionals did worse than the market averages. And this before adding on commission charges and advisory fees.

As I indicated at the time, these were the only samples I had been able to locate. Since publication, with further digging and an excellent research assistant—Ms. Nan Miller—as well as some luck, we have unearthed a large number of additional samples—some fifty-two encompass investment advice given over the fifty-one-year period between 1929 and 1980. The surveys show the favorite stock or portfolio of groups of professional investors. The number participating ranged from twenty-five at the low end to as high as several thousand. The median was well over a hundred. Wherever possible, the subsequent performance of the professional choices was measured against the S&P 500 for the next twelve months.*

*Several studies used different averages or time periods. For details see Appendix I, pages 303–307.

Table 5

EXPERT FORECASTS OF FAVORITE STOCKS AND INDUSTRIES

TIME SPAN	SOURCE OF SURVEYS	TOTAL SURVEYS	PERCENT OUTPERFORMING MARKET IN NEXT YEAR
1929–32	Cowles Surveys	3	0
1953–76	*Trusts and Estates*	21	33
1967–69	*Financial Analysts Journal*	1	0
1967–72	*California Business*	7	29
1969–73	*Institutional Investor*	7	0
1973	*Business Week*	2	50
1974	*Seminar* (Edson Gould)	2	0
1974	Callan Associates	4	0
1974–76	Mueller Surveys	4	25
1980	Financial World "All-Stars"	1	33
Total number of surveys		52	
Percentage of professional surveys *underperforming* market			77

NOTE: Dividends excluded in all comparisons.

The results are presented in table 5. The first column shows the time period for each set of surveys, the second the source of the survey, the third the total number of surveys conducted, and the final column the percentage of each set of surveys that outperformed the market in the next twelve months.

The findings startled me. While I believed the evidence clearly showed that experts make many mistakes, I did not think the magnitude of error was as striking or as consistent as the results make evident.

Eighteen of the studies measure the performance of five or more stocks the experts picked as their favorites. By diversifying into a number of stocks instead of just choosing one or two, the element of chance is reduced. And yet, the eighteen portfolios so chosen underperformed the market on sixteen occasions! This meant, in effect, that when you receive professional advice about stocks to buy, you would be given bad advice nine out of ten times. Throwing darts at the stock pages blindfolded or flipping a coin to decide what to buy would give you a fifty-fifty chance. Using a financial professional would reduce your odds considerably.

The other thirty-four samples did not do appreciably better.

Overall, the favorite stocks and industries of large groups of money managers and analysts did worse than the market on forty of fifty-two occasions—or 77 percent of the time—as table 5 shows.

One of the first studies was done by Alfred Cowles,* among the earliest systematic students of markets, who made three separate studies measuring the forecasting record of investment advisors, large insurance companies, brokers, and bankers between 1928 and 1932. All underperformed the market.†

Another important survey is based on polls conducted by *Trusts and Estates* over a twenty-one-year period. Each year a large number of investment officers with bank trust departments (as a group, the largest institutional common-stock investors) were asked to name their three favorite industries for the next year. Table 6 gives the results for the 1953–76 period.‡ The favorite industry of most bank portfolio managers did worse than the market in fourteen of the twenty-one years, or 67 percent of the time. It's also interesting, since there are dozens of industries to choose from, that one industry—office equipment—was favored so often.

Moving on to more recent times, a number of broad surveys have been conducted by *Institutional Investor,* a magazine widely read by the professionals. In late 1971, for example, the magazine polled more than 150 money managers in twenty-seven states, each of whom chose the five stocks he or she believed would show the best performance the following year. Different types of money managers were surveyed, ranging from the people who ran hair-trigger performance funds to conservative bank and insurance types. The magazine indicated that although four hundred stocks were selected overall, there was a remarkable consensus regarding the top ten favorites, which were weighted toward concepts popular at the time.[19]

The top ten fizzled in a rising market, gaining only 1.3 percent in 1972, a year the averages rose 15.6 percent. For the two-year period,

---

*For those interested in more details of the samples, please refer to Appendix I.

†Cowles was a formidable researcher and a possible precursor of the random walk theory, coming as he did from the bastion of that theory, the University of Chicago. One of his many tests measured all the recommendations of William Peter Hamilton, who you may remember was the editor of the *Wall Street Journal* and cooriginator of the Dow theory. Cowles plotted Hamilton's entire forecasting record between 1904 and 1929 and once again found that if someone had followed each recommendation, he would have done worse than the averages. (Alfred Cowles III, "Can Stock Market Forecasters Forecast?" *Econometria* 1 [1933]: 309-324.)

‡The first poll took place in 1953; no polls were made between 1954 and 1956.

the favorites declined almost eight times as much as the averages. After the top ten that year, fifty runners-up were named. They did even more poorly, declining an average of 5 percent in 1972 and ten times as much as the market in the 1972–73 period.

Another survey was conducted the next year, 1973. It was a down year for the market and the S&P dropped 17.4 percent, hardly a ripple when compared with the average decline of 40.4 percent for the top ten, as shown in table 7 on page 112. Twenty-seven other stocks were also selected for performance that year, and again they did worse than the averages.[20] The surveys were discontinued after 1973.

Table 6
TRUSTS AND ESTATES
Subsequent Twelve-Month Performance of Favorite Industry

YEAR	FAVORITE INDUSTRY	PERFORMANCE OVER THE NEXT 12 MONTHS	
		INDUSTRY	S&P 500
1953a	Electric and gas public utilities	1.0%	− 6.6%
1957	Oil	−16.0	−14.3
1958	Electronics and electric utilities	75.0	38.1
1959	Oil	− 9.7	8.5
1960	Auto and accessories	−26.6	− 3.0
1961	Office equipment and machine group	31.0	23.1
1962	Chemicals, office equipment, banks	−17.1	−11.8
1963	Electric utilities	6.9	18.9
1964	Chemicals	15.6	13.0
1965	Chemicals	4.3	9.1
1966	Oil	−10.6	−13.0
1967	Utilities	4.7	20.1
1968	Office equipment	− 0.9	7.7
1969	Office equipment	15.6	−11.4
1970	Office equipment	−17.5	0.1
1971	Building materials	5.5	10.8
1972	Retail	11.7	15.7
1973	Office equipment	−21.5	−17.4
1974	Office equipment	−37.0	−29.7
1975	Office equipment	27.7	31.5
1976	Petroleum	29.0	19.1
Percentage underperforming market		67 %	

aNo surveys conducted in 1954, 1955, and 1956.

Table 7
THE 1973 TOP TEN

COMPANY	PRICE 1/1/73	PRICE 12/31/73	PERCENT CHANGE	PRICE 12/31/74	PERCENT CHANGE FROM 1/1/73
IBM	321⅝	246¾	−23.3%	168	−47.8%
Polaroid	126⅛	69⅞	−44.6	18⅝	−85.2
ITT	60¼	26⅜	−56.2	14¾	−75.5
Teleprompter	33¼	3⅞	−88.3	1½	−95.5
Eastman Kodak	148⅜	116	−21.8	62⅞	−57.6
Gillette	63⅞	35⅞	−43.8	25⅜	−60.3
McDonald's	76¼	57	−25.2	29⅜	−61.5
Motorola	65½	49¼	−24.8	34⅛	−47.9
Digital Equipment	91¾	101⅞	+11.0	50¾	−44.7
Levitz Furniture	26⅞	3⅝	−86.5	1¾	−93.5
Average change			−40.4%		−67.0%
S&P 500					
(without dividends)	118.1	97.6	−17.4%	68.6	−41.9%

NOTE: All companies adjusted for stock splits.
SOURCE: Reprinted from *Psychology and the Stock Market*, by David Dreman, p. 154.

Table 8
CALLAN ASSOCIATES SURVEY (12/31/74)
Performance Over the Next Twelve Months

Six-stock portfolio to buy	+20.7%
Favorite industry—drugs	+ 2.8%
Worst six stocks	+42.9%
Worst industry—electrical and electronics	+42.0%
S&P 500	+31.5%

A final survey, conducted by Callan Associates, a West Coast consulting firm, is worth noting. Three dozen investment managers were asked at the end of 1974 to pick both their favorite six stocks and favorite industry and at the same time the six stocks and single industry they thought would do worst in the following year. Table 8 shows some rather extraordinary results. The "worst" stocks and single industry did better than the S&P, while the "best" did worse.

More recently, professionals have been reluctant to participate in such polls. When asked to name his favorites, one analyst replied tersely: "We don't make this information available free anymore."

What do we make of results such as these? The number of

samples seems far too large for the outcome to be simply chance. In fact, the evidence indicates a surprisingly high level of error among professionals in choosing both individual stocks and portfolios over a period spanning almost fifty years.

Such evidence, in the first place, is incompatible with the central assumption of the efficient-market hypothesis.* But far more important are the practical implications of what we have just seen: the discovery of a very plausible explanation of why fundamental methods often do not work. The theory demands just too much from man as a configural reasoner and information processor. Both within and outside of markets, under conditions of information overload our mental tachometers appear to surge far above the red line. When this happens, we no longer process information reliably. Confidence rises as our input of information increases, but our decisions are not improved. And from the evidence we've seen in the stock market at least, they appear to deteriorate.

While it is true that experts may do as poorly in other complex circumstances, the market professional unfortunately works in a goldfish bowl. In no other calling that I am aware of is the outcome of decisions so easily measurable.

The high failure rate among financial professionals, at times approaching 90 percent, indicates not only that errors are made, but that under uncertain, complex conditions, there must be some systematic and predictable forces working against the unwary investor to account for such extraordinarily poor results.

The next chapter will look at what these forces are, and how we may try to counter them.

---

*The hypothesis states that it is impossible to beat the market because of the competition among professionals, which results in prices always being about where they should be. But just as the theory holds that even professionals cannot outdo the market over time, it also holds that they cannot do substantially worse. After all, it is their very decision making that keeps prices at their proper level in the first place. The surveys, however, give us a different picture from the one assumed by the theorists. The massive underperformance in both up and down markets indicates that their most crucial assumption is inconsistent with a statistically significant body of evidence. Findings such as these appear to indicate that the hypothesis is made of straw. Further, Betas, the core of the efficient-market hypothesis, have proven to be notoriously unstable over time—which means that the very heart of the theory seems to have disintegrated.

CHAPTER SIX

Avoiding
Bad Market Odds

"It is a great advantage for a system of philosophy to be substantially true," Santayana once wrote. Similarly, it would seem a great advantage for popular investment philosophies to be essentially workable. Unfortunately, as the evidence to date indicates, their workability often appears as elusive as the "truths" of philosophy.

But perhaps even more striking is that the methods not only fail to provide any help to the expert, but prove a positive liability—judging from the record we just viewed. Indeed, the failures appear so widespread that there must be systematic reasons to account for them. And there are. Despite what many economists and financial theorists assume, people are not good intuitive statisticians, particularly under the difficult conditions previously described. Which means they simply do not calculate odds properly when they make investment decisions. Because they don't, repeated and predictable errors crop up in markets—errors that can be recognized and avoided. First, we must attempt to learn why such mistakes occur so frequently. Once their nature is understood, a set of rules can be developed to help monitor investment decisions and provide a safety net against serious mishap. After doing this, we can move into specific strategies that are built precisely upon these intuitive statistical limitations.

Mental Shortcuts

Researchers have found that people, in making many decisions, adopt shortcuts or rules of thumb rather than formally calculating the actual odds of something happening. Called judgmental heuristics, in technical jargon, these are the various learning and simplifying strategies people use to make the processing of large amounts of information possible. Experience over a lifetime shows that most such judgmental shortcuts work exceptionally well and allow us to cope quickly with and organize data that would otherwise prove overwhelming. Driving a car down Broadway, for example, one would (or should) concentrate only on operating the vehicle, other traffic, and pedestrians, screening out thousands of other distracting and disruptive bits of information. The rule of thumb is to focus solely on what directly affects our driving, and the rule is obviously a good one.

We also use selective processes in dealing with probabilities we are facing. In many of our decisions and judgments, we tend to be intuitive statisticians. We use mental shortcuts that work well most of the time. We think our odds of survival are better driving at fifty-five miles an hour than at ninety miles an hour, although few of us have ever bothered to check the actual numbers. A professional hockey team is likely to beat an amateur one, if the "amateurs" are not Russians or Czechs; a discount department store will probably sell TV sets more cheaply than Macy's or Bloomingdale's; and we might expect to get to a city six hundred miles away faster by air than by ground transportation. There are many dozens of such examples one could readily cite to indicate that such procedures are both valuable and immensely timesaving.[1] But being an intuitive statistician has limitations as well as blessings. The very simplifying processes that are normally highly efficient timesavers in most cases tend to lead to systematic mistakes in investment decisions. Here they can make people believe the odds in an investment situation are dramatically different from what they actually are. As a result, they consistently shortchange the investor.

The distortions produced by the subjectively calculated probabilities are large, systematic, and very difficult to eliminate even after people have been made fully aware of them, as we'll see next.

The Short, Happy Life of the "Hot" Advisor

We have already seen how quickly investors flock to better-perform-ing mutual funds, even though financial researchers have shown that the "hot" funds in one time period very often turn out to be the poorest performers in another. Fred Mates was the top fund manager for most of 1968, and close to the bottom of three hundred fund managers in 1969. The subsequent records of Fred Carr and Gerald Tsai were also lackluster at best. Even so, investors are continuously enthralled by such "hot" performance for brief periods. Because of this susceptibility in most people, brokers or analysts who have had one or two stocks move up sharply or chartists who call one turn correctly are believed to have established a credible record and can readily find market followings.

Likewise, an advisory service that is right for a short period of time can beat its drums loudly. "Professor C," for example, is cur-rently advertising week after week in numerous publications how his "market barometers" have never been more negative, and shows the reader how right he has been for one year. Or Hans Frinz, the Swiss monetary gnome and goldbug, runs banner advertisements proclaim-ing the correctness of his recent opinion on the upward movement of gold. The truth of the matter is that both Hans and the good professor have been wrong in their judgments far more often than either would like to remember. In 1974, near the bottom of the market, I remember Frinz telling a seminar of professionals that he felt gold would go to $600 within a year, the level at the time of the Dow. And the Dow in turn would go to 200, near the level at which gold was then trading. Shortly thereafter, gold dropped sharply, and the market increased by nearly 70 percent. And in early 1980, Frinz saw gold moving from its then-current price of $800 to $1,500 "im-minently." Perhaps it is all in the way you define "imminently." Gold proceeded to $385 within a year, and remains near that level at the time of this writing.

However, advisors understand—either intuitively or con-sciously—that the public is convinced that results over short periods are meaningful when they are more often than not simply chance happenings. And those in the public eye usually gain large numbers of new subscribers for being right—for a time. Joe Granville, whom we met earlier, quadrupled his subscribers and increased his income tenfold this way. The principle is central to the subscription game.

This brings us to the first of the major probability errors that this chapter will examine, the one that Israeli psychologists Amos Tversky and Daniel Kahneman called the "law of small numbers."[2] Examining journals in both psychology and education, they found that researchers tended systematically to overstate the importance of findings taken from small samples. The statistically valid "law of large numbers" states that large samples will usually be highly representative of the population from which they are drawn; for example, public opinion polls are normally fairly accurate because of their ability to draw on large and representative groups. However, the smaller the sample used (or the shorter the record), the more likely the findings are mere chance occurrences rather than really meaningful. And yet the Tversky and Kahneman studies showed the typical psychological or educational experimenters gambled their research theories on samples so small that the odds that the figures were simply chance were much too high.[3] This is almost identical to the investor gambling on an excellent but all too brief record of an advisor. The psychologists and educators were far too confident that their results, based on only a few observations or a short period of time, were significant, even though they were trained in statistical techniques and should have been well aware of the dangers.

What is important to note is how readily people can overgeneralize the meanings of small numbers of supporting facts or statistics. Our intuitions seem to be satisfied with quite limited statistical evidence, which may not be at all representative of the real facts. Sometimes the evidence we accept may run to the absurd. I once heard two brokers at Elaine's, a popular New York café, agreeing that the best way of judging Coca-Cola's sales prospects was to talk to a few of the deliverymen. Since the company has many thousands of such men scattered throughout the country, I felt a little sorry for the clients who were to benefit from such incisiveness.

Tversky and Kahneman's findings, which have been repeatedly confirmed, are particularly important to our understanding of some stock market errors and lead to a rule that investors should try to follow:

Rule 1: Don't be influenced by a short performance record of a money manager, broker, analyst, or advisor.

The law of averages indicates that many—usually playing currently popular trends—will have excellent records, often for months and sometimes for a year or more, only to be followed by disastrous ones later. If you buy the record just after a period of spectacular performance, chances are that the manager will not sustain it.

This is the sad lesson to be learned from the "performance managers" of 1968, many of whom forlornly traded in smoking pistols for cab driver's medallions or bartender's aprons after decimating their clients' portfolios. And it was the same lesson that the English and French investors buying the South Sea and Mississippi companies were taught some 250 years earlier.

A Variation on the Previous Problem

A second error, in many ways parallel to the first, also indicates man's shortcomings as an intuitive statistician. People, in making decisions, appear to become overly immersed in the details of a particular situation and neglect the outcome of very similar situations from past experience. These past outcomes are called prior probabilities and logically should help to guide similar choices in the present.[4]

But they tend not to. An experiment showing this rather clearly was made with a group of advanced psychology students. The group was given a brief analysis of a graduate student, said to have been written by a psychologist several years earlier after conducting some tests. Psychology students are taught that profiles of this sort can be enormously inaccurate. And the one here was not only outdated but contained no indication of the subject's academic preference. The study, which follows, was intended to provide them with nothing of practical value.

Tom W. is of high intelligence, although lacking in true creativity. He has a need for order and clarity and for neat and tidy systems in which every detail finds its appropriate place. His writing is dull and rather mechanical, occasionally enlivened by somewhat corny puns and flashes of imagination of the sci-fi type. He has a strong drive for competence. He seems to have little feeling and little sympathy for other people, and does not enjoy interacting with others. Self-centered, he nevertheless has a deep moral sense.

Tom W. is currently a graduate student. Please rank the following nine fields of graduate specialization in order of the likelihood that Tom W. is now a student in that field. Let rank one be the most probable choice:

_____Business Administration

_____Computer Sciences

_____Engineering

_____Humanities and Education

_____Law

_____Library Science

_____Medicine

_____Physical and Life Sciences

_____Social Science and Social Work

Given the lack of substantive content, the graduate students should have ignored the study entirely, and made choices based simply on the percentage of students at the graduate school going into each field—information that of course had been provided for them, and that, it was assumed, they would act upon. At least, according to the laws of normative probability, this was what was expected of them. According to these laws, the more unreliable the available information is in a specific situation (called the case rate—in this example the profile of Tom W.), the more one should rely on past percentages (called the base rate—in this instance the percentage of students enrolled in each field).

Did the group look at the past percentages? No. This experiment and others like it demonstrated that the students relied entirely upon the profile and decided that computer sciences and engineering were the two most probable fields for Tom W. to enter, even though each had relatively few people in them. In spite of their training to the contrary, the psychology students based decisions on unreliable information, ignoring the more pertinent inputs.

A parallel example in the stock market is the emphasis people put on the individual outlook for exciting new issues and concept stocks (the case rate), even though the substantiating data are usually flimsy and uncertain at best. Still, investors rarely examine the high probability of loss in such ventures (the base rate). For example, most buyers of hot new issues in 1968, focusing on the individual story, forgot that over 98 percent of these issues had dropped in price after the 1962 market break; and as we saw by 1981, they had completely forgotten the experiences of 1962 and 1968. Here again, the prior probabilities, although essential, were ignored in the analysis. Which brings us to another rule of investment decision making:

Rule 2: Don't rely solely on the case rate. Take into account the prior probabilities.

The greater the complexity and uncertainty present in the investment situation you face, the less emphasis you should place on your current appraisal alone, and the more you should look to the success or failure of similar situations in the past.

Put another way, rather than attempting to obtain every fact and sliver of information about a difficult investment situation (much of which is contradictory, irrelevant, and difficult to evaluate correctly), the investor should, if it is at all possible, concern himself as much with trying to gauge the longer-term record of success or failure of a particular course of action.

We have already looked at new issues. The same rule could be applied to a number of similar investment situations. For example, if the investor likes a concept stock, he might take a cross-section of favorites of other periods and see how they worked out some years later, or if he decides to try his hand at market timing, examine how well the system he has chosen has worked over time.

In each instance, the information in the particular case being examined should, where possible, be supplemented by evidence of the longer-term record of success or failure of similar situations, the base rate, which should influence the decision made.

Regression to the Mean

The two previous investment biases play major roles in buttressing one of the most important and consistent sources of investment error. As intuitive statisticians, we do not comprehend the principle of *regression to the mean.* Although the terminology sounds formidable, the concept is actually quite simple. This statistical phenomenon was noted over a hundred years ago by Sir Francis Galton, a pioneer in eugenics, and will prove indispensable to the practical investment methods we are coming to next.

In studying the height of man, Galton found that the tallest group had sons whose mean height was shorter than the father's; conversely, in the shortest group of fathers, the mean height of the sons was taller. Since many tall men come from families of average height, they are likely to have children shorter than they are, while the opposite holds true for shorter men. In both cases, the height of the children was less extreme than that of the fathers and closer to the average.

The study of this phenomenon gave rise to the term *regression*, and the principle has since been documented in many areas.

Regression to the mean, although quite alien to us intuitively, occurs quite frequently.[5] Take the example of the reaction we have to a baseball player's batting average. Although a player may be a .300 hitter over some seasons, his record is anything but even. The player will not get three hits in every ten times at bat. There are times when he will be batting .500 or more, well above his average (or mean), and others when he will be lucky to hit .125. Over 162 games, whether the batter hits .125 or .500 in any dozen or so games makes little difference to the average. But rather than realizing that the player's performance over a week or a month is not usually in line with his season's average, we tend to relate only to the immediate past record. The player is believed to be in a "hitting streak" or a "slump." Fans, sportscasters, and, unfortunately, the players themselves place too much emphasis on brief periods and tend to forget the longer-term average.

Regression also occurs in many instances where it is not expected and yet is bound to happen. Air Force flight instructors were chagrined after they praised a fledgling pilot for an exceptionally good landing because it was normally followed by a poorer one the next time. Conversely, when they criticized a bad landing, a better one usually followed. What they did not understand was that at the particular level of training of these student pilots, there was no more consistency in their landings than in the daily batting figures of baseball players. Bumpy landings would be followed by smooth ones and vice versa. In effect, there was a pattern of regression to the mean. Correlating the landing quality to their remarks, the instructors erroneously concluded that criticism was helpful to learning and praise detrimental, a conclusion almost universally rejected by learning theory researchers.

And now, with some understanding of the principle, we can

go back to how it works in the stock market. According to a major study made by Ibbotson and Sinquefield of the University of Chicago,[6] stocks over the last fifty years have returned 9.2 percent annually in price appreciation and dividends (see figure 14, page 124), against a return of about 4.1 percent for bonds. An earlier study by the Cowles Commission showed much the same stock return going back to the 1880s.

However, as the figure shows, the return has been anything but consistent—not unlike the number of hits a .300 hitter will get in individual games over a few weeks or a month. There have been long periods when stocks have returned more than the 9.2 percent mean. And within each of these periods, there have been times when stocks performed sensationally, rising sometimes 50 percent or more in a year. At other times, they have seemed to free-fall. Stocks, then, although they have averaged 9.2 percent over a long period of time, have had their own periods of "streaks" and "slumps."*

For investors, the long-term rate of return of common stocks, like the batting average of a ballplayer, is the important thing to remember. However, as intuitive statisticians, we find it very hard, if not impossible, to do so. Market history provides a continual example of our adherence to current trends.

The investor of 1927 and 1928 thought that returns in the nature of 35 to 40 percent were in order from that time on, although they deviated far from the past mean; and in 1933 and 1934 he believed huge losses were inevitable, although they too deviated sharply from the long-term mean. The same is true of every major market peak and trough. As figure 1 (page 13) on investment advisor buying and selling indicates, most experts are closely tied, if not pilloried, to the current market movement. The belief that extreme returns, either positive or negative, will persist continues, rather than the far more likely probability that they are simply a remote point on the graph charting the distribution of returns and that succeeding patterns will tend to fall in line with historical standards.

The relevance of these long-term returns can be masked by detailed knowledge of the specific trend or fashion and by intense involvement in it.[7] Even those who are aware of these long-term

*As we'll see in chapter 13, this rate should rise with increasing inflation.

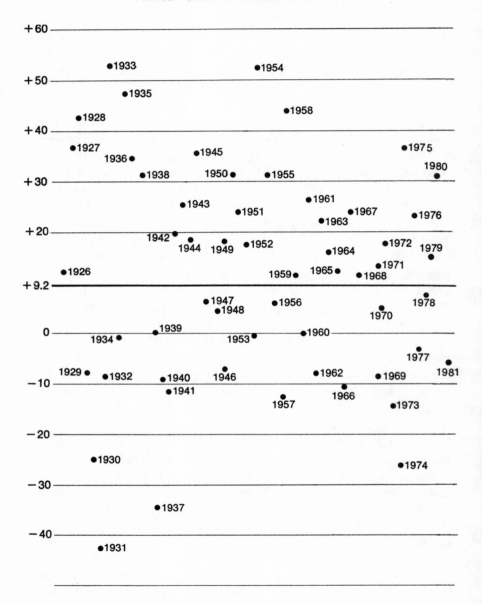

Figure 14.
Annual return on stocks. 1926–81.

standards of value for stocks often cannot see them clearly because of preoccupation with short-term conditions. And this leads to a third protective rule:

> *Rule 3: Don't be seduced by recent rates of investment return for individual stocks or the market when they deviate sharply from past norms (the case rate). For investors, longer-term characteristics of stocks (the base rate) are far more likely to be established again.*

Returns that are extremely high or low should be treated as deviations from long-term norms. The long-term return of the market might be viewed like the average height of men. It is unlikely that abnormally tall men will beget even taller men, just as it is unlikely that abnormally high returns will follow already high returns. In both cases, the principle of regression to the mean will most probably apply, and the next series of returns will be less extreme. As chapter 8 will detail, even as returns deviate sharply from the market mean, dynamic forces on the investment and economic scenes are at work to reduce the deviations.

Because experts in the stock market are no more aware of the principle of regression than others, each sharp price deviation from past norms of value is explained by a new, spurious theory. This, together with other cognitive biases we will examine, leaves the investor vulnerable time and again to the fashions of the marketplace, however far removed prices may be from intrinsic worth.

In bull markets, as Gerald Loeb noted, we tend to congratulate ourselves for boldness as prices move up, and we wish we had taken even greater risks. In bear markets, of course, we rue being in stocks at all. The pattern is ever-repeating.

The Input-Output Blues

Another powerful bias that usually leads to consistent error in the market and encourages investors to accept the biases just discussed is their intuitive belief that inputs and outputs should be closely correlated. Tests have shown, for example, that people are far more confident that a student will regularly have a B average if he has two B's rather than an A and a C. They believe that consistent inputs allow greater predictability than inconsistent ones, although the belief is not statistically valid.[8]

The direct extension of this finding is the manner in which investors equate a good stock with a rising price and a poor stock with a falling price. One of the most common questions analysts, money managers, or brokers are asked is, "If the stock is so good, why isn't it moving?" The answer, of course, is that its value (the input) is often not recognized in price (the output) for quite some time. Yet many investors demand such immediate, though incorrect, feedback—and can make serious mistakes as a consequence.

Another interesting aspect of the latter phenomenon is that investors tend to place high confidence in extreme inputs or outputs, which are often not valid. Computer service stocks in the 1967–68 market had sensational earnings growth (the input), which was confirmed when the price went up astronomically—as much as one-hundredfold (the output). The seemingly strong fundamentals went hand in hand with sharply rising prices for the South Sea Company or for that matter growth stocks in 1972 or early 1973. Extreme correlations look good and many people are quite willing to accept them as likely to continue, but as generations of investors have discovered the hard way, they aren't.

The same thinking is also applied to each crash and panic. Here the earnings estimates and outlooks (the inputs) became notably worse as prices dropped. Graham and Dodd, astute market clinicians that they were, saw this input-output relationship quite clearly. They wrote that "an inevitable rule of the market is that the prevalent theory of common stock valuations has developed in rather close conjunction with the change in the level of prices."[9] The consistency of this behavior leads us to our final market rule:

Rule 4: Don't expect the strategy you adopt to prove a quick success in the marketplace.

Demanding immediate success invariably leads to playing fashions or fads that are currently performing well rather than to investing on a more solid basis. An investment course, once charted, should be given time to work.* In reality, patience is a crucial but very rare investment commodity. The problem is not as simple as it may appear because studies have shown that businessmen and other

*I'll say more on this in chapter 9.

investors abhor uncertainty.* Certainty to most people in the market is a satisfactory explanation of events within a condensed time frame; in short, quick input-output matching.

On Grizzly Bear Attacks and Stock Prices

Further evidence indicates that we consistently misread probabilities intuitively, and just as consistently we get into investment difficulties as a result. The ease and frequency with which we can recall an event affects the probability with which it is judged to occur.[10]

Now, this judgmental shortcut, or heuristic, works well most of the time because we normally recall events more easily that have occurred frequently. However, our recall is also influenced by factors in addition to frequency, such as how recently the events have happened and what their emotional saliency is.[11] People recall good or bad events out of proportion to their actual occurrences. The chances of being mauled by a grizzly bear at a national park are only one or two per million visitors, and the death rate is lower. Casualties from shark attacks probably represent an even smaller percentage of swimmers in coastal waters, although *Jaws* certainly resulted in a noticeable decrease in swimming off the Hamptons, Fire Island, and elsewhere for a time in 1976. However, because of the sensational nature of the dangers, most people tend to think the probabilities of such attacks are much higher than they really are.

And the actual occurrence of disasters, rather than the probabilities of their happening, has an important bearing on our purchase of casualty insurance. Earthquake and airline insurance purchases go up sharply after a calamity, as do purchases of flood insurance.[12]

Statements by experts, crowd participation, and recent experience strongly incline the investor to follow the prevailing trend or fashion in the marketplace. In late 1972 and 1973 the only stocks doing well were the highfliers, companies that month after month continued to climb steadily while more mundane companies dropped sharply. The experience was repeated and salient to the investor, while the disastrous aftermath of the 1961–62 speculation in highfli-

*See, for example, George Katona, *Psychological Economics* (New York: American Elsevier, 1975).

ers or that of 1967–68 had receded far back in his memory. The same is true with last year's new-issue high-tech craze.

A moment's reflection indicates that this judgmental bias reinforces the others. Recent and salient events, whether positive or negative, strongly influence judgments of the future. People, it appears, often become prisoners of such experience and view the future as an extension of the immediate past. The more memorable the circumstances, the more they are expected to persist, no matter how out of line with prior norms.

Just how powerful recent and salient events can be was brought home to me last year in an interview with a national magazine. The interviewer had read the first edition of this book and was familiar with its investment philosophy. In the course of the conversation he asked me to name some stocks that I thought provided good value. I did, reiterating to him that normally our investment strategies called for a holding period of at least two years.

Sure enough, six months later a friend called to say the magazine had reviewed the performance of these stocks. A small fund that was also mentioned in the article, which concentrated on emerging growth stocks at the height of this boiling market, was up sensationally. By comparison, our record "wasn't so good," being ahead of the market through the same period only about 50 percent with conservative stocks.*

What the reporter hadn't checked was the more important longer-term record. If he had, he would have found the same fund was among the worst performers of 500 mutual funds monitored by Arthur Lipper (a service devoted to ranking mutual funds) in the previous year, having declined almost 50 percent. For the one-, two-, or seven-year periods our accounts were far ahead of this fund. But again, recency and saliency (and possibly a reporter's deadline) proved to override the other, more important considerations. As psychologists have pointed out, this is a difficult bias to shed.

The defense here, as in rule 4, is to try to take a longer-term view of events. While there is certainly no assured way to put such recent or memorable experience into absolute perspective, it might be helpful during periods of extreme pessimism or optimism to wander back to your library. If the market is dropping sharply, reread the daily

---

*To update the story, by the end of 1981, as the new-issue high-tech craze cooled, the fund was down more than 30 percent. Over the period we were still ahead slightly, although the general market had declined 10 percent.

and weekly financial periodicals during the last major break. If you can, pick up the *Wall Street Journal,* turn to the market section, and read how negative the opinion was of expert after expert in October, November, and early December of 1974, just before the market began one of its sharpest recoveries. Similarly, if we ever have another speculative market, it would not be a bad idea to check the *Journal* again and read the comments made during the 1967–68 or 1978–80 bubble. While rereading the daily press is not an elixir, I think it will prove helpful.

We might briefly view two other systematic biases that are relevant to the investment scene and tend to fix investment errors firmly in place. They are also difficult to correct, since they tend to buttress the ones we've already viewed.

The first is known as *anchoring,* [13] another simplifying heuristic. In a complex situation, such as the marketplace, some natural starting point, such as current price, is selected as a first approximation of worth from which most people then make adjustments. Fairly typically, the adjustments are not sufficient. Thus, an investor in 1972 might have thought a price of 60 was too high for Levitz Furniture, and that 45 was more appropriate. But Levitz was grossly overvalued at 45, to which it dropped on the way to 5.

Again, the best defense against this bias appears to be in our earlier rule: *If the returns are particularly high or low, they are most likely to be abnormal.*

The final bias is an interesting one. In looking back at past mistakes, researchers have found that people believe that each major error made could have been seen much more clearly at the time than it was if only they hadn't been wearing rose- or dark-colored glasses at the time. The inevitability of what happened seems apparent in retrospect. Hindsight bias seriously impairs people's proper assessment of past errors and places a significant limit on what can be learned from experience. [14]

I remember sitting in an investment committee meeting of a large mutual-fund advisory group in 1971 when its members were particularly bullish on the market—naturally, it was going up at the time. The senior partner, looking at how sharply prices had risen from the depressed levels of 1970, asked, "How could we not have bought stocks then?" In 1975 he asked the same thing after the even sharper drop of 1974. And he'll likely ask it again after the next market rally.

This bias too is a difficult one to handle. That walk to the library appears here to be as good a solution as any. I think you will see that the mistakes made were far less obvious than they appear today.

Decisional Biases and Market Fashions

We saw in chapter 4 the seductiveness of current market fashions, how large numbers of rational and prudent investors could be swept away by the lure of profit from the New World, from bubble companies, or from go-go stocks. Now, with some knowledge of decisional biases, we can understand why the tug of fashion has always been so persistent and influential on both the market population and the expert opinion of the day.

Whatever the fashion, the experts could demonstrate that the particular choice performed in a manner superior statistically to other less favored investments in the immediate past. And sometimes the investment did so for fairly long periods of time. Tulip bulbs appreciated sharply for seven years prior to 1637. A Dutch expert in that latter year could easily show that for more than a decade tulips had yielded considerably more annually than did owning buildings, shops, or farms. The recent record was exciting and rising prices would seem to justify much more of the same.

The pattern continually repeats itself. A buyer of canal bonds in the 1830s or blue-chip stocks in 1929 could argue that though the prices were very dear, each had proved to be a vastly superior holding in the recent past. Along with the Crash and the Depression came the passion for government bonds at near-zero interest rates, which persisted for a decade and a half. A distinguished economist stated at a conference in 1948: "Never in the lifetime of anyone in this room will government two-and-a-halves sell below par." Barring the few unfortunates who, heeding these words, fell on their coupon clippers when bond prices nose-dived shortly thereafter, most found the prediction proved dramatically wrong.

In the 1950s investing in good-grade common stocks again came into vogue, and in 1962 and 1968 an excellent case could be and was made for buying concept stocks. By the end of the decade, the superior record of stocks through the postwar era had put investing in bonds in disrepute. *Institutional Investor,* a magazine exceptionally adept at catching the prevailing trends, presented a dinosaur on the cover of its February 1969 issue with the caption CAN THE BOND MARKET SURVIVE? The article continued: "In the long run, the public market for straight debt might become obsolete."

Stocks as a percentage of institutional portfolios rose dramatically, from 40 percent of assets in 1958 to 74 percent in 1972. So great was the demand for stocks that not only did pension funds—the largest institutional investor—put all new monies into them, they also sold off a portion of their bonds to increase their holdings further. The accumulation of stocks occurred just as their rates of return were beginning to decrease sharply. Of course, bonds immediately went on to provide better returns than stocks through 1978.

And with the poor results in the stock market in recent years, there has been a full swing of the pendulum. Through the end of 1978, stocks were being rapidly reduced as a percentage of total portfolios by institutional investors, and only a small part of their new monies were being committed to them. At the same time, good-quality long-term bonds were being bought almost frenziedly. In 1978, I heard a well-regarded money manager tell an investment group the last decade was only the prelude—bonds would outperform stocks for the next twenty years.

Of course, as we know, it happened all over again. The bond market massacre of late 1979 and early 1980, replayed even more destructively in 1981, was worse than any stock market decline of the whole postwar period. Issues fell almost 50 percent and, unlike the stock market, have not recovered to date.

As always after a major miscalculation, perceptions shifted radically. Money managers are once again leaning heavily toward equities and large amounts of institutional funds have been earmarked for this purpose in the next few years.

And behind the polls of expert failure we saw in the last chapter was the fact that the professionals tended to play the fashions of the day—concept stocks in 1968 and 1971, the top tier in 1972 and 1973, or "Smokestack America" in 1975 and 1976. In the *Institutional Investor* contest of 1972 for instance, the top-tier selections were weighted toward concepts popular at the time, including Bausch & Lomb, Levitz, and TelePrompter. By early 1973 interest had shifted from concepts to growth stocks, and the top ten included IBM, Polaroid, ITT, Eastman Kodak, McDonald's, and Digital Equipment. One fund manager, noting the sharp rise in the price of large growth stocks at the time, said that their performance stood out "like a beacon in the night." Both the growth stocks and the concept stocks were clobbered shortly thereafter.

Although market history provides convincing testimony about the ephemeral nature of recent fashions, they have captivated generation after generation of investors. Each fashion has its supporting statistics, the law of small numbers. The fashions are salient and easy to recall and are of course confirmed by rising prices, the inputs and outputs again. These biases, all of which interact, make it natural to project the prevailing trend well into the future. The common error each time is that although the trend may have lasted for months, even at times for years, it was not representative and was sometimes far removed from the performance of equities or bonds over longer periods (regression to the mean). In hindsight we can readily see the errors and wonder why we did not see them earlier when they were so obvious.

Thus, it helps to have some rules in order not to be swept away by prevailing fashion. Let's briefly review the four rules:

1. Don't be influenced by a short performance record of a money manager, broker, or advisor.

2. Don't rely solely on the case rate. Take into account the prior probabilities.

3. Don't be seduced by recent rates of investment return for individual stocks or the market that deviate sharply from past norms. Longer-term characteristics of stocks, the base rate, are far more likely to be reestablished.

4. Don't expect the strategy you adopt to prove a quick success in the marketplace.

Frankly, the above four rules are going to be a lot harder to follow than you might think, because the cognitive biases are anything but phantoms. However, the effort to understand their pull should prove rewarding and help avoid many a serious error.

Shortcuts to Disaster

We find, then, that the information-processing shortcuts—called heuristics—which are normally both highly efficient and immensely timesaving in day-to-day situations, work systematically against us in the marketplace. Only in recent years has it been recognized that people simply do not follow the principles of probability theory under conditions of uncertainty. The tendency to underestimate or altogether ignore past probabilities in making a decision is undoubtedly the most significant problem of intuitive prediction in fields as diverse as financial analysis, accounting, geography, engineering, and military intelligence.[15] The implications of such consistent errors and cognitive biases are enormous, not only in economics, management, and investments, but in virtually every area where such decision making comes into play.

But the cognitive biases seem to flourish particularly well in the stock market and result in a high rate of investment error. These interacting biases systematically lead us into bad investment decisions. We are too apt to look at insufficient information in order to confirm a course of action, we are too inclined to put great emphasis on recent or emotionally compelling events, and we expect our decisions to be met with quick market confirmation. The more we discuss a course and identify with it, the less we believe prior standards are valid.

And so each trend and fashion looks unique, is identified as such, and inevitably takes its toll. Knowledge that none prevails for long is dismissed.

These cognitive biases, which affect each of us to a greater or lesser extent, are far more firmly locked into place by the group pressures described previously. Our own inclinations are powerfully reinforced when we see other people we respect interpret information the way we do. The failure of professional investors who are normally oriented to current fashions seems telling evidence of this point.

However, we should not be discouraged by these biases. In fact, as was suggested earlier, they can be harnessed to work in our favor. Let's turn to see how, next.

PART III

A WORKABLE INVESTMENT STRATEGY

CHAPTER SEVEN

The
Low Price/Earnings Ratio
Investment Strategy:
What Is It?

In Samuel Beckett's play Vladimir and Estragon sit endlessly waiting for Godot. Having come this far, you may have begun to feel that a sound and workable investment strategy, like Godot, may never appear. Certainly, the problems identified in the last three chapters suggest futility. Man's abilities as an information processor are imperfect, his limitations as an intuitive statistician are disheartening, and his investment decisions are all too often made under the influence of his fellow inebriates.

Fortunately, the story does not end here. Unlike Beckett's play, it has a good chance for a happier ending. Indeed, the very consistency of investor behavior patterns forms a crucial part of the strategy I'm about to propose. These patterns can be translated into a workable investment method that may very well pinpoint excellent opportunities for you.

The Quagmire of Visibility

One of the few things academics and financial practitioners agree on these days is this: earnings are a major determinant of stock prices.[1] Hence the ability to forecast profits with reasonable accuracy should give the professional a decided edge over the crowd. Little wonder, then, that an article of faith among Wall Street research departments has been that nothing is as important in the practice of security analysis as estimating the earnings outlook. The clearer the company's prospects and the better they look at a particular time, the better the visibility. Companies with the best earnings prospects and fastest growth rates are normally accorded higher price/earnings ratios, while companies with poor or lackluster prospects are banished to the lower-multiple tiers. Sometimes the disparity between the price/earnings ratios of the most favored and the least favored companies is immense. In early 1973, for example, investors valued each dollar of earnings of McDonald's or Disney at ten times a dollar earned by U.S. Steel.

In order to make such evaluations, as we have seen, forecasts extending earnings well into the future must be made with extreme accuracy. Forecasting is the heart of most security analysis as it is practiced today.

But from the evidence screened previously, the accuracy of such forecasts should be viewed with suspicion. Investment strategies so based have performed with a great deal of inconsistency, to say the least. What seems apparent is that the companies the experts liked best tended to be the wrong ones to buy. We must therefore ask another question: should one avoid the stocks the experts or the crowd are pursuing, and pursue the ones they are avoiding? The answer, as we shall see, is an unqualified yes. Here we will document the consistent success of an investment strategy over an almost forty-year period—a strategy that dramatically opposes much of conventional wisdom—and the reasons why it works.

For the findings show that *those companies that the market expects will have the best futures as measured by the price/earnings ratios they are accorded have consistently done worst subsequently, while the stocks believed to have the most dismal futures have always provided the best subsequent returns.* The foundation of the strategy is not without an element of black comedy. In fact, to some devotees of contemporary investment methods, the approach may appear to be a form of devil worship. What is believed to be "good" as an investment, according to P/E multiples, almost invariably turns out "bad"—and naturally, what is "bad" turns out to be very "good."

However, the findings are fortunately not in the least magical.

For we know about the immense difficulties, and shortly we will see corroborating statistical evidence, of predicting earnings and economic events with any degree of consistency. Most investors do not recognize this, and when forecasting methods fail, aided in no small degree by the biases enumerated in the last chapter, a predictable psychological reaction occurs.

And here we confront the main irony: *One of the most obvious and predictable variables that can be harnessed into a workable investment strategy is the continuous overreaction of man himself when his assessment of a company's earnings (or the economy itself) proves incorrect.* This works just as surely with the investor today as it has with investors in all markets of the past. Let's turn to just how consistent this overreaction actually is.

The World Turned Upside Down

Beginning in the 1960s, researchers began to wonder if visibility— that crucial pillar of modern security analysis—was actually as solid as generally believed. One of the first to question how accurate the P/E ratio was as a measure of subsequent market performance was Francis Nicholson, who researched the problem while with the Provident National Bank.

In one comprehensive study done in 1968 measuring the relative performance of high versus low P/E stocks, he analyzed 189 companies of trust company quality in eighteen industries over the twenty-five years between 1937 and 1962. The results are given in table 9.

Table 9
PERCENTAGE GAINS, 1937–62

P/E Quintile	AVERAGE PRICE APPRECIATION PERCENTAGES OVER TOTAL PERIOD AFTER						
	1 Yr.	2 Yrs.	3 Yrs.	4 Yrs.	5 Yrs.	6 Yrs.	7 Yrs.
1st (highest)	3	11	21	31	46	65	84
2nd	6	14	24	35	50	65	83
3rd	7	18	30	43	60	77	96
4th	9	22	34	48	65	82	100
5th (lowest)	16	34	55	76	98	125	149

SOURCE: *Financial Analysts Journal* (January–February 1968).

Nicholson divided the stocks into five equal groups solely according to their P/E rankings. The groups (or "quintiles," in statistical nomenclature) were rearranged by their P/E rankings for periods of one to seven years. Recasting the quintiles annually on the basis of the new P/E information resulted in the stocks most out of favor (quintile 5) showing a 16 percent annual rate of appreciation over the total time span. Conversely, switching into the highest P/E's on the same basis resulted in only 3 percent annual appreciation over the period. Although the performance discrepancies were reduced with longer holding periods, even after the original portfolios were held for seven years, the lowest 20 percent did almost twice as well as the highest.

Similar results were turned up by Paul Miller, Jr., who used as his data base the companies on the COMPUSTAT 1800 Industrial Tapes with sales of over $150 million between 1948 and 1964.*

Like Nicholson, Miller divided the stocks into quintiles according to their P/E's. The findings are displayed in table 10. With remarkable consistency, investors completely misjudged subsequent performance. In both studies the results are completely uniform. The second most popular quintile had the second worst results, while the second most unpopular quintile had the second best results.

Miller also found that the lowest 20 percent of stocks according to P/E's did best in twelve of the next seventeen years. The highest 20 percent, by comparison, did best in only one subsequent year and worst in eight.

A third study, this one involving the thirty stocks in the Dow-Jones Industrial Average itself, is cited in *The Intelligent Investor*. The performance of the ten lowest and the ten highest P/E's in the group and of the combined thirty stocks in the industrial average was measured over set periods between 1937 and 1969. In each time span the low P/E's did better than the market and the high P/E's did worse. (See table 11.)

The study also calculated the results of investing $10,000 in either the high- or low-multiple groups in the industrial average in 1937 and switching every five years into the lowest P/E's (in the first case) and the highest P/E's (in the latter). Ten thousand dollars

---

*All fiscal years in the study were between September 30 and January 31. All companies studied had positive earnings. The number of such companies increased from 110 in the former year to 334 in the latter. (Paul F. Miller, Jr., Drexel Harriman and Ripley, Inc., Report, October 1966.)

Table 10

AVERAGE PRICE INCREASE PER YEAR, 1948–64

P/E QUINTILE	PRICE INCREASE
1st (highest P/E)	7.7%
2nd	9.2
3rd	12.0
4th	12.8
5th (lowest P/E)	18.4

SOURCE: Drexel & Co., Philadelphia, monthly review, 1966.

Table 11

AVERAGE ANNUAL PERCENTAGE GAIN OR LOSS ON
TEST ISSUES, 1937–69

PERIOD	10 LOW-MULTIPLE ISSUES	10 HIGH-MULTIPLE ISSUES	30 DJIA STOCKS
1937–42	− 2.2	−10.0	− 6.3
1943–47	17.3	8.3	14.9
1948–52	16.4	4.6	9.9
1953–57	20.9	10.0	13.7
1958–62	10.2	− 3.3	3.6
1963–69	8.0	4.6	4.0

SOURCE: Benjamin Graham, *The Intelligent Investor*, 4th ed. (New York: Harper & Row, 1973), p. 80.

invested in this manner in the lowest P/E's in 1937 would have increased to $66,866 by the end of 1962. Invested in the highest P/E's, the $10,000 would have appreciated to only $25,437. Finally, left in the Dow-Jones Industrial Average itself, the $10,000 would have grown to $35,600 by 1962.

A number of other studies through the 1960s came up with the same conclusion.* One by William Breen, published in the *Financial Analysts Journal,* used the fourteen hundred companies on the

*Francis Nicholson, in an earlier test that eliminated companies with nominal earnings, measured the performance of high and low P/E stocks in the chemicals industry between 1937 and 1954. The results strongly favored the low P/E stocks. James McWilliams used a sample of nine hundred stocks from the S&P COMPUSTAT tapes in the 1953–64 period and found strong corroboration of the better performance of low P/E stocks. McWilliams further discovered that while stocks having the highest individual appreciation in any given year appeared to be randomly distributed, those with the greatest declines were in the high P/E ratio group. (Francis Nicholson, "Price/Earnings Ratios," *Financial Analysts Journal* 16 [July–August 1960]: 43-45; James D. McWilliams, "Price–Earnings and P/E Ratios," *Financial Analysts Journal* 22 [May–June 1966]: 137–142.)

COMPUSTAT tapes for the 1953–66 period.[2] He eliminated all stocks with less than 10 percent annual earnings growth in the previous five years. He then selected a number of portfolios. The first consisted of ten stocks with the lowest P/E multiples relative to the entire market. The second portfolio also consisted of ten stocks, but in this case they had the lowest P/E multiples relative to their own industries. Each portfolio was assumed to be purchased in the first week of January and sold one year later. Both appreciation (or loss) and dividends were included in the return. Randomly selected portfolios were constructed and compared with the results of the two low-multiple portfolios. Table 12 indicates the proportion of randomly selected portfolios in each year that underperformed the low P/E groups. Again, the findings are dramatic. The low P/E's in both cases almost consistently outperformed a large percentage of randomly selected portfolios.

The conclusion of these studies, of course, indicated that low

Table 12
PERFORMANCE OF LOW P/E STOCKS RELATIVE TO RANDOMLY SELECTED PORTFOLIOS

YEAR	LOW P/E RELATIVE TO MARKET		LOW P/E RELATIVE TO INDUSTRY	
------	COMPOUND RETURN	PERCENTAGE OF RANDOMLY SELECTED PORTFOLIOS WITH LOWER RETURN	COMPOUND RETURN	PERCENTAGE OF RANDOMLY SELECTED PORTFOLIOS WITH LOWER RETURN
1953	19.3%	95%	13.3%	95%
1954	57.5	95	92.8	95
1955	45.2	95	35.5	95
1956	19.4	90	7.7	65
1957	−9.9	45	−15.6	20
1958	112.6	95	72.6	95
1959	102.9	95	61.1	95
1960	13.7	90	12.1	90
1961	155.2	95	36.1	70
1962	−4.2	95	−19.8	35
1963	25.5	75	33.8	90
1964	26.1	80	26.7	80
1965	50.5	80	22.0	15
1966	3.4	85	6.1	90
Average	37.5%	—	23.9%	—

SOURCE: *Financial Analysts Journal* (July–August 1968).

P/E stocks were distinctly superior investments over an almost thirty-year period. But theories, like sacred cows, die hard, and the findings created little stir at the time.

Slumbering Success

If the results were analyzed at all, they were criticized. For one thing, the growth school was still dominant among institutional investors during the first half of the decade. Even after the demolition of the two-tier market in 1974–75, many institutional investors could not bring themselves to believe the efficacy of the findings. After all, the results did seem to cavalierly toss aside our years of indoctrination (or perhaps brainwashing) to the contrary. When I published a paper in early 1976 summarizing some of the previous research, a number of professionals told me that such information was only history: "Markets of the 1970s are very different."

And the evidence, of course, was a mere transitory enigma to our financial friends in academe who in the late 1960s were adjusting the final nuts and bolts of the formidable efficient-market hypothesis. According to this university-launched dreadnought, such results simply could not exist because rational profit-seeking investors would not allow them to. Clever investors would immediately jump into the better-performing lower P/E stocks and stay clear of the trickier high P/E multiples until all the extra profits were extracted from the unpopular stocks.

Further academic criticism asserted that low P/E stocks were systematically riskier (in the parlance, had higher Betas) and therefore deserved to provide somewhat higher returns. And for the *coup de grâce,* criticisms of the previous studies were wheeled into action. They were mostly hair-splitting and not convincing—at least to me. But recalling Einstein's dictum that the theory determines the observations, here indeed was evidence that *could not* exist if the dreadnought was to proceed merrily annihilating current investment practice.

Some Newer Work

Buying low P/E stocks appeared successful in studies of past performance. And, as a practical matter, it had worked for me, as I indicated
—no small inducement to belief. Consequently, I thought it might be
interesting to bring the findings up-to-date. Watching the collapse of
the high P/E concept stocks through the early 1970s and finally the
entire two-tier market in 1973–76,* it seemed that things had not
really changed all that much. And a more recent study which I
undertook with the cooperation of Rauscher Pierce Refsnes Securities
again demonstrated the low P/E case.† The work attested to the
overall superior performance of such stocks through the seventies.

The experimental design tried to deal as thoroughly as possible
with the problems of the previous findings.‡ The sample, the largest
to date, was constructed from the COMPUSTAT 1800 Industrial
Tapes, which contain data on the largest publicly held companies in
the country. Included in the sample of 1,251 issues were 70 percent
of the common stocks listed on the New York Stock Exchange as
well as large companies on the AMEX and over-the-counter.§ The
study covered the mid-1968–77 period. As in Breen's study, total
return was measured—capital gains (or losses) and dividends paid—
in each period analyzed.

The stocks were arranged by computer into ten equal groups
(called deciles) strictly according to P/E's. The subsequent performance of each decile was measured. To determine P/E rankings, most
recent twelve-month earnings were used to the end of each period,
along with price on the last day of trading two months later. In effect,
the earnings information was fully public at the time, and the P/E
ratios were the ones currently available in the financial section of any
newspaper.

---

*I've documented some of the evidence on the performance of concept stocks and the
two-tier market in chapter 6 of my earlier book, *Psychology and the Stock Market.*

†I was ably assisted by Kirit Patel, Jane Ruelfi, Bill Avera, and Clifford Atherton, among
others.

‡For details, see footnote on page 149.

§All companies with five-year records and with fiscal years ending in March, June,
September, or December were included. In the high P/E group, a maximum multiple of 75
was used to filter out companies with only nominal earnings, which were put into an eleventh
group and included in the calculation of the overall sample return. Results of this group were
erratic, partly because the sample size varied markedly in the different holding periods.

A large number of different holding periods were used to get as many comparisons as possible of the performance of the various P/E groups. Portfolios were recast according to new P/E information as frequently as every three, six, or nine months, or held unchanged for as long as nine years.

Table 13 gives the results for the entire period of the study. *Even a glance at the record indicates the superior results of the low-multiple groups over the length of the study.* Recasting the deciles quarterly according to latest twelve-month earnings shows dramatic results. Had an investor put $10,000 evenly in the bottom 10 percent of P/E's at the end of August 1968 and switched quarterly thereafter to keep in the lowest P/E's continuously, he would have amassed $32,519 before commissions through August 31, 1977—and these returns occurred during an extremely poor period for the market. By comparison, had the investor switched quarterly on the same basis into the best stocks, the highest P/E's (decile 1), his $10,000 would have diminished to $7,708. In other words, the lowest P/E stocks did more than four times as well as the highest over the entire period of the study.

Had an investor switched annually, he would have received returns of 10.3 percent in the lowest P/E decile; by comparison, the returns in the top P/E decile were –1.1 percent. Even buying and

Table 13
ANNUALIZED COMPOUND RATES OF RETURN, AUGUST 1968–AUGUST 1977 (FULL PERIOD OF STUDY)

| STOCKS RANKED BY P/E MULTIPLES | SWITCHING AFTER EACH | | | | HOLDING ORIGINAL PORTFOLIO FOR |
DECILE	1 QUARTER	6 MONTHS	1 YEAR	3 YEARS	9 YEARS
1 (highest)	−2.64%	−1.06%	−1.13%	−1.43%	0.33%
2	0.92	1.62	0.56	−0.28	1.27
3	0.51	0.62	1.63	0.85	3.30
4	3.06	3.42	3.31	4.87	5.36
5	2.19	4.46	2.93	5.02	3.72
6	4.84	5.33	6.70	4.82	4.52
7	7.90	6.07	6.85	5.89	6.08
8	8.83	8.24	8.56	7.78	6.35
9	11.85	8.40	6.08	7.73	6.40
10 (lowest)	14.00	11.68	10.26	10.89	7.89
Average return of sample			4.75%		

holding the same stocks over the length of the study still distinctly favored the low P/E's. Ten thousand dollars in the bottom 10 percent of stocks in August 1968 held unchanged to August 1977 would have become $19,824; and $10,000 in the top 10 percent, $10,306. Although the superiority of the bottom over the top group is the most impressive, the eighth and ninth normally did far better than the second and third.

"But wait," the skeptical top-tier advocate might say. "What if you used a different starting point—for example, a starting date at the bottom of the 1970 market. Would the top tier (the high P/E's) do better from this point to the end of the 1974 bear market?"

Our numbers cruncher, a large Digital Equipment computer, had the answer in a flash; it is provided in table 14. The low P/E stocks far outperformed the upper deciles: the bottom 10 percent of P/E's over the full four-and-a-half-year period provided returns of 2.3 percent, while the top 10 percent of P/E's returned –1.5 percent. You might certainly ask why returns were so low. The answer lies in the fact that the bottom of the 1974 market was even lower than the bottom of the 1970 market. The S&P 500 (before dividends) was 9.1 percent under its May 1970 level in November of 1974. When allowances are made for sample composition and divi-

Table 14
ANNUALIZED COMPOUND RATES OF RETURN, MAY
1970–NOVEMBER 1974 (MARKET BOTTOM TO BOTTOM)

STOCKS RANKED BY P/E MULTIPLES DECILE	SWITCHING AFTER EACH				HOLDING ORIGINAL PORTFOLIO FOR
	1 QUARTER	6 MONTHS	9 MONTHS	2¼ YEARS	4½ YEARS
1 (highest)	−5.45%	−5.08%	−2.67%	−5.33%	1.54%
2	0.68	0.80	0.59	−6.07	−0.98
3	−2.64	−0.99	−1.91	−2.84	−2.49
4	−1.52	−3.02	−0.82	−2.47	−0.73
5	−4.05	−2.84	−2.39	−2.02	−0.89
6	−1.74	0.87	−0.60	−1.78	−1.80
7	2.34	1.34	0.55	1.52	1.21
8	0.85	0.17	−0.35	4.04	3.32
9	2.00	1.50	−1.04	0.88	−0.65
10 (lowest)	6.01	3.12	2.54	5.04	2.27

Average return of sample   −0.60%

dend reinvestment, results do not appear to be strikingly different.*

We next asked the computer to give us a snapshot of how the P/E investment strategy worked in another time period, this time from the top of the 1968 market to the market top in 1972, using the November 1968 to November 1972 period. Once again, the low P/E deciles produced superior overall results.

After reviewing these periods of bad markets, our tireless electronic colleague deserved a more cheerful question: how did the low P/E strategies work between the market bottom of August 1970 and the end of August 1976? The answer is found in table 15 (page 148), which shows the annualized returns for portfolios held for one to six years. Portfolios were held intact for the four- to six-year periods. As you can see, superior returns—and for a change, far above average ones—were provided for the low P/E stocks in all but the four- and five-year time periods. For example, turning over portfolios every three years provided 15.2 percent annual returns for the lowest P/E decile and 3.5 for the highest. Holding portfolios without switching for the full six years provided annual returns of 12.4 percent for the least-favored P/E stocks, compared with 7.1 percent for the highest 10 percent.

The four-year returns, and to some extent the five-year returns, are much lower than the rest. This is because we were near the bottom of the bear market in 1974, the worst of the entire postwar period, in the first case, and in the earlier stages of the recovery in the second.

Do low P/E strategies always provide superior results? No investment strategy should, and there was one period I was particularly curious about: namely, when it was pretty universally accepted that high-multiple stocks did do considerably better—during the height of the two-tier market between 1970 and 1973. Recall that at the time investing in high P/E stocks was almost obsessional with individual and institutional investors alike. To measure these results, we began at the bottom of the 1970 market once again, as this was the point from which the high P/E concept stocks and the growth stocks caught fire. The results are found in table 16, page 148.

As you can see, the high-multiple stocks did do relatively better than in the previous tables, particularly for the one-year holding

*The larger equally weighted indices, such as the *Value Line* composite average of 1,684 stocks, were down more than the S&P 500 through this period.

Table 15

ANNUALIZED COMPOUND RATES OF RETURN, AUGUST 1970–AUGUST 1976

STOCKS RANKED BY P/E MULTIPLES	SWITCHING AFTER EACH			HOLDING ORIGINAL PORTFOLIO FOR		
DECILE	1 YEAR	2 YEARS	3 YEARS	4 YEARS	5 YEARS	6 YEARS
1 (highest)	6.10%	4.93%	3.50%	−1.45%	5.07%	7.07%
2	6.25	2.48	5.64	−1.42	6.47	8.03
3	8.01	6.72	10.07	−2.49	4.68	8.20
4	8.79	7.60	8.14	−4.95	3.33	7.26
5	7.49	9.52	12.00	−3.42	4.73	9.91
6	11.99	10.91	10.67	−2.81	5.58	9.91
7	12.36	13.28	11.67	1.21	7.69	11.99
8	12.79	12.70	11.64	−0.82	6.34	11.41
9	8.61	11.16	11.50	1.47	7.19	12.30
10 (lowest)	14.13	15.45	15.16	0.09	7.66	12.39
Average return of sample	10.14%	10.14%	10.14%	−1.26%	6.22%	10.14%

Table 16

ANNUALIZED COMPOUND RATES OF RETURN, MAY 1970–FEBRUARY 1973 (TWO-TIER MARKET)

STOCKS RANKED BY P/E MULTIPLES	SWITCHING AFTER EACH				HOLDING ORIGINAL PORTFOLIO FOR 2¾ YEARS
DECILE	1 QUARTER	6 MONTHS	1 YEAR	2 YEARS	
1 (highest)	13.07%	12.51%	15.78%	12.84%	12.40%
2	19.19	20.66	15.05	12.04	13.01
3	14.11	15.49	17.64	16.17	15.86
4	13.95	13.27	14.34	13.12	14.97
5	10.71	10.56	12.66	13.32	16.94
6	13.19	15.88	15.75	12.22	12.98
7	14.83	14.26	13.10	15.39	16.01
8	15.06	14.54	14.19	16.93	17.23
9	16.45	17.83	17.56	19.36	14.20
10 (lowest)	20.35	16.09	15.41	18.56	15.25
Average return of sample			14.54%		

period. In any case, however, even in a period where it was common belief that high P/E stocks were absolutely the buy, the table indicates that such was definitely not the case.

The superiority of the low P/E groups, then, is much more consistent than that of the higher P/E deciles. Although the bottom decile seems to have the best results in just about any period surveyed, the sixth, seventh, and eighth deciles have on occasion outperformed the ninth.

The findings presented here certainly make it appear that the advantage of a low P/E strategy is clear-cut. *In our work, it did not matter whether the investor started near a market top or a market bottom; superior returns were provided in any phase of the market cycle (including the top-tier mania).* And the cycle we measured showed the widest fluctuations of any in the postwar period. The average multiple of the S&P 425 varied sharply—from a high of 21 to a low of 7—yet the findings consistently and dramatically supported the strategy of buying and holding out-of-favor stocks.

The results in the study were certainly more striking than I had expected. If anything, they indicated patterns of investor behavior—and error—far more systematic than one would have believed possible.

But what of some of the past criticisms? Did any of them still have validity?* An efficient-market theorist would legitimately inquire about Beta—that somewhat discredited gauge of risk. "Low P/E groups are more volatile," he might say, "and should return more." We asked the computer this question, and fifty thousand or so calculations, or half a second, later, we had our answer. The Beta measurements indicated that, if anything, the low P/E stocks as a group were slightly less volatile than the higher deciles.† Low P/E stocks not only gave you better performance, but were marginally safer!

Our findings have also been confirmed by other new work in recent years. Two carefully prepared studies by Sanjoy Basu[3] came up with similar results. In his more recent study, published in the *Journal of Finance* in June 1977, Basu used a data base of 1,400 firms from the New York Stock Exchange between August 1956 and August 1971. He took 750 companies that had year-ends of Decem-

---

*Within the experimental design, we adjusted methodological criticisms of previous studies, such as hindsight bias—selecting stocks, as Nicholson did, that had survived to 1962, something an investor of 1937 could not have known; and not using year-end earnings and prices, as previous studies did, when investors could not know earnings until several months later. As I said, I did not think these would markedly change results, and our findings indicate they didn't.

†Average Beta, starting with the lowest deciles, was .9898, .9791, .9648, .9657, .9646, .9785, .9933, .9777, 1.3596, .9396. Average Beta for the bottom 40 percent was .9748; for the top 40 percent, 1.0667. An interesting by-product of this study appeared to be that Betas did not seem to be stable over time.

ber 31 and turned over the portfolios annually, using prices on April 1 of the following year. Like most of the previous studies, he divided the stocks into quintiles according to P/E rankings. The results (again using total return) are shown in table 17.

Basu's conclusions were similar to all the others: "The average annual rate of return declines (to some extent monotonically) as one moves from low P/E to high P/E portfolios."

Basu found, as we did, that the low P/E stocks provided superior returns, and were also somewhat less risky. Again, using his words: "However, contrary to capital market theory, the higher returns in the low P/E portfolios were not associated with higher levels of systematic risk. The systematic risk of portfolios D and E (the lowest) were lower than those for A and B (the highest)."

This and subsequent work, updated and adjusted for previous criticisms through December 1980, thus provides new evidence that links to a chain extending over forty years, documenting the superior performance of low P/E issues.

Buying Out-of-Favor Stocks

The consistency of the previous studies is truly remarkable. Over almost every and any period measured, the stocks considered to have the best prospects (according to their P/E ratios) fared significantly

Table 17
PERFORMANCE OF STOCKS ACCORDING TO P/E RANKING,
APRIL 1957–MARCH 1971

P/E QUINTILE		BETA (SYSTEMATIC RISK)
A (highest)	9.3	1.1121
A*	9.6	1.0579
B	9.3	1.0387
C	11.7	0.9678
D	13.6	0.9401
E (lowest)	16.3	0.9866

A = highest P/E quintile.
A* = highest P/E quintile, excluding stocks with negative earnings.
SOURCE: As adapted from *Journal of Finance* 32 (No. 3, June 1977).

worse than the low P/E stocks, using the same criterion. This leads us to a general observation, or rule if you like:

> *Rule 5: The evidence strongly supports an investment philosophy of buying solid companies currently out of market favor as measured by their price/earnings ratios.*

It is the very unpopularity of such issues—because their visibility seems so poor when contrasted with the high enthusiasm displayed for the prospects of the "best" companies—that makes such an approach possible.

But if the record is so clear, why isn't everybody scouring the stock pages to bag these plump quarries—especially when the season is always open and there is no limit on the number you can bring home?

Needless to say, the reasons are not hard to find. Recall that these stocks violate just about every notion we have about proper investment theory.* In fact, some of the "good old boys" with impeccable backgrounds, faithful to the tried and failing methods of current investment practice, might, as I indicated, find this strategy borders on the heretical. "Do you know what's down there?" a major money manager once asked me, indicating by exhaling a touch more heavily than usual his considerable disgust. "How can any prudent man look at companies like these with such unthinkably poor visibility?" The high P/E's, on the other hand, present the best visibility money can buy. They are the real blue bloods of the investment scene. How, then, can one recommend such a reversal of course?

And here we run into the problem. Despite the record extending over four decades, people still believe they can accurately predict which stocks will perform well and which poorly. They are in no small measure aided by the cognitive biases. The high P/E companies have far higher than average earnings, sometimes for quite extensive periods, and prices advanced in line or ahead of their improving results. Many experts recommend these stocks—usually after they have already made a considerable move. As the P/E ratios move further and further away from those of average companies, many believe the divergence is justified, if indeed it should not be

---

*Although not those of Benjamin Graham. He warned repeatedly, in both *The Intelligent Investor* and *Security Analysis,* of the dangers of overemphasizing visibility, which he also believed would lead to repeated investor errors.

greater. The same factors apply in the opposite manner to the out-of-favor stocks.

People are too sure of their evaluations, which prove wrong often enough to lead to the results we have viewed. *The psychological consistency of the error is remarkable.*

This does not mean, of course, that there are not excellent stocks that justify their price/earnings ratios and others that should command only the slimmest of multiples. But, as the evidence indicates, these are relatively few, and, as we'll see next, the chances of knowing which they will be at the time are very small. Predicting the future is far trickier than most people imagine.

CHAPTER EIGHT

Why Low P/E Strategies Work: The Failure of Forecasting Techniques

As the last chapter indicated, investors are too sure of their ability to judge how well or poorly a company will do. However, an impressive and growing body of evidence developed in recent years appears to demonstrate this conclusion. Earnings estimates and the forecasts of corporate executives and economists that often underlie them just aren't very reliable. Worse than that, the expert consensus about the outlook for the economy or estimate for an individual company is frequently far off the mark—so far off, in fact, that using such forecasts can often prove harmful to stock selection, portfolio performance, and investment health. I think it is important that we review these findings in greater detail, for they are at the heart of why low price/earnings strategies work and why the casualty rate among those using other contemporary methods is so high.

Chapter 5 showed that making earnings estimates is hardly a simple process. Because of our limited ability at configural, or interactive, reasoning and the vast amounts of information we are required to analyze, errors are very common. We have already seen that though they are not confined to the marketplace, the stock market appears to provide a hothouse environment for such errors because of the large number of inputs and assumptions required by the investor to forecast earnings correctly.

Yet reasonably good earnings estimates are essential to contemporary method. Just how important the differences between forecasts and actual earnings may be to the future performance of stock prices was demonstrated in a study by Niederhoffer and Regan. The researchers examined the fifty best- and worst-performing stocks on the New York Stock Exchange in 1970, and a random sample of one hundred other companies. Earnings estimates were taken from the Standard & Poor's Earnings Estimator (which specializes in tracking estimates of major retail and some institutional brokerage houses).

Figures were available for forty-four of the top fifty performers. The median projection called for a rise in earnings of 7.7 percent for the group. In fact, the actual increase turned out to be 21.4 percent. The forecast was off by 13.4 percent, enough to result in the median price of this group appreciating 48.4 percent!

The results in the bottom fifty companies are even more telling. Of the half-hundred worst-performing equities, thirty-four had published estimates. The median estimate was a rise of 15.3 percent. The actual reported earnings: a median decline of 56.7 percent. This "estimate gap" was accompanied by a staggering 83 percent drop in price.

Niederhoffer and Regan concluded that estimates were an important factor in performance: "In sum, the results of this study demonstrate that stock prices are strongly dependent on earnings changes, both absolute and relative to analysts' estimates. . . . It is clear that an accurate earnings estimate is of enormous value in stock selection."[1]

Enter the Economic Forecaster

Since fundamental earnings estimates rely on many underlying economic assumptions, the forecasting record of economists might be a good launching point to begin an analysis of the process.

Although economists have done dozens of excellent studies on the performance of financial institutions and the forecasting records of executives and analysts, they have surprisingly overlooked their own pronouncements. Perhaps judiciously, for while the evidence remains sketchy, what is available does not provide a picture of sibylic accuracy.

A survey of thirty-two major forecasters in December 1973, for example, discovered that only one had projected any decline in economic activity the following year—1974—which saw the worst recession of the entire postwar period until now.[2] In fact, at a conference called in the fall of 1974 by President Ford, the nation's leading economists resoundingly devoted their attention to the problems of curbing inflation. Newspapers pictured many of them happily wearing their large WIN buttons (Whip Inflation Now). They showed absolutely no awareness that the most critical phase of the recession was just about to start. It was almost like watching a professional football player pick up a loose ball, lose direction, and start rushing downfield the wrong way, followed by the rest of the team yelling encouragement. With the passage of time, and more detailed study of recent economic events, history may prove kinder to the economic advisors of Herbert Hoover.

But not to digress. What about the one man who proved correct in late 1973 and actually did see the recession coming? An article reported: "[Mr. X] stopped issuing stock market forecasts several years ago after being wide of the mark time after time."

Was this instance, striking as it is, simply the exception that proves the rule? Apparently not. Other evidence indicates that the forecasting record of the "dismal science" is dismal indeed. In 1947 a group of well-known forecasters predicted that U.S. economic activity would decline approximately 6 percent. The economy that year actually proved to be one of the strongest on record, showing an increase of 11 percent. And a survey of many dozens of economists and business analysts in late 1969, with business already in a downturn, disclosed that few believed a recession would occur in 1970.[3]

If you detect some not-too-subdued delight in such happenings, I am afraid it is the natural reaction of a professional investor. For in building random walk theory, economists have assumed that we professionals can make extremely accurate forecasts using most of the very techniques with which they themselves have floundered so often. I suppose it's always easier to analyze another's performance.

The problem again takes us to familiar ground: the more complex the level of decision, the greater the probability of a high level of error. Recently, albeit slowly, a part of the economic profession itself is questioning the value of forecasting.

These economists foresee the end of what they call "Newtonian economics," with its predictable cause-and-effect relationships. Too many things can go awry to base much faith on a simple one-figure forecast. According to Professor James B. Ramsey of New York University, "Almost all scientific disciplines have been moving in recent years from sure cause-and-effect relationships (deterministic) to (odds-on) 'stochastic' formulations of their theories."[4] Professor Lester Thurow of MIT adds that "to judge economics on its prediction record is to judge it in a way no other science is judged"[5] (except perhaps the way economists judge us poor market professionals). Professors Thurow and Ramsey see the end of simple single-figure estimates and the adoption of much wider ranges by economists to reflect the vast political and economic uncertainty the forecasts actually entail.

Management Forecasts

Since earnings estimates normally rely on many economic assumptions as well as dozens of factors unique to the industry or company, they too can often be far off the mark, frequently accompanied by the even wider swings in price that the Niederhoffer and Regan study indicated.

An article in the *Journal of Business* in October 1972[6] examined the estimates made by executives of fifty corporations published in the *Wall Street Journal* in 1968. Because the thorough analyst or money manager carefully interviews senior corporate officials in making his or her own projections, the results are illuminating. The executives missed actual company earnings by an amazing average of 20.1 percent. The error was downward-biased, since one company—Phoenix Steel, where the forecast of $2.50 in profits turned into a loss of $1.79, a difference of 139.7 percent—was excluded. Also telling was that the average forecast was for a period of under eight months (after eliminating the six forecasts made within a month or less of the end of the time, the average was still only 8.2 months).

An earlier study by Green and Segall (1967)[7] examined the accuracy of twelve company forecasts published during the 1963–64 period, again in the *Wall Street Journal*. Only seven precise dollar figures were given. Because of one large error (268.4 percent), the average absolute error for the seven was 50.3 percent. However, even after eliminating the figure, the mean error was still a formidable 14.0 percent.

A more recent study made by Basi, Carey, and Twark in 1976 measured the estimates of a group of executives of eighty-eight companies published in the *Wall Street Journal* in 1971–72, one of the calmer periods for business in recent years. It concluded: "Given the potential disruptive effects of poor forecasting on investing decisions as a result of current stock market mechanisms, perhaps it would be wise to declare a moratorium on pressures for mandatory published forecasts by firms* until forecasting techniques have been refined sufficiently to assure considerably better accuracy than currently."[8]

As table 18 on page 158 shows, the average error of four management studies was 14.5 percent, or as wide a miss as that of the estimates of the top fifty in the Niederhoffer and Regan survey. In fact, when one remembers that most investors consider earnings increases of 7 to 8 percent normal—and 10 to 15 percent in the above-average-to-growth category—executive forecasting errors of 10 to 20 percent make it impossible for the investor relying on them to distinguish the growth stock from the also-ran.

Analysts' Forecasts

The problem becomes even more complicated for analysts and money managers since most attempt to "fine-tune" earnings estimates well within a 10 percent range. As "Street-smart" investors know, even a 5 or 6 percent "miss" of the projection—particularly for stocks with supposedly excellent visibility, such as Avon, Polaroid, Xerox, or Franklin Mint—has unleashed waves of selling in the stocks, taking the prices down five or sometimes even ten times the amount of the forecasting error itself. Thus, an acuteness in predicting capabilities is called for on the Street that even managements well into the year and aware of their results (if indeed not exercising some control over them) cannot provide.

*The Securities and Exchange Commision has been toying for some years with the idea of making it mandatory for corporations to publish earning forecasts.

Table 18
FORECASTS, ANALYSTS VERSUS MANAGEMENT

Management Forecasts, One Year or Less[a]

STUDY	PERIOD STUDIED	NUMBER OF COMPANIES	MEAN ERROR[b]
Green and Segall, 1967	1963–64	7	14.0%
Copeland and Marioni, 1972	1968	50	20.1%
McDonald, 1973[c]	1966–70	151	13.6%
Basi, Carey, and Twark, 1976	1970–71	88	10.1%

Mean error in management studies: 14.5%

Analysts' Estimates, One Year or Less

STUDY	PERIOD STUDIED	NUMBER OF COMPANIES	MEAN ERROR[b]
Samuel S. Stewart, Jr., 1973[d]	1960–64	14	10–15%
Barefield and Cominsky, 1975[e]	1967–72	100	16.1%
Basi, Carey, and Twark, 1976	1970–71	88	13.8%
Malcolm Richards, 1976[f]	1972	93	8.8%
Richards and Frazer, 1977	1973	213	22.7%
Richards, Benjamin, and Strawser, 1977[g]	1969–72	50	18.1%
Richards, Benjamin, and Strawser, 1977[g]	1972–76	92	24.1%

Mean error in analysts' studies: 16.6%

[a]Managements' estimates taken from the Wall Street Journal.
[b]Minus signs removed so errors do not tend to cancel each other out. The last six analysts' studies use the S&P Earnings Forecaster exclusively or as a major source of estimates.
[c]C.L. McDonald, "An Empirical Examination of the Reliability of Published Predictions of Future Earnings," Accounting Review 48 (1973): 502.
[d]Samuel S. Stewart, Jr., "Research Report on Corporate Forecasts," Financial Analysts Journal (January–February 1973): 77–85.
[e]R. M. Barefield and E. E. Cominsky, "The Accuracy of Analysts' Forecasts of Earnings per Share," Journal of Business Research 3 (July 1975): 241–252.
[f]R. Malcolm Richards, "Analysts' Performance and the Accuracy of Corporate Earnings Forecasts," Journal of Business 49 (July 1976): 350–357.
[g]Richards, Benjamin, and Strawser, Financial Management, Fall 1977.
SOURCE: Adapted from R. Malcolm Richards, James J. Benjamin, and Robert W. Strawser, "An Examination of the Accuracy of Earnings Forecasts," Financial Management, Fall 1977, p. 82.

How well do analysts do at this game, where even slight errors often result in instant wipeouts? We've already seen the record of the *Institutional Investor* "all-stars." The aforementioned Basi, Carey, and Twark study also recorded estimates for the same companies from the Earnings Forecaster made by analysts at the same time. The analysts' error was some 40 percent higher than the executives', averaging 13.8 percent (errors ranged from an underestimation of 38 percent to an overestimation of 126 percent).

Another study, by Richards and Frazer (1977), used the S&P Forecaster for analysts' 1973 estimates on 213 companies, mainly on the NYSE. In addition, forecasts of six other analysts were collected from institutional, brokerage, and bank trust departments (the latter "high-powered" research estimates were not publicly available). The findings indicated that the mean forecast error was a cool 22.7 percent! Moreover, only minimal differences existed among researchers on any particular company. The investigators ended by stating that the small investor was not at a disadvantage because he could not afford the more costly research: "It is unnecessary to pay large sums for certain services when others are available at low cost."[9] The authors graciously did not add, "Particularly since both were so wide of the mark."

Probably the most devastating research spotlighting errant analytical forecasting is also among the most recent. Richards, Benjamin, and Strawser, writing in *Financial Management* (Fall 1977), evaluated analysts' estimates (again from the Earnings Forecaster) for ninety-two companies listed on the New York Stock Exchange. Each concern selected had annual estimates available for the 1972–76 period. For economic comparability, companies with fiscal years ending in the mid-calendar year were eliminated. A subsample of fifty of these companies was also used where estimates were available annually from 1969 through 1972. The results are shown in tables 19a and b, page 160.

Particularly striking is the high average annual error rate: 24.1 percent for the 1972–76 period, and 18.0 percent for the 1969–72 period. The analysts proved especially susceptible to changing economic circumstances. In the recessions of 1970 and 1974, the average estimate was off by a whopping 43.1 percent and 59.6 percent respectively.[10] (In fairness, however, it should be remembered that the analysts were ably assisted by the economic forecasters.)

Were the results due simply to the major errors of a few analysts' forecasts? No. Both Richards and Barefield and Cominsky in previous studies indicated the differential among forecasters on any one company was not significant. The consensus was far off target time and again.

Another shocker is presented in table 20 (page 161), which indicates the average industry forecasting error made by analysts

Table 19a
ANALYSTS' ESTIMATES ON FIFTY COMPANIES

YEAR	MEAN ERROR
1969	8.1
1970	43.1
1971	12.8
1972	8.0

Average annual error 18.0

Table 19b
ANALYSTS' ESTIMATES ON NINETY-TWO COMPANIES

YEAR	MEAN ERROR
1972	7.8
1973	13.7
1974	59.6
1975	22.5
1976	16.7

Average annual error 24.1

SOURCE: Tables 19a and b adapted from R. Malcolm Richards, James J. Benjamin, and Robert W. Strawser, "An Examination of the Accuracy of Earnings Forecasts," *Financial Management,* Fall 1977, p. 82.

annually for the 1972–76 period. Over the entire time span, the error ran to 26.2 percent annually. More significant, some of the industries supposedly with the "highest visibility," such as computers and retail stores, actually proved to have the worst estimates. The average annual analyst error in the office equipment and computer group was an astonishing 88.8 percent.

Since these two samples were taken from the S&P Earnings Forecaster, normally carrying the largest or most widely followed companies, and the companies covered had estimates from five to nine years, the results can scarcely be considered an aberration.

As table 18 indicates, analysts strayed wide of the mark in virtually every study—the mean error of all studies was 16.6 percent, and these studies were for one year or less!

However, investors, notably professionals, attempt to extend their earnings projections out well beyond one year, particularly if the stocks involved sport above-market multiples. The higher the multiple, the greater the visibility of earnings demanded. At the height of the growth mania in 1972–73, the growth rate for the

Table 20
ANALYSTS' FORECASTS BY INDUSTRY

INDUSTRY	1972	1973	PERCENT MEAN ERROR 1974	1975	1976	AVERAGE YEARLY PERCENT MEAN ERROR 1972–76
Banking	5.5	2.3	6.4	6.5	3.7	4.9
Building	12.0	13.7	35.8	28.2	28.1	23.6
Chemical	5.9	17.2	26.4	39.8	14.5	20.8
Drugs	3.3	6.2	10.1	10.7	8.6	7.8
Electrical equip.	13.3	17.5	20.2	30.6	8.4	18.0
Electric utilities	2.9	5.5	13.5	11.6	10.8	8.9
Office equip. & computers	17.1	14.1	391.8	13.1	8.1	88.8
Paper	19.7	20.2	16.1	32.1	10.0	19.6
Petroleum	4.9	19.4	40.6	40.7	10.7	23.3
Retail stores	9.1	7.1	182.6	24.3	10.2	46.7

Average annual error   26.2

SOURCE: Adapted from *Financial Management,* Fall 1977.

highfliers was projected out for five or ten years or longer to justify the prevailing P/E ratios—60 for Avon, 90 for Electronic Data Systems, and 100 for Polaroid. If one-year estimates were off 10 to 20 percent or more, the more distant projections, as you might expect, were certainly no better.

One of the earliest studies analyzing longer-term projections was done by Cragg and Malkiel and published in the *Journal of Finance* in March 1968. The two professors studied the earnings projections of large groups of security analysts working for five important and highly respected investment organizations, including two major New York City bank trust departments, a mutual fund, and an investment advisory firm. Estimates were made for 185 companies for periods of from one to five years. *The researchers found that most analysts' estimates were simply linear extrapolations of current trends, and that the correlations between the actual and the predicted earnings turned out to be very low.* Cragg and Malkiel state that in spite of the vast amount of additional information analysts have, supplemented by frequent company visits, estimates are based on a continuation of past trends: "The remarkable conclusion of the present study is that the careful estimates of security analysts . . . performed little better than those of (past) company growth rates."[11]

In addition, it was discovered that had the analysts made the simple forecasting assumption that the sample companies' earnings would continue to grow near the long-term rate of 4 percent annually, the projections would have resulted in smaller overall errors in the five-year period than the analysts actually made.[12]

Similar results have been found in other studies. One by Edwin Elton and Martin Gruber compared mechanical forecasting techniques (a number of formulas based on the extrapolation of current trends) against the forecasting records of institutional analysts.[13] They found such techniques "do about as good a job of forecasting as security analysis."*

Reviewing the evidence makes it appear that forecasting is far more art than science and, like the creative fields, has as few masters. Excluding the highly talented exceptions, people simply cannot predict the future with any reliability. It seems extremely dangerous, then, for us to depend on methods that require the exceptional.

Et Tu, Earnings?

Some remarkable new research also shows that forecasting earnings provides an extremely wobbly crutch for investors. Oxford Professor I.M.D. Little revealed, in a paper appropriately entitled "Higgledy Piggledy Growth," that the recent earnings trends of a large number of British companies were of no use in predicting their future course.[14] Little's work proved uncomfortable to theoreticians and practitioners alike, and was promptly criticized on methodological grounds. The criticisms were duly noted, the work was carefully redone, but unfortunately, the outcome was the same. Earnings appeared to follow a random walk of their own, with past and future rates showing virtually no correlation. Recent trends (so important

*You may recall here the Meehl studies of clinical psychologists, where it was shown that simple mechanical techniques performed as well as or better than the complex analytical diagnoses in twenty separate studies of trained psychologists. In fact, mechanical prediction formulas have been suggested in a number of fields, primarily psychology, as a direct result of these problems, and they will be a part of the strategies proposed in the next chapter.

to security analysis in projecting future earnings) provided no indication of their actual future course.[15]

The research was repeated in a number of major studies in this country,[16] with the same conclusions: changes in the earnings of American companies also appeared to follow a random walk from time period to time period.

Richard Brealey, for example, examined the percentage changes of earnings of 711 American industrial companies between 1945 and 1964. As in the other studies, he too found the directions of the earnings trends were not sustained but actually showed a slight tendency toward reversal. The only exception was for companies with the steadiest rates of earnings growth, and even here the correlations were only mildly positive.[17]

Thus once again and from quite another tack we see the precariousness of attempting to place major emphasis on earnings forecasts. *In short, it is impossible in a dynamic economy with constantly changing political, economic, industrial, and competitive conditions to use the past as a basis for estimates of the future.*

The Altar of Visibility

We have just seen that an imposing body of evidence demonstrates just how unreliable the future estimates of analysts are. *If one cannot forecast with any degree of accuracy, then the range between high and low P/E multiples should be much narrower.* *But the range usually is not, and because it is not, the road to investment opportunity is wide open to us.*

Even though the evidence seems convincing, most of us feel intuitively that something has to be wrong. After all, we can name companies with years of uninterrupted and predictable earnings progress—Johnson & Johnson, Automatic Data Processing, and

---

*Additional evidence demonstrates that P/E ratios are poor predictors of future earnings growth. Stocks trading at low P/E multiples will have the same probabilities of large positive earnings as stocks trading at high P/E multiples. The experiment discovered that in 76 percent of the cases, there was no significant correlation between the P/E multiple and the future rate of earnings growth. Other work questions the market's ability to make accurate earnings expectations. (J. E. Murphy and H. W. Stevenson, "P/E Ratios and Future Growth of Earnings and Dividends," *Financial Analysts Journal* 23 [November–December 1967]: 111–114; Aharon Ofer, "Investors' Expectations of Earnings Growth, Their Accuracy and Effect on the Structure of Realized Rates of Return," *Journal of Finance* 3 [May 1975]: 509–523.)

Burroughs come to mind easily. However, a few years back this list would have included Polaroid, Avon, Xerox, and Burroughs—companies that were once considered to have outstanding prospects but have since been downgraded by investors.

Polaroid, one of the classic growth stocks, seems to be a particularly appropriate case. The company had an unbroken string of earnings growth between 1964 and 1970. The market anticipated spectacular earnings ahead with the introduction of its revolutionary SX-70 camera, and accorded it a gravity-defying P/E multiple of 100 times earnings in 1972.

I remember clearly the enthusiasm at that time among professionals at a major conference. One of the Street's foremost experts on the stock gave us his best thinking on Polaroid's price parameters for the next eighteen months. He believed the stock, then trading at 100, would be a minimum of 125 by the end of this time period and a maximum of 200. At worst, he said, "you should make 25 percent on your money." He had just put out a bulky research report documenting the earnings explosion he expected.

Unfortunately, problems with the SX-70, the introduction of a competing camera by Kodak (which at the time many photography analysts said would only expand the market), and a badly breaking stock market resulted in the minimum price parameters proving high. The stock dropped to under 15 within twenty-four months. Its vaunted and well-documented visibility had disappeared entirely.

For years, DuPont traded at well-above-average P/E ratios as investors saw the demand for polyester and nylon synthetic fibers outstripping supply indefinitely. It didn't, and the large premium in its P/E multiple was whisked away. The same proved true of Xerox, another exceptionally fine growth company. With the expiration of its plain-paper-copier patents, it began to experience increasing competition, which led to a slowdown in its growth rate and a drastic decline in its multiple.

The two-tier market of 1972–73 saw the stress on the visibility phenomenon carried to an extreme. Not long afterward, the vaunted visibility of not a few of these "religion" stocks was shattered, and the top tier collapsed dramatically.

But Why?

There are many reasons why a company may show outstanding sales and earnings growth for a period of years, followed by succeeding periods of slower expansion. Sometimes an excellent earnings record may be traced simply to accounting legerdemain: National Student Marketing, Memorex, and University Computing might be gruesome reminders to some of you.

In every market there are scores of concept companies, some formed by creative accounting and others by short-lived competitive advantages. Invariably the market, enraptured by the high growth rates, mesmerizes itself into believing this to be a permanent joyride. The showroom-warehouse concept of Levitz Furniture was such a case. At the height of its popularity in 1971, the company sold at one hundred times earnings—before being crippled by management and competitive problems. It then dropped 97 percent in price.

In fact, the more successful a company becomes, the more difficult the task of maintaining its momentum. Competition, government controls, and market saturation all play roles in damping down returns. Safe patents—such as those of Polaroid and Xerox—are suddenly circumvented. Products and markets seemingly invulnerable to competition for years are suddenly inundated with it. Costs rise and cannot be passed on. Management teams skilled at running rapidly expanding companies with $100 or $200 million in sales may prove totally inadequate when volume reaches $300 or $500 million, and so on. Unexpected socioeconomic events, such as the energy crisis, wreak havoc on the soundest of company visibilities.

Within a dynamic and relatively free competitive economy, there are forces at work such as these, which tend to bring down above-average sales, growth, and return on capital over time. Such other forces as reduced competition, improving management, and tighter financial controls tend to improve returns for companies going through difficult periods. These pressures are always moving companies toward average sales and profits rather than abnormally high or low returns.

And here we might refer again to the principle of regression to the mean, which we looked at in chapter 6. Company progress rarely runs in a straight line. In a dynamic, changing environment there will be periods of excellent growth and profitability, which create the seeds that foster greater competition and lower growth sometime in the future. On the other hand, for companies and industries undergoing current difficulties, the very elements of their lowered expansion, reduction of overhead, and belt tightening often bear the fruit of above-average growth once again.

In *Security Analysis* Graham succinctly summed up the problems of analyzing corporate fortunes: "The truth of our corporate venture is quite otherwise [than investors think]. Extremely few companies have been able to show a high rate of uninterrupted growth for long periods of time. Remarkably few also of the large companies suffer ultimate extinction. For most, this history is one of vicissitudes, of ups and downs, with changes in their relative standing."[18]

The push toward average returns is a fundamental if not the fundamental principle of competitive markets. And yet it is one that never seems to have been learned on the investment scene.

The lessons of chapter 6 about our limitations as intuitive statisticians help to explain why it is so hard to recognize the principle. The cognitive biases we reviewed—the law of small numbers, recency and saliency, inputs matching outputs, and hindsight—all combine to make us believe that this time the record of the good or bad company is different . . . this time it will persist. Looking at the case rate—the visibility of the individual company itself—we consistently ignore the base rate—the overall record that visibility is more often than not illusive. Doing so makes the situation seem unique each time and leaves us wide open to exactly the same errors.

Investor Overreaction

And the push toward average returns is precisely why the superior performance of the low P/E stocks and the inferior returns of the high P/E's are so consistent. The phenomenon, though clear and well documented enough, is simply not recognized by investors at large. Thus, great emphasis is placed on forecasting, although indeterminable economic, political, and company-related events make it impossible to pinpoint the future with any degree of accuracy—the reason, of course, that earnings follow a random walk of their own.

Because this is so, the disparity between high and low P/E stocks, as indicated, would be much smaller on average if the investor were the unfailingly rational man the academics think him to be. Unfortunately, he is not. When disappointments take place in the group of stocks whose earnings supposedly have the highest visibility, there follows a negative reaction from disillusioned investors. This occurs often enough for the group to consistently underperform both the market averages and the low P/E stocks.

And with the low P/E stocks, the reaction is the opposite. Such stocks languish in investor doghouses, if not tiger cages, because of their poor near-term visibility. Our analytical tools indicate that these companies offer only the poorest of value on a continuing basis. And we tend to overemphasize the importance of the adverse circumstances they are currently encountering. Because visibility is not nearly as predictable as we would like to believe, enough pleasant surprises occur in these groups (earnings, after all, follow a random walk) to lead to their above-average performance.*

Both the high and the low P/E cases represent extremes. The probabilities are very strong that future returns will be more in line with those of more average companies. But most investors do not see it this way. Instead, they tend to see the current trend as the norm, no matter how extreme the present situation might appear within a probability distribution. The consistent overreaction to current trends opens up a great opportunity for the investor—putting him ahead of the crowd, so to speak. Which brings us back to the theme of the last chapter, and to an important rule:

Rule 6: It is far safer to project a continuation of investor reactions on the basis of what we now know psychologically than it is to project the visibility of the companies themselves.

From the prior performance of the low P/E stocks we have seen this approach work with remarkable reliability over an almost forty-year period.

It is true, of course, that there are excellent companies that will continue to chalk up above-average growth for many years or even decades to come, and there are especially talented investors who will

---

*It is also important to note that the sharpest reactions to news, both good and bad, occur in the shortest time periods after it becomes known. The best performance for the low P/E and the greatest disappointments for the high P/E occur in the quarterly returns, followed by those for six and nine months.

find them at reasonable prices. But for most of us, whether individual or expert, the odds of winning at this game are pretty slim.

The Investor-Overreaction Hypothesis

Since the publication of the first edition, we have uncovered three additional well-documented areas of investor overreaction. In all three cases, investor errors are both remarkably similar and can be taken advantage of. The three appear to validate what I call the investor-overreaction hypothesis of market behavior. As we shall see, they provide further buttressing of the investment methods to be outlined in the succeeding chapters.

Let's look briefly at these cases.

1. The first is found in a study conducted by the Marine Midland Bank of the S&P 425 Industrials between 1948 and 1967. The research indicates that investors systematically overreact to companies' reporting losses. According to what we have learned about investment behavior, we might expect such reactions to companies reporting bad news, and this is precisely what happens.

However, as the record also indicates, the initial reactions are incorrect, for the stocks that have reported losses have consistently outperformed the S&P 425 (now the 400) over the period of the

Table 21
COMPANIES IN S&P 425* REPORTING DEFICITS, 1948–67

HOLDING PERIOD	S&P 425 % CHANGE	STOCK PURCHASED DECEMBER 31, YEAR OF DEFICIT % CHANGE	STOCK PURCHASED DECEMBER 31, YEAR AFTER DEFICIT % CHANGE
1 year	12.1	23.2	25.4
2 years	25.5	47.9	49.6
3 years	38.1	78.9	100.0
4 years	52.0	116.9	127.1
5 years	69.3	159.7	158.1

*S&P 425 has become S&P 400.
SOURCE: Courtesy of Marine Midland Bank, November 1968.

study. As table 21 shows, if you had purchased stocks reporting deficits one year after the deficit occurred, you would have increased your capital an average of 25.4 percent each year and 158.1 percent for the five-year periods, compared to 12.1 percent and 69.3 percent, respectively, for the S&P 425.

2. A second and related example occurs with investor behavior toward the bonds of companies in financial trouble. Investors appear to overreact to bad news about a company without checking whether the developments will affect the bond itself. Often a bond is well secured by company assets, so that the adverse developments may only partially affect the issue, if at all. Even a bankrupt company's bonds may have strong prior liens on assets before other creditors, often many times the size of the bond issue itself.

One such example was Interstate Stores, which went into Chapter XI (bankruptcy) proceedings in the early 1970s. One of its debentures, due in 1987, was secured with liens on inventories as well as by a general obligation. With the credit crunch and panic in both the bond and stock markets in 1974, the debenture traded at under 10 cents on the dollar* (about the same price as Russian Imperial Government Bonds), although the company actually made $13 million that year. Earnings continued to increase and by 1976 the bonds traded at 75, a market appreciation of over 650 percent.[19]

Another case of a serious overreaction was with Con Ed 9⅜ of 2,000, which were rated as BBB and were trading at 106 in 1974. In April 1974 the company eliminated its quarterly dividend and the stock plummeted. The company's bond ratings were subsequently downgraded one rank, from BBB to BB. The result—the bonds dropped nearly 50 percent. In late 1977, after Con Ed restored its dividend, the rating was raised to A–, and the bonds moved back over par to 102. The total return in the swing, including interest, would have been 170 percent in three and a half years.

It's worth noting that Benjamin Graham and many other astute investors took advantage of precisely this overreaction in the 1930s. Very often institutions—and as Graham stated, particularly insurance companies—would sell the bonds of companies in trouble at any price, which often meant a pittance at best. By getting them off the books the investment officer "got rid of the bodies," thus perma-

*Ten cents on every dollar the company was obligated to repay on the debenture.

nently burying his mistakes. Graham made substantial profits by recognizing this pattern.*

Other statistical evidence also confirms similar investor reactions in the bond market. A study by BEA Associates, a major New York advisory firm, showed that buying bonds with lower credit ratings in periods of tight money yielded returns of over 30 percent. Thus, once more there appear to be major overreactions that seem to be even larger than that for low P/E stocks.

3. The third discovery is particularly interesting and well documented. Some recent work produced at the University of Chicago by Rolf Banz and Marc Reinganum and presented in *Fortune* magazine[20] provides strong supporting evidence for the investor overreaction hypothesis. Banz did a study of the performance of companies listed on the New York Stock Exchange according to the market value of their stock. Stocks were placed into five equal groups strictly by this market value for five-year periods from the late 1920s to the late 1970s. Banz concluded that the smallest 20 percent of capitalization did significantly better over that time than the other groups.

Why did smaller companies do better? To quote Banz: "There is no theoretical foundation for such an effect, we do not even know whether the fact is size itself, or whether size is just a proxy for one or more but unknown factors correlated with size."

Although admittedly unsure of what this finding signified, both Banz and his colleague, Mark Reinganum, spent considerable time publicizing it in lectures around the country. To quote him again in *Pensions and Investment Age,* a periodical widely read by pension fund and money managers: "We still do not know why the [size] effect exists . . . however, no other thesis such as Dreman's Contrarian Investment Strategy explains the effect."[21] With all due respect to the new professors, I disagree.

My curiosity more than a little whetted by his statements, I undertook my own research on the subject. My findings indicated that some of his figures were right. But look out! The reasons are far different from what you might think, and once again illustrate the danger of using statistics blindly.

Small capitalization companies did well not because they were

*Institutional investors still continue to act in much the same way today. An explanation of why will be given in chapter 12.

rapidly improving market share and profitability, as most people, including Banz, conjectured, but for precisely the opposite reason—many were in severe financial and operating difficulties at the time they were in the smallest capitalization group. Subsequently, a good number recovered, accompanied by dramatic increases in price.

This point comes out clearly in the 1931–35 period of the study, which indicated that the smallest capitalizations did substantially better. The figures show that the smallest New York Stock Exchange companies were up over 100 percent, handily beating their bigger brothers throughout this period, though many companies—and in particular smaller ones—were in serious financial trouble in this period, which included the bottom of the Great Depression.

What had happened was that Banz's computer sort automatically placed large numbers of troubled companies in his bottom group. Some of these capitalizations had shrunk drastically in the process—the average company value at year-end 1930, for example, was only $2.3 million. The study had also unintentionally been geared to measure only New York Stock Exchange survivors, while omitting those companies delisted and going down for the third time.

Some of the reasons for survival were not a little strange. For example, the Electric Boat Company, now a part of General Dynamics, came through this period with giant gains, because it won an $8 million settlement in the World Court from the German government. The reason: the Imperial German Navy had "borrowed" a number of its submarine patents without permission in 1911 and 1912. Without this windfall, the company would have submerged permanently.

At the beginning of 1931, although they were still listed on the New York Stock Exchange, some companies were in receivership, and many traded at a fraction of a dollar—a number going to as low as ¼ or 1/16. The average price of the bottom 20 percent of capitalizations was only about $2. Subsequently, by 1935, well over 30 percent of these companies were delisted. It took only three survivors to improve the average performance of each remaining stock in the bottom fifth by 35 percent.

The 1940–45 period, the best in the sample, demonstrates this point even more strikingly. Only two companies by themselves appreciated enough to boost the results of the entire group of low-capitalizations stocks by 75 percent in this five-year period.

In fact, if one were to eliminate these two controversial periods from the study, the low-capitalizations stocks do not do better than the high caps—in fact, they do worse. Reinganum's findings, worked in tandem with Banz's, also seem to support the investor overreaction hypothesis.*

In his work, Reinganum divides his P/E's into 10 deciles. His lowest P/E decile has a P/E ratio of only slightly over 1, compared to 6.5 for his next lowest decile. A P/E of 1, of course, indicates serious trouble. Most of these stocks are also very small. Twenty-two percent of his sample have market values of $13 million (which are inordinately small capitalizations in recent years), and fully 65 percent have market values under $68 million by P/E. By comparison, only 2.4 percent of companies in the largest capitalization decile trade at P/E's of 1. Again, the small companies that recover bounce back sensationally; those that don't are delisted.

What these findings bring out clearly is that investors react sharply to the financial difficulties of smaller companies. The fear of bankruptcy or severe operating problems drastically shrinks their price. This reaction is even more severe than for larger companies, which was demonstrated by the low P/E findings.

However, the point—and this, I believe is crucial—is that *the cause—the stress by investors on near-term visibility—is identical in both cases.* But, once again, as it turns out, visibility is not nearly as predictable as investors think. More small companies survive and eventually prosper, just as many low P/E companies have better results than people believe at the time, and subsequently are awarded higher prices.

This factor of serious financial difficulty seems to be similar to

---

*Time out for a gripe! Both Banz and Reinganum first officially published their results in April 1981. However, the preliminary findings were leaked almost a year earlier to *Fortune* magazine—a strong efficient-market backer. The reason, as the *Fortune* article made clear, was to discredit "Dreman's trumpeted low P/E findings" because they, in the magazine's words, presented "the strongest challenge yet" to this hypothesis originated by the University of Chicago.

Since the two researchers did not release their methodology or studies at this time, it was impossible to analyze their work. The two spent a considerable amount of time promoting their conclusions long before their formal reports were released, which is not exactly in the highest traditions of scholarly research. This is disappointing, since it suggests that the authors' primary interest is in protecting the efficient-market hypothesis (as these conclusions attempted to do) rather than in the research itself.

The academic journals in the financial area have been closed for a decade to publishing reasoned, though dissenting, arguments and quantitative evidence that contradict the efficient-market hypothesis. Perhaps my partner, Arthur Gray, put it best: "It's a new form of burning the books." I hope this is a passing phase of "publish or perish," which will soon be behind us.

that of the overreaction to bonds. The financial-distress reaction and the reaction to companies reporting losses appear to stimulate even larger investor overreactions, as I indicated, than does the low P/E phenomenon. Psychologically, this is quite understandable; since the stimulus—fear—is greater, the magnitude of the reaction should thus also be greater.

Thus, the investor-overreaction effect appears to be very powerful, one we can see demonstrated in four distinct forms. All four can be used in successful investment strategies. (The latter three will be discussed in chapters 9, 10, and 11.)

However, although the three just reviewed hold out hope for higher rewards, they also require far greater investor sophistication and have a greater degree of risk than the low P/E strategy itself, since many of the smaller companies do eventually sink under the waves.

The low P/E approach, then, appears to be best suited for the average investor, offering both well-above-average returns and significantly higher safety.

The Low P/E Investment Strategy

All of these findings lead very naturally to the strategy of buying companies out of favor as determined by their current P/E ratios. The investment strategy is built on the assumption that most investors will continue to value stocks as they always have, placing the most stress on how good or bad the company's outlook or visibility currently is. And, if this is the case, investor expectations will continue to change frequently, often to a far greater extent than changing company fortunes. The investor has only to be aware of this psychological phenomenon and act on it.

It's like betting on a marathon race where a prize is given to all who finish. We know that the great bulk of a thousand or more major competitors (the large corporations in this case) will do so, although most will run unevenly—the pace quickening or slowing for each at different times. But the crowd, surprisingly, isn't able to remember what the race is really about. Forgetting that most will finish, they concentrate only on those ahead at the moment, betting heavily on them and heavily against the marathoners doing poorly at the time. We have seen that the evidence strongly favors betting against the crowd. The low P/E approach is the first instrument that appears to be reliable and systematic enough to guide the individual investor successfully through the market dangers by now so obvious. Perhaps there are other and better strategies yet to be devised that will make this one look crude by comparison. Nevertheless, this strategy works where nothing else appears to. Knowing that it works, we can now safely move on to outlining how to use it in detail.

CHAPTER NINE

How to Use
Low P/E Investment
Strategies

In markets, as in the world of espionage, there is a flood of information to cipher through, most of it inconsequential, misleading, or even contradictory. The separation of the monumental from the trivial is no easy task. In fact, the intelligence services of World War II conspicuously demonstrated how good information could be totally ignored. We know today that the Germans had information on the exact time and place of D-day. And, closer to home, there were advance and repeated warnings of a probable attack on Pearl Harbor.

And so with the information that was described in chapter 7. The conclusion was clear. Buying low P/E stocks would have provided above-average returns over the last forty years. However, as we have seen, although a good part of the evidence has been available for well over a decade, many a sophisticated investor who has viewed the results didn't really believe them.

Such conclusions, after all, seem too easy—too pat. Low P/E strategies are simple, in many respects mechanical, downgrading or eliminating entirely complex judgmental factors. Can the complexity of the modern investment scene be reduced to such an approach?

Common sense says no. There must be any number of methods that should provide superior returns to the investor. But if we examine the actual results, such methods are not in evidence. No other system appears to work as consistently, or for that matter, at all.

This is not to say that there are not numbers of investors who have run up large gains, sometimes fortunes, investing in growth or concept stocks, selling short, or a dozen other ways. But their success rests far more on their judgmental abilities than on the systems themselves.

Although it translates into a relatively simple and easy-to-follow method, we have seen how the low P/E investment strategy is rooted in new and fairly complex psychological and statistical findings that, even if well documented, are antithetical to most security analysis as it is practiced today—with its heavy emphasis on presumably accurate forecasting.

In the present chapter, we'll examine the practical application of the low P/E strategies in building a stock portfolio. There are a number of possible approaches. Some totally disregard security analysis because of its inherent problems with forecasting, information processing, and decisional biases. Others rely on some of its traditional principles that have demonstrated their value, while de-emphasizing or excluding entirely those that have proven problematical.

In short, the work will be laid out in a manner that I believe will make it possible to use low P/E strategies to improve your investment results.

Some Rules for the Low P/E Investor

The initial problems confronting any investor are how to select individual stocks and the number of stocks he should hold in his portfolio. Let's start with a few simple rules that have proven their worth over the years:

1. *The investor should buy only low P/E stocks because of their superior performance characteristics.* However, he has a number of choices in exercising this rule, which will be discussed later.

2. *Ideally, a portfolio should be invested equally in fifteen to twenty stocks, diversified among ten to twelve industries.* This is important if your means allow it.* Diversification is essential to conduct the low P/E strategy properly. Because returns among individual issues will vary widely, it is dangerous to rely on stocks in only a few companies or industries. By spreading the risk, you have a much better chance of getting a return fairly similar to the average for the quintile or quintiles chosen, rather than one substantially above or below this level.†

In our 1968–77 sample, for example, exactly half of the 3,870 stocks in the lowest decile over the entire period performed better than the S&P 425.

3. *The low P/E investor should attempt to buy medium or large-sized companies* (such as those on which the studies have been based), which means stocks listed on the New York Stock Exchange, or larger companies on the American Stock Exchange or traded over-the-counter.

Such companies are usually subject to less accounting gimmickry than smaller ones, which provides some added measure of protection. Accounting is a devilishly tricky subject and has taken a heavy toll of investors—sophisticates as well as tyros.

The larger and medium-sized companies also present another advantage to the investor: they are more in the public eye. A turnaround in the fortunes of Bethlehem Steel (which occurred several years ago) is far more noticeable than that of a publicly owned five-store auto-parts chain buried in the snows and pollution of Buffalo. And finally, the larger companies have more "staying power." The failure rate among them is substantially lower than among smaller ones or start-up situations.

Should We *Abandon Security Analysis* Entirely?

As we have seen, selecting stocks strictly because of their low P/E multiples, with no reliance on security analysis, has turned up better-than-average returns over long periods of time. Should we, then,

---

*For investors with very limited capital, alternative strategies will be discussed later in the chapter.

†Financial studies have indicated that well-diversified portfolios of as few as sixteen stocks have an excellent chance of replicating approximately 85 to 90 percent of the return of the group from which they are selected, even if the group is the stock market as a whole.

consider abandoning security analysis entirely? A pertinent question, I think, for the evidence we've seen certainly shows it doesn't help much. However, I would not go quite this far (and not just because I've been thoroughly steeped in the doctrines of the Old Church). I believe parts of it, which we'll look at next, can be valuable within the low P/E framework. Too, using the low P/E method eliminates or downgrades those aspects of traditional analysis, such as forecasting, that have been shown to be consistently error-prone. By recognizing the limitations of security analysis, the investor, I believe, can apply it with a good chance of achieving even better results within the low P/E universe.

In the next sections, I'll attempt to show in some detail how these fundamental screens can be used to supplement the three basic rules of low P/E investing we just looked at. Following this analysis, we'll examine other P/E methods that do not depend on security evaluation at all. These too should provide above-average market results. After viewing the various methods, you should be in a position to decide for yourself which seems to suit you best.

An Eclectic Approach

In my own application of the low P/E approach, I have used the bottom 40 percent of stocks according to P/E's for stock selection. The four lowest deciles provide a broad universe to apply the ancillary selection criteria that follow. The analysis of the results that we saw in the last chapter indicated that this group, when viewed together, has shown consistently superior returns.

For those of you who are brave enough to dabble in security analysis after what you've seen, here are the ancillary criteria that I believe are most helpful:

Indicator 1. A strong financial position. This is easily determinable for a company from information contained within its financial statements. (The definitions of the appropriate ratios, current assets versus current liabilities,* debt as a percentage of capital structure,

---

*Previously defined in chapter 3.

interest coverage, etc., can all be found in any textbook on finance, as well as in material provided free of charge by some of the major brokerage houses.)*

A strong financial position will enable the company to sail unimpaired through periods of operating difficulties, which low P/E companies sometimes experience. Financial strength is also an important factor in deciding whether a company's dividends can be maintained or increased.

Indicator 2. As many favorable operating and financial ratios as possible. This would help to ensure that there are no structural flaws in the company. The definition of such ratios again can be found in standard financial textbooks.

Indicator 3. A higher rate of earnings growth than the S&P 500, both in the immediate past and projected into the near future. Such future estimates are an attempt not to pinpoint earnings, only their general direction. We must remember that we are dealing with stocks in the bottom deciles, for which only the worst is expected. By assessing industry and company conditions, we can point to the path of earnings movement. We do not require precise earnings estimates like those of conventional forecasting methods; we should merely note their direction, and for short periods of time, usually about a year or so. If we are wrong, there's probably little downside risk, since the market has already discounted the worst, but if we are right and earnings are growing faster than the averages, the stock may well outperform the lower P/E groups in general. On a risk-reward basis, there is little cost for error and a good deal of upside if you are on target.

The important distinction between forecasting general direction of earnings and trying to derive precise earnings estimates is that the former method is far simpler and therefore more likely to be successful.

Indicator 4. Earnings estimates should always be made to lean to the conservative side, which ties in with Graham and Dodd's "margin of safety" principle. By relying only on general forecasts, and keeping them conservative, you are reducing the chances of error even further. If these standards can be met and the company still

---

*Merrill Lynch publishes a booklet, entitled "How to Read a Financial Report," which provides a brief introduction to corporate accounting and outlines most of the important financial ratios the average investor would require.

looks as though its earnings are growing more quickly than the
S&P's for a term such as a year or so, this may prove to be an
excellent ancillary criterion.

Indicator 5. A high-dividend yield, which the company can
sustain and probably increase. This is a crucial indicator and is
dependent on indicators 1 through 4 all being favorable. Because of
its importance to the investment strategy I'll propose, let's look at
it in some detail.

Since publication of my earlier book, I have run studies to
pinpoint the contributions dividends make to overall results. The
findings turn out to be striking. The studies show conclusively that
conventional investment thinking about dividends is far off the mark.
Current wisdom holds that low P/E stocks should provide higher
dividend yields but a lag in capital gains. According to the good
books, the two goals are not compatible. You must go for either one
or the other of these targets.

Since most investors are in the stock market for capital appreciation, the usual way to attain it is by selecting fast-growing companies, at the price of lower dividends. The good book continues:
widows, orphans, and others who require current income should
stick to solid companies that pay high dividends. Such issues will
undoubtedly lag in the appreciation race but one hopes they will
provide steady and increasing income and give some appreciation to
boot.

To measure the dividend effect, we again used the 1,800 largest
industrial companies in the country for the years 1968 through 1977.
The format is the same as in tables 13 to 16. All aspects of the study
were identical to those described on pages 144–145. The sole addition
is that total annual return is broken down into its two components
—yield (dividends) and appreciation.

A glance at table 22 indicates just how far off target the conventional wisdom is. What our studies indicate is that, far from being
incompatible, the pursuit of higher income and the quest for superior
capital gains go hand in hand.

As you can see, to no one's great surprise, an examination of the
dividend return (the second column in each group) reveals that low
P/E stocks provide higher dividend income. What is surprising is
how much better the dividend returns of these stocks are in every
period measured.

In the lowest P/E decile, for example, returns range from

Table 22

ANNUAL PERCENTAGE RATE OF RETURN, 1968–77

STOCKS RANKED BY P/E MULTIPLES	3 MONTHS			SWITCHING AFTER EACH 1 YEAR			3 YEARS			HOLDING ORIGINAL PORTFOLIO FOR 9 YEARS		
DECILE	TOTAL ANNUAL RETURN	YIELD	ANNUAL APPRECI-ATION	TOTAL RETURN	YIELD	APPRECI-ATION	TOTAL RETURN	YIELD	APPRECI-ATION	TOTAL RETURN	YIELD	APPRECI-ATION
1 (highest)	-2.64	1.17	-3.81	-1.13	1.15	-2.28	-1.43	1.22	2.65	0.33	1.17	-0.84
2	0.92	1.76	-0.84	0.56	-1.70	-1.14	-0.28	2.28	-2.56	1.27	2.96	-1.69
3	0.51	2.17	-1.66	1.63	2.21	-0.58	0.85	2.25	-1.40	3.30	2.32	0.98
4	3.06	0.94	2.12	3.31	2.78	0.53	4.87	2.95	1.92	5.36	2.89	2.47
5	2.19	3.21	-1.02	2.93	3.21	-0.28	5.02	3.31	1.71	3.72	3.00	0.72
6	4.84	3.65	1.19	6.70	3.67	3.03	4.82	3.43	1.39	4.52	3.39	1.13
7	7.90	4.00	3.90	6.85	4.06	2.79	5.89	3.93	1.96	6.08	3.82	2.26
8	8.83	4.19	4.64	8.56	4.18	4.38	7.78	4.05	3.73	6.35	4.44	1.91
9	11.85	4.28	7.57	6.08	4.22	1.86	7.73	4.27	3.46	6.40	4.21	2.19
10 (lowest)	14.00	4.26	9.74	10.26	4.06	6.20	10.89	4.26	6.63	7.89	4.83	3.06

three and a half to four times as high as the top P/E group. Even if the same portfolio is held for nine years without change, the bottom group yields 4.83 percent annually versus 1.17 percent for the top. (For this period, the dividend return on $10,000 would have been $5,288, versus $1,103 for the highest decile.) The next three lowest deciles (7, 8, and 9) also provided markedly higher dividend returns than the top three (2, 3, and 4) in just about every time frame. On this score, then, the widows' and orphans' stocks breeze ahead easily.

What shouldn't happen, but does, is that the low P/E stocks also provide considerably better appreciation than the high P/E groups in almost every period measured. If the portfolios are turned over annually, the lowest P/E group appreciate 6.20 percent compared to minus 2.28 percent for the highest. Even holding the same portfolio for nine years shows better returns for the lowest P/E deciles than for the highest (+3.06 vs. −0.84).

These findings play a cruel joke on the supposed "visibility" of companies. Rather than high multiples reflecting better prospects, appreciation in most cases is almost directly inverse to the P/E ratio. Although the superiority in appreciation of the bottom group over the top is most impressive, the next three lowest deciles again do significantly better than the next three highest. The stocks that widows and orphans should buy thus appear to hit a clean sweep.

The study also indicates the stronger defensive nature of large dividend-payers. In periods of poor markets, the substantially higher yields of the low P/E stocks are the major reason for the better overall returns. If the original portfolios were held through the nine years ending in 1977—certainly not the most enthralling of markets —about 65 percent of annual returns of the lowest 20 percent of P/E's would be provided by income. However, since yields were significantly better in the lower P/E groups, total return on the lowest 20 percent of stocks was eight times that of the upper fifth.

You might ask if the results hold up through both bull and bear markets. Our computer came up with dozens of different holding periods. It didn't matter much if we started at the market bottom or market top. Both the annual appreciation and dividend components of return were always higher in the lower P/E groups. The low P/E stocks were able to beat the market in up and down years alike.

Table 23 demonstrates the returns for a period of better mar-

Table 23
ANNUAL PERCENTAGE RATES OF RETURN, 1970–76

STOCKS RANKED BY P/E MULTIPLES	1 YEAR			SWITCHING AFTER 3 YEARS			HOLDING ORIGINAL PORTFOLIO FOR 6 YEARS		
DECILE	TOTAL ANNUAL RETURN	YIELD	APPRECIATION	TOTAL RETURN	YIELD	APPRECIATION	TOTAL RETURN	YIELD	APPRECIATION
1 (highest)	6.10	1.25	4.85	3.50	1.25	2.25	7.07	1.30	5.77
2	6.25	1.80	4.45	5.64	1.83	3.81	8.03	2.46	5.57
3	8.01	2.36	5.65	10.07	2.38	7.69	8.20	2.06	6.14
4	8.79	3.02	5.77	8.14	3.06	5.08	7.26	1.59	5.67
5	7.49	3.40	4.09	12.00	3.47	8.53	9.91	5.62	4.29
6	11.99	3.95	8.04	10.67	4.08	6.59	9.91	3.89	6.02
7	12.36	4.40	7.96	11.67	4.20	7.47	11.99	4.37	7.62
8	12.79	4.43	8.36	11.64	4.60	7.04	11.41	4.25	7.16
9	8.61	4.34	4.27	11.50	4.25	7.25	12.30	4.24	8.06
10 (lowest)	14.13	3.84	10.29	15.16	3.64	11.52	12.39	4.21	8.18

kets, those between 1970 and 1976. Its construction is identical to that of table 22, showing the annual rates of return of turning portfolios over for one- and three-year periods, and for holding the original portfolio for the full six years. Again, the annual return is broken down into its two components of dividends (yield) and appreciation. The results once more markedly favored the low P/E stocks in every period. In the stronger markets the low P/E's showed substantially better appreciation than the higher deciles, in addition to higher income. By turning the portfolio over every three years, appreciation of 11.52 percent in the bottom decile is about five times that of the top. The annual income pattern is also remarkably similar to the previous table, with the bottom decile providing dividend returns three to four times as large as the highest P/E decile. Another easy win for the out-of-favor stocks.

You can see that low P/E stocks give you the best of both worlds—higher appreciation and higher dividends. The stocks, then, that widows and orphans should choose will work just fine for the more aggressive businessman, and vice versa. Yield and the prospect of increasing dividends thus play a major role in our stock selection process, as we shall see.

This section has examined some important screening criteria that, we have found, have significantly improved our performance when used in conjunction with the primary rule of buying low P/E stocks.

Next, let's look in some detail at how to make stock selections using these criteria. To do so, I'll draw on some actual written recommendations that I made several years ago* as well as others that were made for my investment counseling firm. While one can be accused of telling "war stories," remembering only the victories while forgetting the setbacks (not to mention the routs), I think that it is important to present the investor with practical examples of how the criteria outlined were often clear-cut even at the time—not only with 20/20 hindsight.

I presented, in the first book, an overall record of how such recommendations fared, updated to April 1979. The record of the

*In a formal report outlining the low P/E strategy for a multiple-branch investment house.

Table 24

LOW P/E INVESTING VERSUS "THE MARKET," APRIL 1976–DECEMBER 1981

DATE RECOMMENDED	COMPANY	PRICE ON DATE RECOMMENDED[a]	DJIA	PRICE 12/31/81	% CHANGE IN STOCK PRICE	% CHANGE[b] IN DJIA
4/30/76	General Tire & Rubber	18.2	996.85	21½	+ 18.1	− 12.2
5/24/76	King's Department Stores	9⅝	971.53	4⅜	− 54.6	− 10.1
5/26/76	Old Republic International	625	970.83	19½	+212.0	− 9.9
6/14/76	General Cinema	9⅜	991.24	36½	+289.3	− 11.8
12/9/76	Macmillan, Inc.	8½	970.74	16½	+ 94.0	− 9.9
2/11/77	Dennison Manufacturing	12⅞	931.52	22¼	+ 72.8	− 6.1
8/3/77	Aetna Life and Casualty	24.6	886.00	44	+ 78.9	− 1.3
12/22/77	Mohasco Corporation	12⅝	821.81	12⅜	− 2.0	+ 6.2
4/28/78	Honeywell, Inc.	51	844.33	70	+ 37.3	+ 3.7
7/13/78	Burlington Industries	18	824.76	24⅜	+ 35.4	+ 5.8
				Average change	+ 78.1	− 4.6

DJIA was 875 on 12/31/81.
[a]Prices adjusted for stock splits and stock dividends through 4/23/79.
[b]Dividends not included.

recommendations (thus assuming no changes could be made) has been extended to the end of December 1981, as shown in table 24 (page 185). Let's move on to the stock selection process itself. The first example is Bache.

Bache (BAC)

To say brokerage house stocks were in disfavor in mid-1980 is to understate the case by a lot.

These stocks—Merrill Lynch, Bache, Shearson Loeb Rhoades, Paine Webber, to name a few of the majors—were trading at extremely low P/E's. In fact, the industry was one of the half-dozen or so in greatest disfavor at the time.

Not only were the brokerage house stocks at exceptionally low P/E's, but most had high dividend yields, and many were trading well under book value. Moreover, earnings in spite of the low P/E's were actually increasing, ofttimes significantly, while financial strength was improving. Given these fundamentals, we recommended Bache to our clients.

The market was particularly negative on this company at the time because the Hunt family had used Bache as its chief commodities broker in its massive silver speculation.

When the silver bubble broke in January 1980, the Hunts were hard-pressed to come up with cash, and as a result, investors thought Bache might inherit huge liabilities. The stock had paralleled the Hunts' misfortune, plunging from a high of 14 to slightly above 7 by May 1980. At this price, it traded at a P/E ratio of 3.6 times the latest twelve months' earnings and yielded 7.8 percent.

All of the important indicators outlined in the previous section looked good. By mid-April, Bache had made an announcement—carried in the *Wall Street Journal*—that the Hunts' margin debt had been reduced to under $1 million—less than 1 percent of its net book value of $150 million at the time. The danger of serious financial impairment to Bache by the Hunt manipulations had thus passed entirely.

The stock traded at a greater than 50 percent discount from its book value, and its financial strength was improving because of a rapid buildup in earnings—our indicator 2 was clearly flashing green.

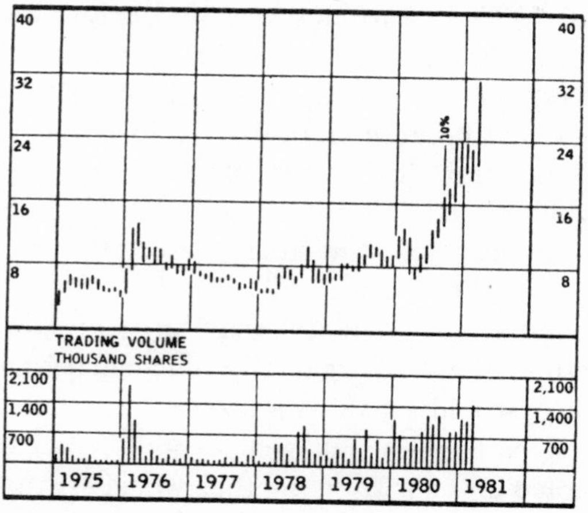

Per-share data ($) Year-end July 31	1980	1979	1978	1977	1976	1975
Book value	17.40	15.37	14.44	15.00	14.50	13.43
Earnings	2.82	1.55	0.62	0.55	1.41	1.20
Dividends	0.59⅛	0.45½	0.36½	0.36½	0.27⅜	0.18¼
Payout ratio	21%	29%	59%	66%	19%	15%
Prices—high	24	11	10½	8½	13⅜	6⅝
low	6¾	6	4½	4⅞	4⅜	2¾
P/E ratio—	9-2	7-4	17-7	15-9	9-3	6-2

SOURCE: *Standard & Poor's Stock Reports.*

Moreover, indicator 3 was also very strong. Bache's earnings had grown at a better than 20 percent rate in the past five years and in the current year (fiscal 1980) were 120 percent ahead of the first six months of 1979. The company has taken substantial write-offs against these higher earnings (without such write-offs, earnings would almost have tripled the six-month earlier total).

If this were not enough, Bache's rapidly increasing profits were coming at a time when market trading volume was relatively slow. Since Bache derives about 60 percent of its income from brokerage commissions, if trading volume picked up again, company earnings were likely to increase even more rapidly. Thus, following the guidelines of indicator 4, and using extremely conservative projections, we estimated that earnings would be well ahead of those of the previous year.

The company also passed our crucial indicator 5 with flying colors. The current yield was 7.8 percent, and the percentage of dividends paid out from earnings was well below previous years, making it appear that dividends would be raised again. (Subsequently, dividends were increased by 32 percent in 1980.) By all the indicators, then, and because of an extremely low P/E, here was a stock to which investors had overreacted sharply.

Market volume picked up in June and July, Bache's earnings increased substantially, and the stock soared. By year-end 1980 it was 23—a gain of 200 percent.

On its fundamentals, Bache looked attractive to some savvy Canadian investors, the Belzberg family, who had been accumulating the stock for a year and a half as a takeover candidate. There was no love lost between Bache's management and the Belzbergs, and the company accepted an offer from another wooer—Prudential Insurance—at a price of $32 in March 1981. The total appreciation since May of the previous year had been 326 percent.

Although the takeover was an "extra perk," it is one that is not uncommon in low P/E stocks. Tough-fisted corporate treasurers are interested in bargain acquisitions and follow criteria very similar to those of the low P/E investor.

Perhaps also worth noting is that most other brokerage stocks, even without takeover offers, moved up 250 percent or more in the same period because of their strong underlying fundamentals. The brokerage stocks provide a good example of how low P/E investing, although safe, need not always be "ho-hum."

Honeywell (HON)

Honeywell was recommended in a written report on April 28, 1978. The company is the nation's seventh largest computer manufacturer as well as the largest producer of industrial and environmental controls for both residential and commercial markets. Once thought of as a prime growth stock, it was at the time on the "hit list" of many institutions, which couldn't abandon it fast enough.

Why? Primarily because its computer business was not meeting the profit criteria of some of its competitors. Shortly before our recommendation, the cover story of one of the nation's leading business magazines speculated that Honeywell might soon dispose of these operations. The stock reacted by quickly dropping 20 percent on stepped-up individual and institutional selling.

Again, upon examination of the facts, it appeared that the stock presented good value. The summary page of the report written at the time follows:

(1) Honeywell was a leading growth stock in the dozen years prior to 1973 because of the bright prospects anticipated for both its computer and control operations. With the collapse of the two-tier market in 1973–74, few companies suffered as severe price attrition. HON shares dropped 88% from their 1972 high to the 1974 low. Earnings, by comparison, declined only 27% to 1974, to $3.74 a share. Since that time, the company has regained its earnings momentum, reporting record income of $6.39 a share in 1977, a 24% increase over the previous year.

(2) The company's strong and expanding positions in environmental and industrial controls, and its improving computer operations (which had proved problematical since the General Electric acquisition) make us believe above-average earnings growth is likely to continue. We are projecting a 13% increase in primary earnings to $7.20 a share in the current year, with further gains ahead.

(3) Honeywell increased its annual dividend rate to $1.90 a share in 1977 from $1.60 in 1976. However, the current payout ratio is well below the long-term norm, and we project an increase of at least 25 cents a share in 1978. The stock yields 4.2% based on an anticipated $2.16 a share rate.

(4) Trading at a 13% discount from book value ($58.49 at year-end) and at 7.1 times our current year's estimate, we believe HON represents excellent value at current levels. Purchase is recommended.

Honeywell stacked up well by the criteria outlined. Its financial position was good and improving. According to indicator 4 (which keeps earnings estimates on the lean side), its earnings were still increasing at a rate well ahead of the S&P 500. The earnings for 1978 were actually $8.48 per share, some 18 percent above our estimate made in June of the same year.

Dividends were expanding in accordance with the analysis outlined in indicator 5, and by mid-1981 the dividend rate had in fact risen some 80 percent.

What had been overlooked by both the magazine and many analysts was the importance of its major environmental and industrial control businesses to total profit. Together, they accounted for over 60 percent of the income, with environmental controls being by far the largest contributor. Moreover, these earnings were growing at a rate of better than 20 percent at the time.

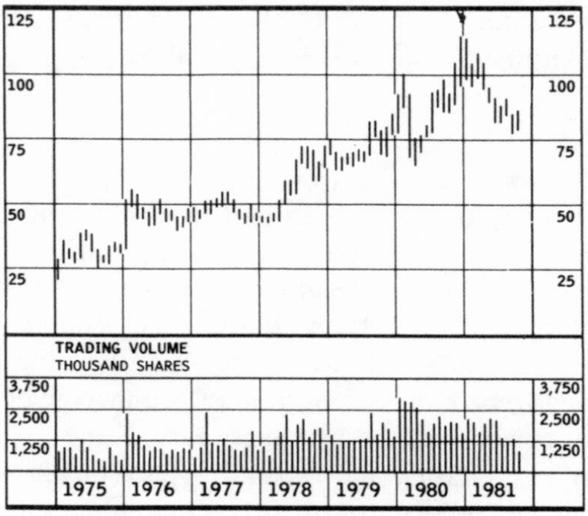

Per-share data ($)

Year-end December 31	1980	1979	1978	1977	1976	1975
Book value	79.51	69.94	61.21	57.37	51.56	47.68
Earnings	12.57	10.95	8.48	6.39	5.12	3.89
Dividends	2.80	2.40	2.05	1.75	1.50	1.40
Payout ratio	23%	22%	24%	27%	30%	36%
Prices—high	115¼	85⅜	73	55¼	56⅛	40½
low	65¼	63¼	43	42⅝	32¾	20⅞
P/E ratio	9-5	8-6	9-5	9-7	11-6	10-5

SOURCE: *Standard and Poor's Stock Reports.*

Even its computer operations, which were supposed to do poorly that year, improved profitability by almost 70 percent. The excellent earnings performance resulted in a reassessment of the stock, with the focus now placed on the profitable controls sector. From a low of 42 in May 1978, the stock traded as high as 110 by December 1980.

Summing up, Honeywell not only was priced at a low P/E and ranked well by almost all the supplemental indicators outlined, it also had businesses that once were considered exciting and could again capture the investor's fancy—and this in fact did happen.

General Cinema (GCN)

General Cinema was a stock particularly appealing to me because it had taken a classic "round trip." Several years earlier it had been a major institutional favorite, trading at a P/E of over thirty times earnings. At the time of the report it was very much on the outs with the institutions and the rest of the market, at a P/E of only 6.6 times latest reported twelve-month earnings, again well below that of the S&P 500. And yet, in spite of the fact that it was in the market doghouse, the analysis indicated it was still the exciting company it had been earlier.

General Cinema is the nation's largest operator of movie theaters, most of which are located in or near shopping centers, as well as one of the major bottlers of Pepsi-Cola and Dr. Pepper. In its 1975 fiscal year (ending October 31), bottling operations accounted for approximately 60 percent and theaters 30 percent of earnings. The company also had smaller investments in two radio stations and a furniture warehouse.

Although General Cinema had a long record of earnings growth (in the 1970s, it was 20 percent annually), the stock suffered severely after the 1974 credit crunch. Investors were alarmed by the fact that

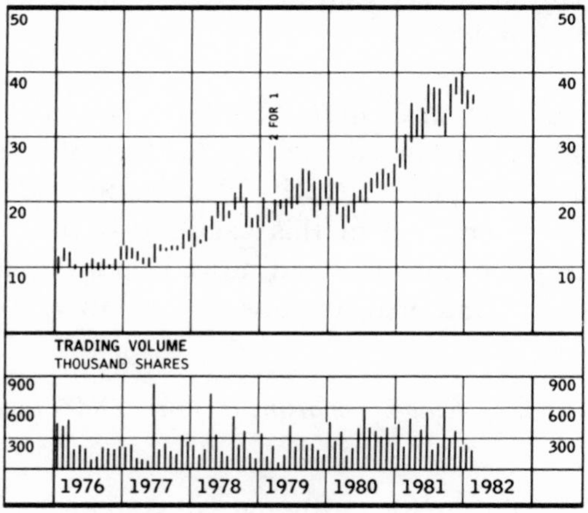

Per-share data ($)

Year-end October 31	1981	1980	1979	1978	1977	1976	1975
Book value	NA	10.17	8.03	6.42	4.97	4.57	3.69
Earnings	3.99	3.03	2.79	2.22	1.82	1.52	1.34
Dividends	0.84	0.71	0.59	0.47	0.36½	0.28⅞	0.23⅜
Payout ratio	21%	23%	21%	21%	20%	19%	17%
Prices—high	40½	25⅞	25⅛	22⅞	15⅞	13⅜	12
low	25	16	16⅜	13¼	10⅜	8½	3⅞
P/E ratio—	10-6	9-5	9-6	10-6	9-6	9-6	9-3

SOURCE: *Standard & Poor's Stock Reports.*

debt constituted a high percentage of the capital structure. The P/E dropped from 32 in 1972 to as low as 3 in 1974–75 (although earnings were actually 53 percent higher in the latter year, indicating once again how dramatic shifts in investor sentiment can be).

Evaluating the company in mid-1976, I thought that rapid earnings growth would continue in spite of the company's abnormally low P/E ratio. As important, not only was it reducing its debt absolutely, but it was doing so more quickly as a percentage of the capital structure because of the fast pace of earnings growth. By 1975 debt had declined to a more acceptable 47 percent of the capital structure from 60 percent in 1972, and by fiscal year-end 1976 it had dropped to 39 percent (the earnings buildup made it apparent that this was occurring at the time of the report). Indicator 1 was turning convincingly positive.

Thus we had a situation where the P/E was again low, the financial position was improving rapidly (indicator 1), and earnings were expected to outpace the market (indicator 3). For added measure, the company was very well managed.* The stock also proved to be a rewarding holding.

The previous text on General Cinema was written for the first contrarian book. At that time it had doubled from its original recommendation and to the present (early 1982) is up fivefold.

Particularly interesting in this example is that in spite of a threefold rise in price, earnings had moved up so rapidly that into 1981 the company continued to trade at a below-market multiple.

One That Didn't Work: King's Department Stores (KDT) (now KDT Industries)

Here is one that didn't work—although all systems looked go at the time. Let's look at the original analysis as presented in the first book:

King's, a discount department store chain (114 stores), was selected in late May 1976. The company had a low P/E ratio (less than eight times earnings

---

*I suppose I could add management as a further criterion, but the assessment is almost metaphysical—like the input-output relationships of chapter 6, it seems we all consider companies well managed when the stocks are going up.

at the time), with earnings expected to be up fairly sharply in 1976 and again the next year. Again, a number of important fundamentals I favor, along with a low P/E multiple, were present.

Indicator 1: One of the strongest relative balance sheets in the retail industry—giving the investor a high degree of safety. (The report speculated that because of the company's exceptionally strong financial position, it was in an excellent position to make a major acquisition, something it actually did in mid-1977, taking over Mammoth Mart, a forty-unit discount department store chain. That should eventually improve KDT's earnings growth.)

Indicator 2: Excellent pretax margins and returns on capital when compared with the industry leaders. (The higher the pretax margins and return on equity, the better.)

Indicator 3: Accelerating earnings expansion in the near future. (As indicated, the estimates had been made conservatively.)

Indicator 5: A high-dividend yield (5.1 percent). Because of its strong financial position and the anticipated earnings increase that was projected,

Per-share data ($) Year-end January 31	1980	1979	1978	1977	1976	1975
Book value	10.11	12.17	10.98	10.48	9.35	8.15
Earnings	0.53	2.08	2.00	2.21	1.70	1.26
Dividends	0.90	0.87½	0.75	0.60	0.52½	0.40
Payout ratio	17%	42%	38%	27%	31%	31%
Prices—high	12½	16¼	18	14½	13⅝	9¼
low	7¾	11⅛	11½	11	8⅝	5½
P/E ratio	24-15	8-5	9-6	7-5	8-5	7-4

SOURCE: *Standard and Poor's Stock Reports.*

we believed it would be upped again. The dividend was in fact raised from a 50-cent rate to 60 cents annually in late 1976 and to 80 cents by spring 1978.

Earnings and dividends went up for some time after the recommendation and the stock moved as high as 16, or 60 percent above the original price. But then some strange things began to happen. The majority of its officers and directors sold controlling interest to an outsider at a price of 17 when the stock was trading at 15. However, the offer was not extended to all the shareholders. I was curious about the legality of the situation and more that a little ticked off by the controlling groups' disregard for the average stockholder.

The new controlling group merged a group of stores they previously owned with King's at a price their hired "outside experts" considered "fair value." The new acquisition did not work out well, and was eventually disposed of.

To end this tale of woe, earnings dropped precipitously, from $2.08 a share in 1979 down to 53 cents in 1980. Subsequently, in mid-1981, the directors omitted the high dividend.

Currently, the stock is trading at under 4 or 60 percent under our original recommended price.

It is interesting to note with this group that even a low P/E selection that becomes almost a "worst case," the loss was made up many times over by other low P/E stocks that have worked out, as table 24, on page 185 indicates.

Indicator 6. A rule of thumb that is usually helpful in such situations is this: if you see management behaving in a way that is puzzling or appears to be in its own flagrant self-interest, it is best to part company with the stock, even if you do so at a loss (we sold ours at about 13).

Aetna Life and Casualty (AET)

A final example using the eclectic approach was the giant Aetna Life and Casualty Company,* the nation's largest publicly owned insurance company, recommended in August 1977. Company earnings had grown at a 15 percent compound rate over the prior ten years—albeit growth had been anything but in a straight line be-

---

*Discussed in evaluating analytical techniques in chapter 5.

cause of the inherently cyclical nature of the property-casualty business.

The recommendation was made as the domestic property-casualty industry was undergoing a dramatic recovery from the 1973–75 debacle, the most traumatic on industry record. Overcompetition and an exceptionally high rate of inflation resulted in staggering operating losses for most of the industry in these years—$2.4 billion in 1974 and $4 billion in 1975. The huge losses caused capital impairment for some companies. The capital squeeze became so intense that a number of larger insurance companies were forced to liquidate major portions of their stock portfolios to raise cash almost at the precise bottom of the 1974 market.

Because of these problems, the industry instituted large rate hikes commencing in late 1975, and these increases continued through 1976 and part of 1977. Since it takes almost two years on average for new rate hikes to filter to the bottom line in the property-casualty industry, the significantly improved operating situation was expected to continue to produce sharp earnings gains in 1977 and again in 1978.

Aetna reacted more quickly than most companies to the problems facing the industry during the 1973–75 period. Management introduced tighter controls and responded faster to the accelerating inflationary conditions. As a result, its property-casualty losses were far less severe than those of the industry at large. (In 1976 AET's combined ratio was 95.8 compared with 102 for the industry.)*

Faster rate adjustments and quicker claim processing also made Aetna's reserves adequate to meet rising claim costs. The necessity of having to increase such reserves had been a major factor in the poor industry underwriting record in recent years.

After a $5.9 million pretax loss in 1975 (and a combined ratio of 106.3), AET's property-casualty earnings rebounded to $243 million in 1976 and represented 60 percent of total earnings—the remainder of income coming from life, health, annuity, pension operations, and other businesses. Even sharper earnings improvements

---

*The combined ratio is the addition of the loss and expense ratios. The combined ratio of 95.8 indicates that Aetna recorded 95.8 cents of expenses and claim costs for every $1 of premiums written and brought 4.2 cents down to pretax underwriting profits. For the industry, the ratio of 102 indicated that it lost 2 cents for every $1 of premiums it wrote. This fits under indicator 2, as a low combined ratio for an insurance company is like a high profit margin for an industrial corporation.

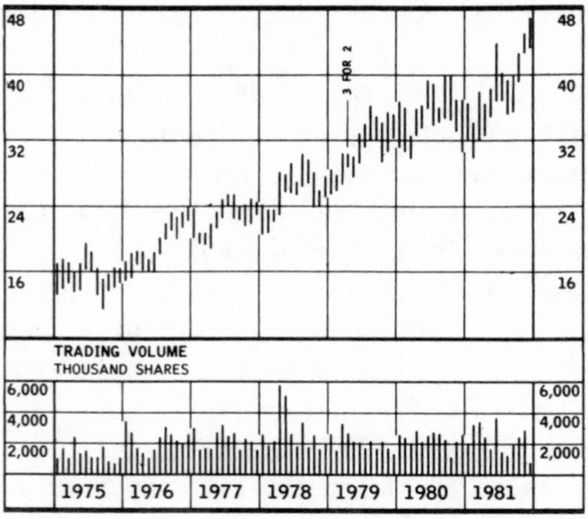

Per-share data ($)

Year-end December 31	1980	1979	1978	1977	1976	1975	1974
Book value	40.77	35.56	30.28	25.33	21.65	18.73	16.79
Earnings	6.30	6.93	6.39	5.17	2.61	1.27	1.90
Dividends	2.12	1.80	1.48	1.00	0.74	0.72	0.72
Payout ratio	34%	26%	23%	19%	28%	57%	38%
Prices—high	40⅛	36⅜	30½	25½	24⅛	19½	26⅛
low	29⅞	25⅝	20⅝	18⅞	15	11½	10⅛
P/E ratio	6-5	5-4	5-3	5-4	9-6	15-9	14-5

SOURCE: *Standard and Poor's Stock Reports.*

were recorded in 1977, with earnings rising 98 percent to $7.75 a share from $3.91. (This perhaps indicates the importance of direction rather than precision—the original 1977 earnings estimate made in June of that year was $6.50, undershooting the actual by 16 percent.)

Once again, most of the major indicators were strong. The stock had an extremely low price/earnings multiple, a reasonable and increasing dividend (at the time, the dividend yield was 4.3 percent), and the probability of continued increases in earnings.

To update the story to early 1982, although Aetna's price has moved up from 24¾ at the time of its recommendation to as high as 47 in 1982, or some 90 percent—earnings have also increased and dividends have almost tripled. Thus, the company continued to remain cheap by our criteria. It currently trades at a P/E multiple of 6, and yields 6 percent. Too, with the worst part of the latest underwriting cycle now behind it, earnings, which had declined about 20 percent from their peak in 1979, should again move ahead, possibly significantly, accompanied by a continued increase in the dividend rate.

Naturally, you won't find all these indicators favorable all the time. Stocks don't trade at low P/E's under A-O.K. conditions. Still, if you look, you will be surprised at how often you will find many of these favorable indicators, as the Bache, Honeywell, General Cinema, and Aetna examples indicate.

A Beneficial Side Effect

Four of the previous companies—Bache, Honeywell, General Cinema, and Aetna—are good examples of a beneficial side effect involved in this strategy. Often low P/E stocks can move substantially higher in price and still be good holdings. The reason: earnings are moving up rapidly enough so that the P/E remains low. This produces a substantially lower turnover rate than most investment strategies.

A lower turnover rate is beneficial to you for a number of reasons.

1. You will have lower capital gains taxes. This is particularly important for gains under one year that are taxed as ordinary income.

2. You will also have lower commission and transaction costs. Transaction costs are often not recognized by investors but can be very expensive. These are the eighths and quarters it costs you to buy or sell a stock. For example, if the stock is trading at 35–35¼ and you wish to buy it, you would probably pay 35¼. If you want to sell it, you would probably receive 35. Such costs can often total 5 percent or more of total capital in a year.

The more commissions and transaction costs can be reduced, of course, the better the overall results will be for the investor. Our experience indicates that by using the low P/E approach, transaction costs and commissions are reduced substantially.

Old Republic International (OLDR)

For investors who enjoy being higher rollers, there is one subcategory of the low P/E strategy that might be considered—buying companies after they have reported losses. According to what we have learned about investor reactions to bad news, we might expect overreactions to companies reporting current losses—and as table 21 (see page 168) indicates, this is precisely what happens.

Investors have always shunned stocks reporting losses, and as a result these stocks have consistently outperformed the S&P. As table 21 shows, if all stocks reporting deficits had been purchased one year after the loss, they would have appreciated 25.4 percent on average in the next twelve months, and 158.1 percent for the full five-year period compared with 12.1 percent and 69.3 percent respectively for the S&P.

Which brings me to Old Republic International. This company was originally a pioneer in credit life insurance (insurance taken out on major installment purchases, such as cars or home durables). However, through the 1970s, it became a major entity in a new and rapidly growing business—workmen's compensation for the coal-mining industry. With changes in federal and state legislation in 1971, giving miners greater coverage, these premiums skyrocketed. OLDR, by far the largest factor in this field, saw this business rise from 3 percent of its premiums in 1972 to 33 percent in 1975 (the business was almost 50 percent of revenues in 1977, a phenomenal rate of growth of over 75 percent annually since 1972). Indicators 1, 2, and 3 were all quite positive.

However, as we have seen time and again, in a dynamic economy nothing is certain, and in 1975 the company incurred substantial losses in its small accident and health line—which it immediately decided to dispose of. After doing so, it lost $3.90 a share in 1975 versus a profit of $2.88 in 1974.

A number of large funds responded to the news in rather predictable fashion by attempting to sell (the more appropriate term is "dump") large amounts of OLDR stock. In this case, approximately 150,000 shares were placed on the market, which normally traded about 5,000 shares a day. The price, not surprisingly, plummeted. The stock dropped from 16 to under 7 the day the news was released.

When the smoke had cleared, it seemed to me that the company's appraisal of its losses was very probably correct, and that there would be no other write-offs forthcoming—statements, incidentally, that the management made publicly.*

*It indicated that the sale of most of the accident and health line had already been negotiated.

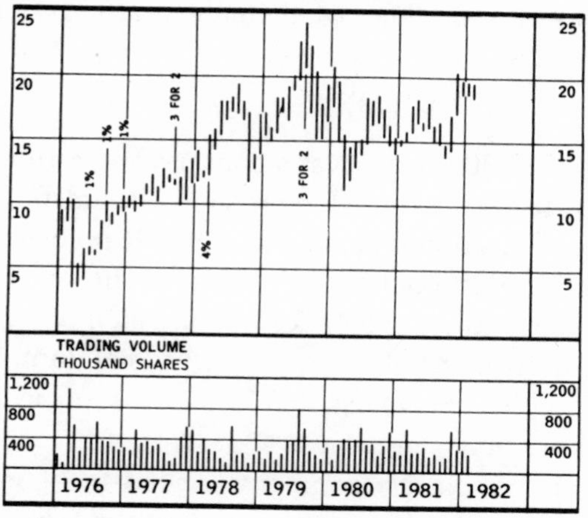

Per-share data ($) Year-end December 31	1980	1979	1978	1977	1976	1975	1974
Book value	17.56	18.18	15.05	12.96	10.11	4.92	6.50
Earnings	3.67	4.31	3.89	3.34	2.99	−2.60	1.92
Dividends	0.92	0.87	0.58¾	0.37⅜	0.18¾	0.32¾	0.32¾
Payout ratio	25%	20%	15%	11%	6%	NM	17%
Prices—high	20⅞	24⅜	19½	13½	11½	9⅞	13¼
low	11¼	15	11⅞	9½	3½	4¾	6¾
P/E ratio—	6-3	6-3	5-3	4-3	4-1	NM	7-3

NOTE: NM = not meaningful.
SOURCE: *Standard & Poor's Stock Reports.*

The stock appeared to be quite attractive. It had the potential of large earnings in 1976 and still had considerable financial strength.

Part of the recommendation ran as follows:

Some of the most profitable investment opportunities have arisen from companies with good records that have stumbled temporarily. Our Investment Strategy Report of April 1976 indicated that companies reporting deficits subsequently outperformed the S&P 400 with regularity [table 21]. While the danger exists that an unfavorable change in a company's fortunes is permanent, for larger corporations in the vast majority of cases it is not, and a resurgence in earnings power normally occurs, resulting in the better performance of the deficit group.

Old Republic, a medium-sized life insurance company, appears to us to provide investors with an excellent opportunity to benefit from this phenomenon. Our analysis leads us to conclude that the problems that caused its large 1975 deficits have been resolved and earnings of $3.30 per share are estimated for 1976. Currently trading at only three times this estimate, and with the likelihood of continuing earnings buildup over the next several years, we believe the stock presents a particularly attractive speculation.

Earnings of $3.30 a share was a conservative estimate, much too conservative as it turned out. (Under such circumstances, however, a very cautious projection is called for.) OLDR reported net earnings of $4.48, and in addition tax and other credits of $2.00 a share, bringing total cash flow to $6.48 for 1976, which was more than the stock traded for at the height of the institutional dumping. (The low reached was 5½.) The next year, 1977, the stock earned $5.21 a share before special credits.

Upon examination the company looked too good to be true. Here was the classic investor overreaction in the face of good fundamentals. I wondered, more than half-seriously, if this might not be the exception that proved the rule. Fortunately for me, it wasn't. The stock proved to be an extremely rewarding holding, rising 184 percent by April 1979. Even after this appreciation, the stock traded at a modest 3.8 times earnings and, I believed, continued to represent good value—this time as a straight low P/E investment.

Indicator 7. As noted previously, buying stocks showing losses is of course considerably riskier than simply buying low P/E stocks. An investor doing this must be very sure of the company's financial strength and should use only a small portion of his portfolio for this purpose, while diversifying into a number of issues to spread the risk.

An Overview of the Eclectic Approach

Indicators 1, 2, 4, and 5 used in accordance with the low P/E rules are all clear-cut and require reasonably straightforward calculations, avoiding the major portion of the configural and information-processing problems previously discussed. And indicator 3, which projects only the general direction of earnings, is much simpler and safer to use, and consequently should have a far better chance of success, than the type of precise estimates ordinarily made by security analysts.

The eclectic low P/E approach that I presented worked exceptionally well through the period 1976–81. While I would be the last to argue that the record is definitive, it does indicate the successful performance of this strategy even through a period of moderate market decline. The results also fit in with the above-average success we have had with our managed portfolio.* Although the degree of success will certainly vary among different individuals and for the same individuals over differing time periods, the eclectic low P/E approach seems to be an extremely workable investment strategy, eliminating most complex judgments. Obviously, this is the method that I most favor.

However, as an investor, you may choose either to follow this strategy as I have laid it down, or perhaps to use a variety of mechanical low P/E approaches that avoid security analysis entirely, yet should show superior performance over time. Let's look at some of these strategies next.

Other Approaches Using the Low P/E Strategy

Since tables 9 through 17 indicated pretty conclusively that the low P/E's normally provided the best returns and the high P/E's the worst, the investor might reasonably ask why mechanical strategies based solely on buying stocks below the market multiple couldn't be used without any of the screening criteria described previously.

I believe such strategies are quite feasible, but once again general rules 2 and 3 apply: namely, the portfolio should be made up of fifteen to twenty stocks, diversified into ten to twelve industries; and the low P/E investor should attempt to buy medium- or large-sized companies.

Buy-and-Hold Strategies

First, we might consider a strategy remarkably similar to one advocated by our efficient-market friends—that of "buying and holding" a well-diversified portfolio of securities over a long period of time. Their strategy took no notice of P/E multiple. However, since the record shows that low P/E stocks provide better returns over

---

*From early 1976 to the end of 1981 this portfolio was up 78 percent, or 17 percent annually, about double the performance of the S&P 500 (both including dividends).

long holding periods, why not buy and hold portfolios of low P/E stocks instead?

As table 25 indicates, both the Nicholson and the Miller studies showed superior performance for the low P/E stocks for periods ranging from three to seven years. The periods tested in our work, from three to nine years, came up with very similar results.

From the table you can see that buying the lowest 20 percent of stocks in this manner and holding them gives you a very good chance of outdoing the market. Buying the bottom 40 percent of stocks according to P/E ratios should still give you superior performance, albeit probably reduced from the bottom 20 percent. However, there is an added measure of safety in the latter case because the investor has double the number of large, high-yielding companies to choose from.

The buy-and-hold strategies eliminate all commissions, transaction costs, and capital gains taxes. *For the ultraconservative investor, they would be the safest way to apply the low P/E strategy.*

You might ask how one determines P/E deciles and quintiles. Brokerage firms, advisory services, and financial publications often advertise long lists of low P/E stocks (the *Value Line* survey, for example, runs lists of high-yielding stocks with P/E ratios under 5

Table 25
AVERAGE ANNUAL RETURNS FOR HOLDING PERIODS OF THREE YEARS OR MORE

| | SWITCHING AFTER EACH | | | | HOLDING ORIGINAL PORTFOLIO FOR | | |
| | 3 YEARS[a] | | 5 YEARS[a] | | 7 YEARS[a] | 8 YEARS[b] | 9 YEARS[b] |
	MILLER[c]	NICHOLSON[d]	MILLER[c]	NICHOLSON[d]	NICHOLSON[d]	1968–77 STUDY	1968–77 STUDY
Highest 20% of P/E's	8.5	6.6	9.3	7.9	9.1	−1.3	0.8
Second 20%	8.9	7.5	9.8	8.5	9.0	3.0	4.4
Third 20%	11.4	9.2	10.9	9.9	10.1	2.7	4.1
Fourth 20%	12.5	10.3	12.0	10.6	10.4	5.5	6.2
Lowest 20%	16.6	11.6	14.1	14.7	13.9	7.2	7.2
Sample return	11.6	9.0	11.2	10.3	10.5	3.5	4.8

[a] Appreciation only.
[b] Total return.
[c] 1948–64.
[d] 1937–62.

almost weekly at the present time), and *Financial Weekly** lists the
P/E deciles for all stocks on the New York Stock Exchange, the
American Stock Exchange, and over-the-counter weekly. However,
if this information isn't available to you, some simple rules of thumb
should suffice. First, take a broad market index, like the S&P 500,
for which the current P/E ratio on latest twelve-month earnings can
easily be found from a variety of sources, including brokers, newspapers, and the S&P stock guide. The current ratio of the S&P 500 is
about 8. We next pick well-established companies paying good dividends and trading below this multiple. One rule of thumb might be
to use a 20 percent discount or more from the S&P 500 (6.4 times
earnings and down at the present time). The deeper the discount
from the S&P 500, the further down you are moving in the low P/E
range.

There is nothing magical about picking the bottom 20 or 40
percent. For a computer, it was simply a good cutoff point. And, as
we found in the most recent study, at times the returns in the second
lowest quintile were better than those in the bottom one.

This simple method should work fairly effectively if you do not
have the actual deciles of low P/E stocks. Next, how do you find the
P/E ratios themselves? This too is easy: the *Wall Street Journal,
Barron's,* and the financial sections of most major daily newspapers
will have the P/E ratio right next to the stock, calculated on latest
twelve-month reported earnings. It is a relatively simple matter to
run down the column and find stocks at a 20 percent discount from
the market multiple (more or less as you choose).

Making Changes in the Low P/E Portfolio

Another twist on this approach, which also appears quite workable,
would be to buy a portfolio of low P/E stocks and weed it periodically as stocks move up to the market P/E multiple or above, or if
they fail to perform as well as the market over a certain period of
time.† An overview of the studies indicated that returns normally
diminished with longer holding periods. Thus, some method such as
the above would serve to enhance overall return above that of the
simple buy-and-hold strategy.

*Box 26, Richmond, VA 23201; tel. (804) 649–6586.
†For sell rules, see page 207.

While this strategy introduces transaction costs, they should be quite small, since the investor should, on average, have only a few trades a year. The pruning process should also allow the investor to maintain a portfolio of low P/E stocks with above-average yields.

But once again, remember the two important rules of portfolio construction: diversification into fifteen or twenty stocks, and medium- to large-sized companies. As noted earlier, the deeper the discount from the average, the more you are moving into the lower deciles.

In any case, whichever of the mechanical strategies you choose, you should have a good chance of outdoing the market with minimal time spent making selections and with only average risk, if that.

Turning over the Bottom 20 Percent of Low P/E's Annually

For those who are willing to take some additional risk and who can get a list of the bottom quintile, the analysis of the findings in chapter 7 indicates that purchasing the bottom 20 percent of stocks and turning them over annually enhances return.*

Table 26 shows the superior performance of the bottom 20 percent of stocks in each study compared with the average return of all stocks in the samples. In all cases, the stocks were turned over on an annual basis. The four studies were conducted in time periods overlapping a forty-year period. Viewing the findings over the entire 1937–77 span, one would certainly conclude that an investor could buy a portfolio of the bottom 20 percent of P/E's and turn them over annually.

"Ah!" you might say, "but what about recent years? Certainly some of your own tables in chapter 7 show that if you tried this method, transaction costs would eat you alive because of the low returns."

It is true that returns will vary widely with different time peri-

---

*Investors without such a list who are willing to put up with an hour or two of work can approximate the bottom 20 percent fairly easily from the stocks on the New York Stock Exchange. There are approximately 1,450 common stocks listed on the exchange, so 140 would be the bottom 10 percent and 280 the bottom 20 percent. Running down the column of P/E ratios, start with the lowest multiples (the 1s, 2s, 3s, and 4s) and tick off the number of each multiple on a sheet of paper. In this manner a data base can be accumulated that should approximate the bottom 20 percent (although not absolutely the same, it is quick and should approximate the sample we are looking for). This need be done only once or twice a year.

Table 26
AVERAGE PERFORMANCE OF BOTTOM P/E QUINTILE VERSUS
SAMPLE MEAN

TIME PERIOD	NAME OF STUDY	AVERAGE ANNUAL RETURN OF BOTTOM QUINTILE	AVERAGE ANNUAL RETURN OF MEAN	SUPERIORITY OF BOTTOM QUINTILE RELATIVE TO SAMPLE MEAN
1937–62	Nicholson[a]	16.0%	8.2%	+45%
1946–64	Miller[a]	18.4	12.0	+53
1957–71	Basu[b]	16.3	12.1	+35
1968–77	Dreman[b]	8.2	4.8	+71

[a]Figures reflect appreciation.
[b]Figures reflect total return.

ods, from the 18.4 and 16.0 percent returns of the Nicholson and Miller studies to the 10.3 percent return we received in table 13, on page 145 (not to mention the 2.0 percent of the May 1970–November 1974 period).

In the final chapter I'll present arguments I hope will convince you that returns should prevail at higher rates than those of the overall past and certainly will be above those of the last twelve years. Ibbotson and Sinquefield, the financial researchers whose evidence we viewed in chapter 6, have projected future rates of return for stocks of 12.5 percent for the next several decades. Suppose we accept this figure and assume a continuation of approximately 50 percent superiority in the returns of the bottom 20 percent of P/E's. This would lead to a total return approximating 18.5 percent annually.

Next, let's look at the specter of turnover costs. We found that 54.4 percent of the bottom decile turns over annually. However, from our observations, most stocks normally move into an adjoining decile. This should reduce turnover somewhat, but to be conservative, let's assume it continues to stay relatively high for the lowest 20 percent, say 45 percent annually. Remember that past annual turnover strategies generated appreciation as high as 18.8 percent, and if we are on target about better future markets, we should be in a position to absorb some added transaction costs, particularly when some brokers have discounted commissions to as low as 10 to 20 cents a share.

Now, let's make some assumptions to see how large the annual transaction costs would be. First, let's assume a portfolio of $100,000 and an average stock price of $25 a share, equally placed into twenty positions. (Each holding would then be two hundred shares.)

Using the 45 percent annual turnover rate, we would buy and sell nine positions a year on average. If we go to our neighborhood discount broker and are able to wangle 20-cents-a-share commission on our transactions,* the cost and commissions would be $360 to sell and an additional $360 on average to replace the positions. If we assume other transaction costs at double these figures, total costs would be $1,440, or 1.44 percent annually.

Using the 12.5 percent rate of return as the future mean, we see that the portfolio average return would be $18,750, less the $1,440 in transaction costs, or $17,310. In other words, the net return would be 17.3 percent, versus 12.5 percent, or some 38 percent more. Obviously, this is a strategy that could only work for individual investors —the size of institutional blocks would markedly increase transaction costs because of their effect on market price.

Remember, again, that these are only assumptions, but I think they are practical ones, and they are based on studies of the returns of low P/E stocks over a forty-year period. The evidence indicates that superior results should be garnered from an approach such as the one just recommended.

On the Drawing Board Only

One potential strategy that intrigues me is based on turning over portfolios on latest twelve-month earnings on a quarterly basis. Quarterly turnover resulted in by far the best returns in the lowest P/E decile and the worst in the highest in virtually every test we ran. For example, even though our studies covered an exceptionally poor period for markets, the average return on the lowest decile on a quarterly basis was 14.0 percent over the nine years of the study. This compared with a return on the highest P/E decile of −2.64 percent on the same basis and a long-term average return on common stocks of 9.2 percent. Returns of up to 20 percent were achieved in some of the better time periods through this interval, which makes me

---

*At the time of this writing some discount brokers were giving the public commissions as low as 12.5 cents a share on two-hundred-share lots.

wonder just how high such returns could be in a bull market. Even adjusting for the significantly higher portfolio turnover on a quarterly basis (about 120 percent per year for the lowest decile) using our prior portfolio and transaction cost assumptions, this would reduce returns by only 3.3 percent annually on average. In more normal markets, quarterly turnover might certainly prove to be an exciting strategy.

However, I must caution you that the strategy is far too wild for my blood. It's based simply on our findings, which cover a single nine-year period, as well as on the assumption that similar results would hold in the future. It would also require a large number of transactions and extensive bookkeeping. To avoid Valium (or at the least increasing your intake), I think I'd leave this approach to a mutual fund to try first.

Realistically, then, there are a number of approaches to the low P/E strategies, all of them with substantial statistical documentation, in addition to the eclectic approach that I personally favor. While I don't believe low P/E investing need necessarily be the final answer to stock selection for everyone, it has consistently provided better performance in both good and bad markets.

To the present time it is the only system I know of that effectively and systematically checks investor overreactions—by far the largest and most important source of investor error.

However, there are still a number of questions that must be answered before you use these strategies, not the least important of which is deciding when to sell.

When to Sell

Regardless of the investment strategy you use, one of your most difficult decisions is when to sell.

There are almost as many answers to the problem as there are investors, but even among professionals the number who follow their own sell rules scrupulously is very limited. Psychological forces appear to impact most sell decisions, often with disastrous consequences. Given what we know of the subject, it seems that the safest approach is once again to rely on mechanical guidelines, which serve to filter out much of the emotional content of the decision.

The general rule that I have been using is that *stocks should be sold when their P/E ratio approaches that of the overall market, regardless of how favorable prospects appear.* These stocks should then be replaced by other low P/E stocks. For example, if the market P/E today was 9 and one of our stocks, say General Cinema, went up to the multiple, it should be sold and replaced by another low P/E stock.*

A further question may at times arise with sell strategies using the eclectic approach. Suppose an investor has a portfolio of twenty stocks and finds a new one that ranks much higher by the indicators previously outlined while also trading at a lower P/E ratio than a number of stocks he owns. A switch might then be made, but he must keep in mind the principle of a fixed number of stocks in the portfolio: each time one is purchased, another one should be sold. And, because he is bringing in more judgment in switching, changes of this sort should be relatively rare in order to avoid the danger that overtrading inhibits results.

A supplementary rule is that a stock that attains a high P/E multiple solely because of a decline in earnings should not be sold. It is true that by using the low P/E approach a number of clinkers will be acquired which, whether because they are cyclical or for other reasons, are approaching peak earnings and will incur earnings declines. However, we know the overall superior record of the low P/E group, which contains numbers of such companies. Thus, if you have adequate diversification, both by the number of stocks and by industry, this should not be a major problem.

Also, the price drop will often be an overreaction to the anticipated decline in earnings. Take the case of General Motors in the high 40s in 1973. At the time it was trading at a P/E of 5, well under the S&P 500. Earnings declined in 1974, and GM's multiple rose above the market's as the stock fell to 29. However, by late 1975, the stock was over 60, and by early 1976 it had moved up to 74—rising far more than the S&P over the period.

Another question is how long an investor should hold a situation that has not worked out. Again, there are many partial answers to this problem. The one that seems to work best is to adopt a two-year holding period.† My criterion is that if the stock has not

---

*Naturally, as prices change over time, the weightings of stocks in the portfolio will differ. When stocks are sold, the effort should be made to bring the weightings more into balance with one another.

†For a cyclical stock with a drop in earnings, this might be stretched to two and a half or three years.

done at least as well as the market after this time, it should be sold and replaced with another.

What the Low P/E Strategy Won't Do for You

Whether you opt for the eclectic low P/E strategy or take the bit between your teeth and head straight for low P/E methods without any form of security analysis, keep in mind that the strategies are relative rather than absolute. This means, in effect, that they won't help you decide on when to get in or out of the market. Whether the market is very high or very low, you will receive no warning signals to sell in the first place or buy in the second.

What the low P/E strategy should do is give you the best relative opportunities for the money you have invested in the stock market. Which means that in a rising market, your stocks ought to do better than the averages, and in a falling market they should decline less.

Alternatives to the Low P/E Philosophy

Mutual Funds and Closed-End Investment Companies

Some investors may wish to participate in the stock market but for various reasons do not wish to make their own investment decisions. Others believe their capital is too limited to get a fully diversified low P/E portfolio.

With a limited amount of funds, the best approach would seem to be to purchase a no-load or low-load mutual fund with a broad portfolio. Select a fund that has come at least reasonably close to the market averages over a period of years (which probably means that it has not done an excessive amount of trading). This should provide you with results pretty much in line with returns received on common stocks in general.

Since studies have shown that no-load funds and low-loads have performed as well over the years as full-load funds, it is silly to pay the extra commission, which goes not to management but to the fund salesman. Brokers are not happy to recommend no-load funds, since those up-front sales charges run as high as 8¾ percent and are their bread and butter. If you do have trouble, as many investors have, finding one that suits your needs, you can get further information on no-load funds by writing to the No-Load Mutual Fund Association, 655 Third Avenue, New York, NY 10017.

A broad portfolio can also be acquired by purchasing a closed-end investment company. These companies, unlike mutual funds, do not continuously issue and redeem shares: their number of shares outstanding is fixed. The larger closed-end funds are usually traded on the New York Stock Exchange, normally at a discount from the value of their assets. Table 27 indicates the average discount over the last five years.

Table 27
CLOSED-END INVESTMENT COMPANIES

COMPANY	ASSET SIZE[a]	AVERAGE DISCOUNT 5 YEARS, 1981
Adams Express	$303.9	17.6%
General American Investors	209.7	11.6
Lehman Corporation	573.7	17.6
Niagara Share Corporation	155.1	12.0
Tri-Continental Corporation	767.0	20.4
U.S. & Foreign Securities	157.9	23.0

[a]In millions of dollars, year-end 1981.

SOURCE: Wiesenberger Investment Companies Service. Copyright 1982 by Warren, Gorman & Lamont, Inc., Boston, Mass.

The discounts provided on a weekly basis in the *Wall Street Journal, Barron's,* the *New York Times,* and various financial publications usually vary between 10 and 20 percent. If the discounts are larger than the average, as they tend to be during periods of market decline, interesting buying opportunities are available.*

Dual Funds

One interesting variation of the closed-end investment companies is the dual-fund concept. These funds pay all income to their income shareholders and all capital gains to the capital stockholders. The

---

*In April 1979, for example, with widespread market disillusionment, the discounts on many of the leading closed-end funds ran well over 20 percent, making them appear particularly attractive relative to equity mutual funds at that time.

capital shareholders thus get a larger play on the market than the portfolio behind the fund itself because they also get the appreciation or loss on the portion underlying the income shares.

Dual funds, like closed-end funds, normally trade at a discount from their net asset price. This price can usually be found in the *Wall Street Journal* every Monday.

An investor who believes the market is going up can get as much as 1.4–1.5 play on the market through owning such a fund because of the combination of a discount-to-asset value and the leverage on the income shares. Thus, if the market went up 50 percent and the fund did no more than match the market, the capital shareholder would see his investment go up 75 percent—and all the capital gain.*

One of my favorites is Gemini Capital, because it is somewhat similar to us in investment philosophy, well diversified, and has a good record outperforming the market for over a decade. Gemini Capital (GEM) is traded on the New York Stock Exchange.

Dollar Cost Averaging

As you receive new money over time, and assuming you've decided the proper percentage to allocate to equities, simply follow the low P/E philosophy. However, suppose you receive a large sum at one time. What should you do? In such cases, you might try a simple and effective method called dollar cost averaging. As an example, take the pleasant case of having just inherited $50,000. After reviewing your financial position, you decide you can afford to put almost all of it into the market.

To be prudent, you should do so over a period of time, possibly two or three years. You might invest each quarter over a two-year period in eight equal installments. When the market is high, you will buy fewer shares; when it is low, more. You will thereby avoid the risk of getting in entirely at the top—and sacrifice the euphoria of buying at the lows. However, it is a safer approach, since your purchases will more closely reflect market movements over a two- or three-year period. The guessing game is something you should leave to the market timers—and you've already seen their record.

*But remember that leverage is a "double-edged sword," as many a poor soul has learned. If you're wrong on direction, the fund will go down more than the market.

In this chapter we have reviewed some of the practical variations on the low P/E approach. Next, let's turn to some widely
discussed investments outside of the stock market—how some can
benefit you, and what, if you're not careful, others might do to your
capital.

CHAPTER TEN

Your Broker
and the Fastest Games
in Town

The last three chapters laid out the strategies that I believe provide the average investor with the best chances for success. While the low P/E approach is certainly not an investment panacea, it does appear to solve many of the problems of selecting the right equities—in a stock market which, as the final chapter will attempt to show, provides excellent value today.

Still, the poor performance of stocks in the past decade and a half hardly qualifies for LeBon's image of instant wealth. Not surprisingly, then, after what we've seen of crowd reactions and cognitive biases, interest has shifted elsewhere. Because the psychology of markets is basically the same, many of the traps and pitfalls that we have already viewed are also present in these other arenas.

In the following sections, we'll look at a number of the other investments that have become very popular today and what your chances are in playing them. Some, fast-paced and barely regulated, are extremely risky. And, as we'll see, although enormous returns are promised, the odds at times are not quite as good as those offered by the old Ponzi scheme.

However, on a more refreshing note, there have been other investment developments in recent years that can be of real help to you, both in rounding out your portfolio and in providing tax savings.

While the examination necessarily will be brief, it should help you delineate some of the new investments you should examine and others you would be well advised to stay clear of.

Before beginning our survey of the investments themselves—not infrequently called "products" in the trade—we'll look at what role the principal merchandisers should play in helping to screen them.

The Role of Your Broker

Your friendly broker knows only too well that stocks have not been the most exciting investment ploys to attract new clients. His management is even more aware of the problem. Many a brokerage firm now states proudly in its annual report how little, not how much, it depends on stock commissions. The more important its other "products" to its total revenues, the better.

Should you rely on a broker primarily for his advice? The answer here, I think, is by and large no. There are many outstanding exceptions, of course (and almost every broker will tell you he is one of them). But how do you spot them? Certainly not by appearance, dress, or manner. Brokers are paid for the commissions they generate, not for the performance of their clients' accounts. They may look successful, but Gucci shoes, Polo suits, and Pierre Cardin ties have far more to do with good merchandising than with ability in the marketplace. The real exceptions, and this applies to all advice givers, should be able to document a successful record of performance, supplying you both with the performance of all stocks and investments they have recommended over an extended period and with the results of a number of their major clients' accounts (make sure they are not relatives or friends).

I don't mean to be cynical. Many salesmen will try to do an honest job, not just to keep the account but to get referrals from the client's friends and associates—essential to expanding business. But even if he is not affected by current fads, his clients undoubtedly are. The account executive's lifeblood is commissions, and because of this, except for those rare exceptions, he is dealing in fashion no less than a high-style boutique, which nudges him toward selling products that are currently "in."

Some brokers will sell anything that has a large commission attached to it, no matter how ill-suited it may be to the client—bad new issues, slow-moving secondaries, or other high-commission products. But is this really much different from the clothing salesmen who try to pocket extra commissions by selling you slow-moving, ill-fitting items? And it would be hard to make the case that the business ethics of insurance or used-car salesmen are much better. In any event, the customer's man can always argue that he gave the account a "shot" at making money, which of course does sometimes pay off.

You should be aware that despite federal statutes and stock exchange regulations going back to the 1930s, there really is no way of stopping an unscrupulous salesman from generating large commissions from the unwary. Unless he has gone to incredible extremes, as sometimes happens, such as "churning" a widow's portfolio from $100,000 to $8,000 in a couple of years while pocketing $150,000 in commissions, he won't be caught. You have to be careful, because many a dishonest type can be extremely soft-spoken and articulate, and dress and act like a banker.

When the exchange does discipline its brokers, the connection between the offense and the public interest is sometimes mystifying, as Alan Abelson once noted:

As a frequent critic of the Big Board, we must, in fairness, bow to its new and uncommon zeal in protecting the nation's investors. Last week, for example, it disclosed a number of disciplinary actions against errant brokers and other wretches whose activities come within its purview. We are particularly heartened by the Exchange's suspension of one fellow who allegedly committed the heinous crime of engaging in an outside business without approval: he was engaged in—grip the arms of your chairs now—a trout hatchery. The poor fish got a year's suspension. We were also relieved to see the powers-that-be at the Big Board crack down on brokers who agreed to share their customer's losses. Imagine if that sort of thing proved contagious. It would destroy a two-hundred-year tradition of sharing everything of your customer's—except his losses.[1]

Remember that the nature of the game makes it necessary for many brokers to turn over their accounts fairly rapidly. Account upgrading, as it is sometimes called, is a common maneuver for many brokers in a slow market or when commission business is slipping.

"Upgrading" means upgrading the broker's commissions, with the probability of only a questionable change (and possibly one to your detriment) in the composition of your portfolio. Some firms expect a minimum turnover in commissions from each salesman, depending on the size of the client's account. So unless there really is a good reason for making a suggested change, be careful.

More recently, with the rising interest in the faster-paced newer games, the commissions the broker can make have increased substantially. A tremendous amount of trading can be generated, much of which is old-fashioned "churning" but disguised in a highly sophisticated manner through the buying and selling of various computerized spreads.*

The salesman is an independent producer, after all, and must exist on his commissions. A few years back, I attended a meeting of a large national brokerage firm. One of two conflicting themes was presented by all the major speakers, and sometimes the same speaker presented both: first, always work in your client's best interest (which often means doing a minimal amount of trading); and second, your client always needs your help, his portfolio always needs some revision (in other words, a good salesman can find an opportunity to trade, or discover a new product). It's not hard, then, to see the danger that the unsophisticated investor has to face.

Unless you really think you can find that ideal broker who both is independent and has an excellent record, you had better use yours in the following manner:

1. As a source of information as to the credit worthiness of various fixed-income securities. He'll know call provisions, bond ratings, available yields, and information of this sort, and he can be useful in doing the bond shopping for you. But watch him; he can also lock in very large commissions on your bond transactions, especially if they are not New York Stock Exchange- or AMEX-listed.†

2. As a source of investment information on companies. He can probably supply you with long lists of high-yielding low P/E stocks and perhaps the lower deciles or quintiles themselves. If you don't

---

*See page 231.

†Particularly with infrequently traded issues, he may buy them at 95 and sell them to you at 98. Shopping around various brokerage houses is not a bad idea. In any case, let your broker know in your conversations that you are aware of such markups. You'll probably save yourself a good deal of money by doing so.

subscribe to a comprehensive statistical service, such as *Value Line,* very likely he does, and he can send you detailed information on the industries and companies you are interested in. He also has the Standard & Poor's statistical sheets. S&P prepares these on all companies on the New York Stock Exchange and American Stock Exchange, and also on major companies traded over-the-counter and on regional exchanges. The sheets contain excellent background data and brief synopses of the companies' major businesses, as well as recent developments. The broker should also be able to provide you with detailed information in any area that interests you. In short, he or she has statistical backup and information-gathering capabilities that can be invaluable aids to you. Brokerage firms spend substantial amounts in obtaining such information, so it certainly pays you to avail yourself of the sources.

The Discount Broker

If you already receive a comprehensive advisory service, you might decide to save on commissions by using a discount broker, particularly if you try some of the mechanical trading strategies mentioned in the last chapter.

In using a discount broker, you should remember a number of points. First, you can't be an odd-lotter. Usually a discount broker charges $25 to $30 minimum commission per transaction, so your volume has to be large enough to warrant the expense.

Second, he offers few or no frills. His only responsibility is prompt execution of orders, which in a good firm will be on a par with brokers charging regular commissions.

It's also important, if you are a large account, to make sure he has federal insurance up to $300,000. Most do, but a few carry it only up to $50,000. You can ask to see his financial statements, which he must provide on request. . Make sure he is profitable and has at least $2-3 million in capital. If a firm "bellies up," your account, even though insured, can be frozen for months, which could cost you dearly if you have to take immediate action. If you glance at the *Wall Street Journal,* Sunday *New York Times,* or *Barron's,* you will see numerous ads for discount brokers.

However, several notes of caution are important. As a *Forbes* article noted: "Don't let the advertising fool you. When a discount broker promises that you will save up to 65%, it doesn't necessarily mean you save 65% across the board on all trades. To get a 65% discount from the pre-May 1, 1975, fixed-rate benchmark against which most discount rates are figured, you have to buy 900 shares of a $30 stock. The biggest savings naturally are keyed to the largest orders."[2]

Although commission costs are significantly less than for a full-line broker, as tables 28 and 29 indicate, the rates can vary markedly even among discounters and change periodically, so it pays to shop around.

A second important point the *Forbes* article noted is that "cheapest isn't always best." It doesn't make sense to save $25 on a one-hundred-share transaction and receive a bad execution that costs you half a point or $50 on the trade. As an investor, you'll do well to look around for the best combination of good executions and low commissions.

Thirdly, it's important to examine the level of service the discounter gives you. Some of the more sophisticated have invested millions in computer operations, and they provide good statements and quick confirmations of executed orders. Fidelity, for example,

Table 28
SOME FULL-SERVICE BROKERAGE RATES

FULL-SERVICE BROKERS	PRICE PER SHARE ($)	TOTAL COMMISSION ON NO. OF SHARES TRADED			
		100	500	1000	2500
Merrill Lynch, Pierce,	10	$36.85	$137.76	$251.66	$512.29
Fenner & Smith	30	69.44	266.21	461.85	667.93
	50	87.00	372.45	575.34	667.93
	100	87.00	460.00	575.34	667.93
E. F. Hutton & Co.	10	34.00	135.00	240.00	497.50
	30	66.00	255.00	442.00	760.00
	50	81.00	355.00	548.00	1,017.30
	100	85.00	425.00	791.00	1,662.50
Shearson Leob Rhoades	10	34.75	143.75	252.50	512.00
	30	69.85	269.25	469.00	809.50
	50	97.00	377.50	581.00	1,089.50
	100	97.00	485.00	861.00	1,789.50

SOURCE: "Picking a Discount Broker," copyright *Financial World,* February 1, 1981.

Table 29
SOME DISCOUNT BROKERAGE RATES

DISCOUNT BROKERS	PRICE PER SHARE ($)	TOTAL COMMISSION ON NO. OF SHARES TRADED			
		100	500	1000	2500
Charles Schwab & Co.	10	$30.00	$ 66.00	$ 87.00	$132.00
	30	54.00	102.00	147.00	225.00
	50	66.00	132.00	207.00	264.99
	100	87.00	207.00	225.00	452.97
Quick & Reilly	10	30.00	52.38	117.49	210.53
	30	30.00	127.73	219.95	209.45
	50	39.72	178.99	149.78	238.96
	100	44.40	222.00	224.30	470.26
Fidelity Brokerage Services	10	33.00	64.00	84.00	149.00
	30	48.00	114.00	144.00	286.50
	50	64.00	149.00	224.00	N
	100	84.00	224.00	374.00	N
Rose & Co.	10	20.00	69.56	128.16	174.88
	30	25.00	110.00	200.00	279.20
	50	25.00	110.00	200.00	312.50
	100	25.00	110.00	200.00	312.50
Andrew Peck Associates	10	39.50	62.50	82.50	132.50
	30	39.50	62.50	82.50	132.50
	50	39.50	62.50	82.50	132.50
	100	39.50	62.50	82.50	132.50
Brown & Co.	10	29.00	45.00	65.00	117.50
	30	32.00	60.00	95.00	122.50
	50	33.00	65.00	105.00	137.50
	100	33.00	65.00	105.00	137.50
Muriel Siebert & Co.	10	25.00	53.35	96.12	170.00
	30	26.95	116.12	179.95	235.00
	50	35.75	162.69	199.70	300.00
	100	40.36	181.64	261.68	310.00
Tradex Brokerage Service	10	35.00	45.00	75.00	137.50
	30	35.00	95.00	115.00	225.00
	50	35.00	130.00	145.00	287.50
	100	45.00	162.50	220.00	475.00
William Aronson & Co.	10	40.00	42.68	64.09	N
	30	40.00	92.89	119.97	N
	50	40.00	130.15	149.97	N
	100	40.00	149.74	206.55	N

SOURCE: "Picking a Discount Broker," copyright *Financial World,* February 1, 1981.
NOTE: N = Negotiated rate.

normally phones the client shortly after the execution. Good record-keeping, including thorough monthly statements, is important to avoid problems later. The quality again varies, from first-class, for firms that have invested heavily in the latest data-processing and communication equipment, to poor, for some of the smallest firms.

Some discount firms also offer a variety of services that are given by a full-service firm. Fidelity, for example, also provides a number of money market funds, ranging from standard funds to those investing only in government securities or tax-free instruments. Clients can put their money into any of these without charge when the funds are not invested in the market. As the discounters gain market share (today estimated at under 10 percent, but eventually likely to expand to 15 or 20 percent or more of the total market), they may provide even more of the services currently offered by the full-line firms.

My preference would be to steer toward the largest well-capitalized discounter noted for both good executions and some additional services, rather than the cheapest guy on the block. With the latter you may save a few bucks on commission, but lose more than that through poor executions, not to mention the heartburn factor.

Next, let's turn to some of the games themselves and your odds if you choose to play.

Investing in Junk Bonds

Before we move on to the more popular games, some of which appear at times to have hawkers at every street corner, let's start with one that is not popular and for this reason may present some good opportunities for you—the interesting but more speculative one of investing in low-quality bonds. This form of investment has never gained a wide following.

Just as low P/E stocks have unfavorable outlooks, so junk bonds, as this group is appropriately named, are considered the poorest of corporate credit ratings*—investors are not sure that the issuing companies will be able to make future interest payments and eventually pay back the face value of the debt.

*If you are unfamiliar with the characteristics of bonds and debentures, please refer to Appendix II, which provides details of contractual obligation, types of risk, etc.

Such companies are at the bottom of the barrel of corporate credits—firms too small to be given credit ratings by S&P and Moody's, the predominant rating agencies;* those which have low credit ratings because of large amounts of debt outstanding, poor or cyclical operating records, or deteriorating financial positions; and at the very lowest tier, companies that are in bankruptcy proceedings. They're anything but hot items, so you won't often worry about a salesman trying to market them to you.

However, it is precisely because of the poor conditions existing or anticipated for such bonds that attractive opportunities often exist. As I noted in chapter 8, I've found that investor overreactions to such bonds seem very similar to overreactions to low P/E stocks.

Although it seems that psychological reactions very often do exist in bond markets, unfortunately rules cannot be formulated nearly as systematically here as in the stock market. Unless you become well trained in assessing credit risk, I would advise you against playing junk bonds on your own. You might find a good advisor who specializes in this area and has a long-standing record of success, or perhaps you could place a small percentage of your portfolio (because of the added risk to come from the equity portion) in a junk bond fund that will give you a widely diversified portfolio of such issues. Two no-load funds investing in junk bonds are listed in table 30 (page 222).

Now let's turn to some of the more popular games.

Commodities

In recent years, the prices of gold, silver, platinum, and diamonds have skyrocketed. Other commodities, industrial as well as agricultural, have also moved up sharply. Not surprisingly, tens of thousands of investors see commodities as the road to instant wealth—once again, that simple but effective image.

What are your odds in this game—certainly one of the most spectacular in town? I think it is useful to examine the question in some detail, for while commodity markets are soaring and may very well continue to do so, the majority of investors are not making money; indeed, most take losses. The reasons for failure are not

*Again, for details on credit ratings, please refer to Appendix II.

Table 30
JUNK BOND FUNDS—NO-LOAD

MUTUAL FUND	TOTAL RETURN	MINIMUM INITIAL INVESTMENT	SIZE OF FUND
American Investors Income P.O. Box 2500 Greenwich, Conn. 06830 Telephone: (203) 622–1600	17.4%[a]	$400	10.5 million
Fidelity High Income 82 Devonshire Street Boston, Mass. 02109 Toll-free number: (800) 225–6190	12.8%[b]	$2,500	71.5 million

NOTE: Includes dividends, capital distributions, and assumes reinvestment of all income.
[a] Annualized return, June 30, 1975, to June 30, 1981.
[b] Total return, November 30, 1977, to November 30, 1981.

terribly different from those that apply to many other fast-paced and seemingly unbeatable games, from high P/E stocks to options.

There are two principal tiers of commodity speculation. One consists of the large and legitimate firms that are members of the various exchanges and thus are subject to some regulation, particularly if the firm is a member of the New York Stock Exchange. The second group is comprised of a wide range of firms often belonging to no exchanges and governed by minimal regulations, if any at all.

The legitimate brokerage firm normally deals in futures contracts. Margins in these contracts are quite low (usually under 10 percent of the total value of the commodity itself), resulting in highly leveraged profits and losses. Expiration dates are brief, running from a day or two to about a year. Because of the short period of time involved, trading techniques have traditionally been based on technical analysis and market timing. From what was seen of the success rate of these methods, you might guess that the scorecard is not good. If you do, you're right.

My father is a commodities futures broker. In the late 1920s, his first job was as a bookkeeper for a commodities brokerage firm. Watching the eager if sometimes frenzied trading of the firm's clientele and listening to their boasts of profits, he began to examine the record to determine how well they had actually done. He was amazed to find that almost without exception none of them made money over time. His advice is that if you are an outsider, stay out. Unless you have that one expert in a thousand to advise you (and you can't know beforehand), you are headed for trouble.

His experience is not unique. One commodities broker quoted recently in *Forbes* said he had had one thousand clients over a period of years; not one of them made money. And an article in *Money* magazine estimated that 90 percent of small investors lose money, with the life span of the average individual account only four months.[3]

Even the pros—armed with years of experience, sophisticated trading techniques, and extensive computer backup—have taken their lumps. Recall the plight of two funds of Conticommodity, the largest commodity broker, both of which went down in flames— losing most of their investors' capital in 1980. Unfortunately, large losses on managed accounts are anything but a rarity.

Commodities are an excellent, almost ideal, revenue source for brokers. Contracts, as noted, are short, there are innumerable spreads,* and thus commissions (the rates are high in themselves) relative to client investment are usually many times those generated by the average stock account. Small wonder there has been such a rush by the brokerage houses to get into this excellent profit center.

However, most legitimate brokers at least try to give the client the best of their insight—whatever such "value added" is actually worth. But in recent years another breed of operator has moved into the game who is not unaware of hype, as the advertisements on page 224, taken from *Commodities* (a magazine dedicated to commodities trading), indicate.

The goals of other new entrants are even more straightforward —find as many customers as you can, dazzle them with the thought of quick gains, and take them for every cent they can be persuaded to put up. As commodities regulation is only in its embryonic stage, such schemes are quite within the law.

Without regulation the smooth operator of "products" from

*Buying or selling one month in a commodity (or one commodity against another) and hedging this by doing the opposite in another month or commodity. This limits profit but also limits loss.

458% PROFIT
IN 15 WEEKS

Yes-this is the actual certified profit realized on one of our own trading accounts shown by our NY broker's equity statement (including both open and closed positions) during a 15-week period last

Commodities, October 1978

7 WINNERS OUT OF EVERY 8 TRADES ACHIEVED AN OUTSTANDING $687,942 GAIN

SURE THING COMMODITY TRADING

Commodities, October 1978

In 1978 (through July) [our company] Signaled 678 Positions in 32 Commodities. 238 Achieved Profits of 50% or More. 141 Showed Gains of 100% or More!

Commodities, August 1978

$887,676.90 PROFIT in four-and-a-half years

These fantastic profits are the result of a unique commodity trading system that is now being offered to a limited number of serious traders.

- Completely mechanical
- No decisions to make
- Easy-to-follow rules
- Double-your-money-back guarantee

Anti-Loss Trading
A TRADER'S DREAM

THE ULTIMATE SYSTEM FOR SMALL AND MEDIUM COMMODITY TRADERS SHOULD HAVE THESE FEATURES:

- **100% safety of original capital**
- **reasonable profit of 80 to 120%**
- **be simple and self administrative**
- **take only 10-15 minutes a week**
- **no automatic trading system**
- **no moving averages to keep**
- **free from worry, fear of loss**

Both from *Commodities*, January 1978

commodities to Persian carpets can bilk you for all or most of your investment.* People who will carefully examine matters when committing relatively small amounts for a car or a television set will often invest $10,000 or $20,000 based on no more than a salesman's pitch.

Let's turn to one commodities scheme that was very popular as an example. Hundreds of salesmen sold the "product"—and why not? If the plan is properly executed, the commodity house is virtually guaranteed 100 percent of the customer's investment.

Although these plans go under a variety of names, the schemes are all fairly similar. One firm calls its plan "Limited Risk Forward." The literature begins by impressing customers with the inherent dangers of speculating in commodities:

LIMITED RISK FORWARD

Commodity markets are notoriously volatile. They can rise or fall the equivalent of thousands of dollars in the matter of a few days, even a few hours. It is just this volatility and its attendant *open-ended risk* which keeps conservative investors out of commodity positions. However, volatile price action can mean windfall profits to those aligned on the right side of any given market. The *question* is: How can a conservative investor enter the commodities market and not risk any more than a set, up-front amount? The *answer:* By taking a position in *Limited Risk Forwards.* [Italics theirs.]

It then goes on to advise the investor:

[We] believe that the trend of the markets favors those commodity speculators who assume medium or long-term positions in a particular market (like coffee, sugar, or copper) and then hold on. It is our experience that fast, in and out, jiggle trading creates lots of commissions for a broker and very few profits for the client. Since LRF's *cannot* be traded on a daily, in-out basis, we believe they are highly suited to a winning trading strategy. This fact coupled with their inherently limited risk makes them an *ideal* trading vehicle for the uninitiated or conservative commodity speculator.

---

*Even the formidable Dr. and Mrs. Henry Kissinger, while on a visit to Iran, were taken. Nancy was shown Persian carpets at the home of the U.S. ambassador by one of the country's supposedly most reputable dealers. She bought several beautiful carpets, investing more than $11,000, after being told they were over fifty years old. On returning to the United States, she had them reappraised; the embarrassed appraiser told her that they were in reality only ten to twenty years old, and that chemical rather than natural dyes had been used. The value was only about one-third of the price they had paid.

It certainly sounds prudent enough; in fact, the company appears to be trying to save you from those naughty brokers who conduct "jiggle trading," creating lots of commissions for themselves at the poor client's expense. Here we seem to have a firm dedicated to your best interests, especially if you're "uninitiated." Now, what does this LRF do for you? Well, first of all, the client's risk is limited to only 100 percent of his investment, *the purchase price he pays for the LRF, not a penny more* [their italics]." If 100 percent loss of investment is considered conservative, this plan is conservative indeed.

Moving on to the mechanics of the LRF itself, the company allows you to buy or sell any commodity contract you choose, domestic or foreign (including foreign exchange). They then immediately buy an offsetting one. Using their example, suppose you placed an order to buy sugar—then trading at 8 cents a pound—for one year, purchasing two contracts for $9,000 (110,000 pounds per contract). The company, at the time of your purchase, would offset your two contracts with two sales for the same time period of one year. By so doing, the company guarantees you will not be called for further margin, because of the hedge. If sugar dropped a cent, it would cost you $1,100 in a regular commodities contract or $2,200 for the two. Sugar would have to drop 50 percent for you to lose your entire equity in a standard contract, as contrasted to an LRF. The only advantage of an LRF is that it protects you against an additional margin call (in this example, if sugar drops more than 50 percent) and maintains your position throughout the further decline. Thus, if the market nose-dives, you will never be sold out.

What is the cost of the privilege? Simply 100 percent of your capital—the amount the company automatically deducts for its service. If the market goes down or stays even, you lose everything. If it rises 2 cents, or 25 percent from the 8-cent price, you still lose. In this case, the $4,400 profit would be deducted from the $9,000, so you would show a $4,600 loss, *or over half your capital.* In other words, although you've made almost a 50 percent profit on the actual investment (as you would in a regular commodities contract),* you realize a greater than 50 percent loss because of their charges. Not particularly exciting odds in your favor. The company then asks:

---

*Commissions on the standard contract would be several hundred dollars.

WHY NOT SIMPLY BUY THE FUTURE ITSELF WITH NO AVAILABLE OPPO-
SITE POSITION, IF YOU THINK THE PRICE WILL GO UP?

Good question. The answer:

LRF's have many advantages over buying commodities with no available
opposite position, but the principal advantage LRF's offer are *increased
leverage* and *limited risk*. . . .*

The many advantages are not spelled out, with good reason. They
don't exist. The only way you can benefit is to have a very sharp drop
in the commodity, putting you deeply into the additional margin the
company provides, followed by a far sharper recovery, which not
only offsets the loss and then your entire original investment but also
leaves some to spare. And all this in a relatively short period of time!
A very rare flight pattern indeed.

You may ask if the house doesn't have some risks. After all, if
additional losses are incurred above the original investment, the firm
must make them up. But as you may guess, these people are no fools.
If the firm is shrewd, why should they bother taking any risk at all?

Salesman A may think London gold futures contracts a year out
are a good buy, and he relates this to Dr. A or Lawyer A. At the
same time, Salesman B surprisingly arrives at the opposite conclusion, and believes gold has shot up far too quickly. He then advises
Dr. or Lawyer B that it should be sold twelve months ahead. In
short, the house can be fully hedged and pocket 100 percent on both
sides. The commission scale, running up to 35 percent and sometimes
more on this type of sale, would of course fail to influence the
salesman's advice.†

Are the salesmen low-keyed? The question is only rhetorical.
With commissions being what they are, and with the lack of regulation, a client can be told virtually anything with little danger. Financial reporter Kathryn Welling wrote of the hype delivered by one
salesman (in a scheme as zany as the one described here—buying
gold options issued by a New York metals dealer). She was repeatedly phoned by the eager promoter, who was unaware of her real
purpose. One version of the hard sell: "Most of my clients have

---

*Which means, as we've seen, you can lose only 100 percent of your capital.
†In recent months a number of indictments have been brought in against a few of the
many operators in the field.

doubled their money in gold options in the last six or eight weeks, and that's just the beginning. I want to get your $5,000 up to $10,000. I feel the worst we should do is 100 percent in a year . . . but the timing is critical. We really have to make a move by Friday."[4]

Just how numerous commodity scams are today was indicated by a 1981 survey by Erdos & Morgan, Inc., a marketing research firm. Their study showed that 40 percent of the readers of the *Wall Street Journal* have been contacted by high-pressure salesmen who promised big profits from dubious commodities investments. Efforts to halt these practices are hampered by sophisticated sales techniques and the origination of new contracts that fall outside the regulator's purview.[5]

Recent commodity scams have been extended to a variety of nonesoteric minerals, including coal. In mid-1981 the Commodities Futures Trading Commission (which regulates commodities trading) investigated a number of such scams. One involved National Coal, accused of absconding with over $15 million of investors' money. The investors were told they were buying freely traded contracts when in effect they were not transferable and could only be exercised by taking physical delivery of the coal on the investors' premises. The idea of taking possession of 300 to 1,000 tons or more of coal on their front doorsteps discouraged more than a few investors with paper profits.

A complaint was filed recently by the New York State Attorney General's office accusing thirty firms and thirty-seven individuals of illegally selling oil futures in sophisticated schemes to the tune of $50 million. According to one New York State official, "It went into somebody's pocket or to the banks in Switzerland, Panama, and the Bahamas. We're trying to trace the funds, but it looks like a total loss."[6]

The previous examples should give some idea of how dangerous it is to enter any game with which you are unfamiliar, particularly one governed by minimum legislation. Barracuda are always looking for you, the next victim. Are the odds any better in options?

Trading Stock Options

Options became the hottest game around after the 1974 break. There are now three or four dozen books out on them, some telling investors how to use them and others of the breathtaking returns possible by following the writers' strategies. First, I'd advise you to avoid the get-rich techniques. Like all others, from commodities to stop-loss orders, they don't work and you'll probably wind up on the losing end. If they are played like commodities, you have about the same chance of success.

But there are, I think, a number of secure ways of using options that, rather than increasing your market risk, should actually decrease it and quite possibly enhance your overall return.

A call contract gives the buyer the right to buy (at his option) a stock at a specific price, called the striking price, for a specific period of time. For selling the contract the seller gets a premium based on such factors as its length, nearness of striking price to market, volatility of the stock and market, and so on. A put is precisely the opposite mechanism. The buyer has the option of selling the stock at a predetermined price for a predetermined time period. For the privilege, the seller again gets a premium dependent on the factors just outlined.

Options are normally listed on stock exchanges, and prices can be found daily in the financial newspapers; they are usually traded in the largest or most active stocks in price intervals of five dollars. Thus if a stock is trading at 45, there may be calls to buy it (and puts to sell it) at 40, 45, and 50. The more volatile the stock, the larger the number of option prices outstanding. Options on listed exchanges are traded for fixed periods up to nine months. Each contract has a definite expiration date—the third Friday of the month the option is due, for example.

Speculators love them because they greatly increase their leverage. If, for example, a chartist believes Travelers is ready to make a major move in the next six months and it is currently trading around 45, he might buy the options instead of the stock. Suppose in this instance he decides to purchase calls on the Travelers 45 options six months out. The call might cost $2.50 per share (more or less, depending on the current volatility of the stock). Each call represents one hundred shares; thus, if he decided twenty calls, or two thousand shares, would do the job, it would cost him only $5,000 (plus commissions), rather than the $90,000 he would have to put up for the stock.

If the stock ran beyond 47½, he would make money. At 50, he has doubled his investment. The stock itself moving from 45 to 50 rises only 11 percent. Thus, options provide leverage, dramatically increasing your bang for the buck. Every point move from the original price is a 2.2 percent move in the stock and 40 percent in the option. The action increases nearly twentyfold.

But of course you have to be right, and in a short period of time: if the stock stays where it is or goes down, your investment is wiped out.

Large numbers of investors use options as a massive crap shoot in an all-or-nothing manner. From the previous indications of market timing and stock selection, most often it is nothing.

However, conservative option strategies can be used in quite different ways. Some can help you to minimize your taxes. You can, for example, use an option to protect a short-term capital gain. Suppose you bought Honeywell (which has listed options traded) at 80, and you had a sudden sharp run-up to 110 in eight months. You might want to take profits but not the short-term gain because it would be treated like ordinary income. In this case, you would buy a put at 75, which would allow you to sell the stock at this price for a period long enough to give you a long-term capital gain. The put might cost $8 to $10 (depending again on the stock's volatility). If the stock goes up, you have an even larger capital gain; and it is long-term, with the option deductible as a short-term loss. If it goes down, $8 to $10 might prove cheap insurance.

Another possibility—one I've tried myself—is to use options in an attempt to reduce taxes if you have large short-term gains in any year. In 1977 I used them to try to offset some short-term gains that would have put me in a higher tax bracket than I was comfortable with. At the time, it seemed there were some excellent low P/E stocks with listed options in them. I bought calls "deep in the money" in Honeywell, Aetna, and Travelers. (A deep-in-the-money call is one where the stock is trading well above the option price. Honeywell, then trading at 48 with a 40 option outstanding, would be such a case. Deep-in-the-money options normally trade at the smallest premiums of any contracts because of the larger downside risk.)* The calls were bought in August 1977, due to expire early in 1978. If they had gone up, the profits would have been realized in 1978, making my 1977 tax bill more palatable. And if not, the loss could be deducted from the taxes on the short-term gains.

As it turned out, the market went down and the calls resulted in a loss. I sold them near year-end and switched ahead, keeping the position intact in options expiring later in 1978. Because of the short-term loss in these options, the 1977 taxes were reduced. And, in a falling market, premiums were lowered in buying the new options.

In the market rally of spring 1978, the options went up sharply, well above the original cost the year before. Once again, there was a choice of selling them and taking short-term profits (if the tax position allowed it) or converting them into long-term profits by exercising the option and then holding the stock for the required time period.†

A final example would be to use options as an adjunct to the low P/E approach when dollar cost averaging. Suppose you wish to put money into the market over time and have found attractive low P/E companies with listed puts on them. You might sell a put expiring six months ahead. (This is the opposite of the first strategy, where puts were bought.) If, for example, Aetna was at 40 and you wanted to dollar-cost-average, you might sell a 40 put, which would result in the stock being delivered to you if the stock dropped below the

---

*If, in the Honeywell case, the stock had fallen to 42 at expiration date, I would have been out $6 and commissions.

†A more common method of shifting gains from one year to the next is by employing option or commodity spreads in the following manner: the investor selects a volatile commodity or stock and then buys and sells offsetting contracts but for differing time periods (or in the case of options, for the same time period but at differing prices). Suppose, for example, HON is volatile, currently trades at 70 and has "deep-in-the-money" options outstanding, say 55s and 60s. The trader might sell the 60s and buy the 55s. For simplicity, let's eliminate premiums and assume the cost of 15 on the 55s and proceeds of 10 on the 60s. It doesn't matter which way the stock moves as long as the move is fairly significant. If HON rose to 80, the 60 call would be bought in at year-end, resulting in a $10 loss that year. To avoid market risk, the 55 call would be sold the first day of the following year, resulting in a $10 profit. If the stock fell to 60, the 55s would be sold at year-end at a $10 loss and the 60s bought in the first day of the following year at a $10 profit. While there are many variations on this strategy, in its simplest form it postpones short-term gains until the following year. But once again, as I've learned from my own earlier experience, you have to be careful with option and commodity spreads that you watch both the prices and the commissions beforehand, or you can wind up with heavy additional costs.

striking price. You would pocket the premium and get a somewhat cheaper price, trading into the position you wanted in any event. If the market went up, you would keep the premium and simply go out and buy the stock you intended to buy in any case,* following through on the principle of dollar cost averaging.

These are but several examples of the numerous option strategies that can be fitted into a conservative investment philosophy. The point to remember is that rather than using them as quick-kill vehicles, they can be tailored to assist your current investment objectives.

Good option strategies are sophisticated and often complex. For readers interested in more than this brief overview, I would recommend a number of publications of the Chicago Board of Trade (provided free) on understanding options. A couple of good books on the subject are Gary Gastineau's *The Stock Options Manual*† and Max G. Anspacher's *The New Option Market.* ‡

Financial Futures Markets

Financial futures were developed first in Chicago in 1976 and later by the New York Futures Exchange (named, appropriately, "Knife") in 1980.

A financial futures contract, like a commodities contract, allows the buyer to buy or the seller to sell a fixed amount of a specified financial instrument at a stated future date. Contracts exist in treasury bills, ten- and twenty-year government bonds, and "Ginnie Mae's" (government-guaranteed mortgage notes). The minimum contract is $1 million for the treasury bills and $100,000 for the other instruments.

If, for example, in September 1981 a speculator thought that long-term interest rates would decline, he could buy a contract at the Chicago Board of Trade to purchase a government 8 percent bond maturing in twenty years. The contracts expire at three-month intervals from September 1981 extending out three years. Naturally the further out the buyer goes, the greater the probability that the inter-

---

*If Aetna was still at a reasonable P/E to the market. If not, you could buy another stock. The risk in this strategy is if the market moves down sharply—more than the gain you received from the premium.

†2nd ed., New York: McGraw-Hill, 1979.

‡New York: Walker, 1975.

est rates will come down (or at least so the market believes) and the greater the premium over current bond prices he must pay for the contract. Thus, if he bought a contract expiring in December 1981, for example, at 57, a contract due in December of 1985 might cost 62, or an additional $5 per $100 of bonds.

Margin requirements are small (and can be posted in the form of interest-bearing treasury bills). Normally no more than 4 percent is required initially, so $40,000 can get you a play on $1 million of intermediate or long-term bonds. If interest rates do go down sharply, as they did in 1980, you can make huge gains on the capital employed because of the tremendous leverage. So, if you call the shot correctly, the leverage can be sensational because the volatility in interest rates futures in recent years has been greater than in stock options or most commodities.

However, volatility, as we know by now, is not always the speculator's friend. In fact, in the bond market, for most it has proved to be a form of Black Death to their capital. Many speculators, including professionals, thought long-term interest rates had peaked in March 1981 at 12 or 13 percent instead of the current October government rates of 14½ percent. The difference cost investors some ten to twelve points, or from two and a half to three times their initial margin, unless they had already been mercifully wiped out by margin calls, thereby losing only 100 percent. Unfortunately the extra margin was often posted, with the disastrous consequence.

Interest rates are obviously very tricky (just how tricky we shall see in the final chapter), depending not only on the money supply, inflation, economic activity, balance of payments, deficits, foreign exchange rates, and a host of other factors, but also on the far more indeterminable phenomenon of how an administration or the Federal Reserve will react to the figures. In a word, an almost impossible forecasting situation—one that has left a long line of thoroughly battered victims. Financial futures have no place in the portfolio of a conservative investor and should be looked at only by masochists or the wildest of dice players.

However, as with stock options, they can be used in a hedging operation. Institutions with large holdings may use such futures to protect their positions in bonds or treasury bills. Say, for example, an institution is holding $10 million of twenty-year bonds and wants to receive the high interest rates available today but does not want to be exposed to market loss if interest rates go even higher. It can sell the futures contract short against its position. If the market goes down, the portfolio is in the red, but the institution has a profit on its futures contract. If the bond market rises sharply, the bonds will go up while the futures will go down by a roughly equal amount. The institution thus avoids losses on its invested capital at the cost of the possible gains. By hedging, it receives the current high rate of return while protecting itself against market risk.

In my opinion at least, financial futures are best used in this manner to protect capital, not as a vehicle to try to increase it.

Tax Shelters

These have most often proven to be fairly rewarding investments—for their promoters. And there are large numbers of salesmen, both inside and outside brokerage firms, pushing them. Many people who have dabbled in tax shelters have not fared well, and some have been badly burned, such as the herds of investors who purchased broker-age-house-sponsored cattle tax shelters in the early 1970s and saw their investments eaten to the bone. Overall, some estimates placed investor losses in cattle shelters in the twelve months ending October 1974 at $2 billion. However, brokerage houses fared somewhat better, receiving front-end fees of up to 18 percent.[7]

Tax shelters might be looked at from two points of view:

1. As investment write-offs designed simply to reduce your current tax, with little hope of recouping much of the investment—the saving in current taxes offsetting the costs of the shelter. But to do this you must be in a high tax bracket. An investor with $40,000 or more of income in a 50 percent bracket investing $20,000 in a shelter designed to give him an immediate $20,000 write-off will have the shelter entirely paid for by the government. Any gain is gravy.

2. Primarily as an investment, but one that should shield you from some of your current tax load.

Large numbers of tax shelters exist, some legitimate, others that skirt the boundaries of fraud. As an investor, you should re-member two things: first, you will at times (as in some of the com-modity schemes) be paying extremely high sales charges to participate. The people selling the most accessible of these packages are usually exceptionally smooth and well-heeled, often making six figures a year plus lavish expenses. Second, you should never consider a tax shelter unless you are in a very high tax bracket—60 percent or more.

There are naturally some very good shelters—in a wide range of investments from real estate to airplane and even railroad rolling-stock leasing—that shield income, provide comparatively high returns, and charge only a moderate load. But these are usually not available to average investors. Minimum participation can range to $100,000 or more, and benefits may extend only to people in very high tax brackets.

When you put half a million dollars into a tax shelter, you can afford a $10,000 examination by your own experts. When you are investing $5,000, you can afford a prayer.

Because the laws are extremely complicated, you must have a good understanding of the mechanics of the shelter and your income prospects or you may wind up with a form of tax alchemy that can turn your gold into lead. Dollars you shield at 45 or 50 percent one year may come back to haunt you at 65 or 70 percent tax rates a few years later.

The following check list of dubious deals, prepared by *Business Week,* [8] indicates a group of shelters to steer away from—if you're audited the IRS will in all probability throw out all the types in the "avoid" group. You should stay clear of the "beware" group because they are lousy investments, usually burdened with very large commissions taken from the initial investment by high-pressure salesmen.*

> *Avoid:*
> · commodity "deferred delivery" contracts
> · commodity tax straddles
> · tax shelters featuring "nonrecourse" financing
> · federal oil–lease lottery schemes
> · oil and gas partnerships with royalty or drilling prepayment
>   provisions

*The question of tax shelters has become so controversial that the IRS has set up a service that helps to guide potential investors. Anyone can send a copy of a prospectus to the Office of the Assistant Commissioner, Technical, at the IRS in Washington and receive a tax ruling that should provide some guidance.

Beware:
· highly leveraged real estate investments
· gem and art tax shelters with high appraised valuation and
  low liquidity
· futures speculation on foreign exchanges
· letter-of-credit tax shelter financing

The dangers of dubious tax shelters have been magnified many times by the passage of Reagan's tax act in 1981, which applies to all returns filed after December 31 of that year.

The law contains a new nondeductible penalty aimed at "exotic" tax shelters built around art, books, lithographs, and records and specifically designed to penalize those shelters that overinflate the value of the underlying property, thus offering the investor tax deductions far in excess of the actual money put up.

The new penalty tax that has been created is graduated, depending on the amount of overvaluation of the asset, moving from 10 percent for overvaluations of 200 percent to 30 percent for overvaluations of 250 percent or more.

Not only would investors have to make up the original tax deduction resulting from overvaluation of the tax shelter, but they would also have to pay the current rate of interest being charged by the IRS—now 20 to 21 percent—as well as the additional penalty tax, which may be as high as 30 percent. (The same penalties will also apply to people who overvalue property in charitable donations.)

According to William G. Brenna, an authority in the field, "the impact could be shattering. Legal opinions and appraisals will not protect you. Many investors could easily incur tax payments of $50,000 a year for four or five years because of the overvaluation of aggressive tax shelters."[9]

Unless you are a very large investor, or have expert knowledge at your disposal, tax shelters constitute another area best to stay clear of. Finally, let's turn to some other schemes, all of which can definitely be of benefit to you.

Keogh Plans and Individual Retirement Accounts (IRAs)

In 1974 Congress passed ERISA, the Employees Retirement Investment Security Act. Although it has proven almost mystical to money managers in interpreting the investments they can prudently make, the act has provided vastly improved safeguards for the pension rights of employees.

At the same time Congress established two other types of pension protection: Keogh plans for people who are self-employed (doctors, dentists, lawyers, artists, accountants, etc.) and who are not covered by other pension plans; and Individual Retirement Accounts for people already employed but not participating in pension plans.

The Keogh plans currently allow you to contribute up to 15 percent of your earnings each year to a maximum of $7,500. A $750 contribution is allowable regardless of the level of income. These contributions come off the upper level of your tax bracket. The IRA allowed a contribution of 15 percent of income each year, with a limit of $1,500.

The Reagan Economic Recovery Tax Act of 1981 increased the eligibility for an IRA. Now anyone, regardless of pension or other retirement provisions, can deduct $2,000 a year right from the top gross income if single ($4,000 if married and the spouse is employed) and place these funds in such a plan, which is tax-free until the person retires and begins to withdraw the funds or reaches the age of seventy and a half.

In both cases, no minimum requirement is necessary in any one year, and any amount up to the maximum may be invested. Contributions need not be made each year, but if they are omitted in any one year they cannot be made up in subsequent years.

Money in either plan must be invested with an authorized trustee. Investments can be made in a variety of alternatives ranging from savings bank certificates to life insurance plans to money market funds to common stock mutual funds. Such plans can be tailored to the individual's personal investment needs. The advantage of these plans is that all interest, dividends, and capital gains are tax-free throughout their lives.

For a person in a high tax bracket this money can compound quickly, particularly with today's soaring rates of interest. Four thousand dollars, for a working couple, for example, invested in an IRA each year at 15 percent becomes $93,360 at the end of ten years and $2,007,960 at the end of thirty. Or, in a Keogh plan, if you have income high enough to take the full $7,500 deduction and do the same thing, you will show a mere $3,764,942 at the end of the thirty-year period. Even with inflation, not all that bad!

Now for the catches. The rules say you cannot begin to with-draw funds from these plans until you are fifty-nine and a half, although you are not required to do so until you are seventy. Since most people retire by sixty or sixty-five, they should be paying taxes at significantly lower rates when they begin their withdrawals.

If money is taken out before the age of fifty-nine-and-a-half, there is a 10 percent penalty on withdrawal, and the entire amount, including the 10 percent, is taxed at your regular income rate. But because "top dollar" for some contributors can lie in the 60 percent tax bracket or above, and all interest and dividends in the interim are invested tax-free, the possible penalty does not turn out to be a particularly onerous burden. Chances are in any case that if money need be withdrawn, your income will be down fairly sharply by that time. Thus, such plans are excellent tax shelters and should be used as investment vehicles for people who can qualify.

Bond Swaps

The soaring interest rates of recent years have triggered a virtual free fall in bond prices, leaving unfortunate investors with billions of dollars of losses. As Vartanig G. Vartan, of the *New York Times,* notes, "some 30-year A-rated bonds of Municipal Electric Utilities, for example, were marketed four or five years ago with a 7% coupon. Currently many of these bonds are worth only sixty cents on the dollar."[10]

Vartan continues: "The process of turning lemons into lemon-ade, so to speak, involves bond-swapping." Bond losses can be used to offset capital gains in other investments. In essence, the investor sells the bond in the red and buys another bond of comparable credit rating and yield.

For example, if an A-rated municipal bond yielding 7 percent has declined to 60, the investor sells this issue and buys another municipal (but not from the same issuer, because the tax laws prohibit what is known as a wash sale—the repurchase of the same or substantially the same bond without a thirty-one-day waiting period). Usually he can receive an almost identical yield, maturity, and credit rating.

Government bonds or the bonds of corporations can also be sold and offset with comparable issues (again, if it is a corporate bond, the investor should buy the bonds or debentures of another corporation). Such losses thus can be used against profits from stocks, real estate, collectibles, and so forth. Moreover, losses on bond holdings of less than one year may be used to offset ordinary income on a dollar-for-dollar basis up to $3,000 in a year if you file a joint return, with any balance carried forward against future taxes.

Two important caveats:

1. If your bonds are municipals or corporations not traded on a major exchange, be very careful of the prices you are quoted. Often the broker can make two or three points on the swap. It's best to get at least two separate bids from different brokers to ensure that this does not happen.

2. In the case of municipals, do your swapping early—normally no later than September, since fewer good swaps are available as the year progresses. Greater pressure is placed on the markets because larger numbers of people look to their losses as the December 31 tax deadline approaches.

While nobody wants a loss, the fact that the bond market is near its all-time lows indicates that there are plenty of opportunities to take advantage of them to restructure your portfolio in a more beneficial manner.

In this chapter we have reviewed the role of the broker, and a number of important financial instruments. Next, in chapter 11, let's continue our examination of financial instruments, concentrating on some recently introduced financial tools, which can prove extremely beneficial to you.

CHAPTER ELEVEN

How You Can Benefit from Innovative Financial Tools

Think back to early 1979. How many of us would have believed then that the prime rate would reach 22 percent or that "interest rates would be higher," as West German Chancellor Helmut Schmidt said, "than at any time since Christ walked the earth." These developments have resulted in a virtual flood of new financial instruments devised by ingenious (or, perhaps more accurately, desperate) corporate and municipal officials because of their urgent need to raise large sums of new money.

More innovation has taken place in secure financial instruments in the last three years than in the last thirty. As James Sullivan, the fixed-income manager of American General Life Insurance Company, expressed it: "Financial history ended in 1979 and a new history started in 1980. The message we have gotten over the past couple of years is that traditional means of planning financings are over and done with."[1]

It is important for investors to know of some excellent new ways to put their money to work with almost no risk, exceptional rates of return, and first-rate tax benefits. In this chapter, we will review a number of the more interesting developments.*

---

*For the new investor, who needs some basic background in insurance, treasury bills, and bonds, it is advisable to read Appendix II first.

Money Market Funds

A decade ago they didn't exist, today money market funds are an integral part of the daily lives of more than seven million Americans. These funds are the prime beneficiaries of the record inflation and interest rates of recent years. The initial trickles of money into the funds, started in 1972, have become a tidal wave in the last few years.

Just how important money market funds have become can be gauged by the following figures. The funds totaled $75 billion at year-end 1980 and reached the astronomical figure of $203 billion by April 1982. Currently savings deposits in commercial banks total only $165 billion and those in savings and thrift institutions $185 billion. At present, there are more than 125 such funds in operation.

Through the seventies, as money market funds first doubled and eventually more than tripled the interest received on savings accounts, the awareness of the much higher returns available (recently as high as 17 percent versus about 5½ percent) became increasingly widespread and dramatically changed the savings habits of millions of Americans.

Money market funds provide a number of advantages over savings deposits or even six-month bank certificates of deposit.

1. Yield as indicated is considerably higher than savings accounts, and sometimes higher than six-month certificates. The latter also contain provisions that will penalize the investor, at times substantially, if they are cashed prematurely.

2. The funds are cashable on a day-to-day basis without penalty. Many large funds also offer the advantage of allowing their holders to write checks on their balances over $500. As an investor you receive interest until the check clears. Since out-of-state-checks sometimes take a week, or more, to clear, the additional interest can add up. Savings accounts, on the other hand, normally have restricted check-writing provisions.

3. The usual minimum investment is only $1,000 to $2,500, compared to $5,000 for a treasury bill or the $5,000 to $10,000 required for a six-month certificate by most banks and other thrift institutions.

Although the funds are not government-insured (as are funds in the banks and thrift institutions), they normally invest in highly secure short-term debt instruments—treasury bills, certificates of deposit of large banks, Eurodollar deposits, commercial paper (short-term notes of large corporations with excellent credit ratings), and the like. There is no sales charge, only a management fee (calculated before, not after, the yield is stated).

If you buy a money market fund, yields can vary as much as 2 to 3 percent because of the differences in the average maturity of the portfolio. It is safest to stay in shorter securities and prime quality investments such as treasury bills, the certificates of deposit of large banks, and A-1–rated commercial paper. A number of funds provide higher yields by downgrading their portfolios slightly or lengthening the maturities. Since the differences in yield are small, I would avoid the increased risk of these funds and stay with the safest.

Three of the largest funds are Merrill Lynch Ready Assets, which has about $18 billion under management and 2,200,000 investors, Dreyfus Liquid Assets (with check-writing privileges), with $6.4 billion in assets and 400,000 investors, and Fidelity Daily Income (also with check-writing privileges), with $3.7 billion and 200,000 investors. These all have toll-free numbers.* A listing showing the current interest each fund pays, such as that in table 31 (pages 244–245), is often found in the financial section of larger newspapers.

One thing to remember is that money market funds are far more responsive to interest rate changes than are savings banks. If interest rates shift suddenly, the funds will quickly reflect this. So you will have to be fairly careful in watching the yields, moving out of the funds into other financial instruments as the occasion requires.

What other dangers exist in money market funds? Really, very few if you don't foresee a doomsday scenario such as our major banks crumbling, our prime corporations being unable to meet their very short-term commitments, or our government defaulting on its debt. As I tell my clients, they are a first-rate place to keep their short-term balances.

*Merrill Lynch, 800-631-0749, ext. 7976; Dreyfus, 800-223-5525; Fidelity Income, 800-225-6190.

Table 31

Money Market Mutual Funds

Money Funds with assets of $100 million or more that are available to individual investors. For period ended May 5, 1982.

Fund	Assets ($ million)	Average Maturity (Days)	7-day Average Yield(%)	30-day Average Yield(%)
Alex Brown Cash Res.	560.1	30	13.8	13.8
Alliance Capital Reserves	1,535.5	25	13.7	13.6
Alliance Governmental Reserves	177.1	16	12.6	12.8
American General	338.2	20	13.5	13.5
American Liquid Trust	361.4	25	13.3	13.3
BIRR Wilson Money Fund	116.5	23	13.6	13.7
Boston Company Cash Mgmt.	266.6	28	13.8	13.8
Capital Cash Mgt. Trust	149.5	22	13.9	13.9
Capital Preservation	1,835.8	24	12.2	12.8
Capital Preservation Fund II	972.6	3	12.9	13.6
Cardinal Govt. Securities	319.8	8	13.8	13.9
Carnegle Gov't Securities	171.6	10	13.0	13.3
Cash Equivalent Fund	3,858.8	38	14.3	14.3
Cash Equivalent Gov't Fund Only	318.8	13	13.7	13.5
Cash Mgmt Trust	617.8	20	14.3	14.3
Cash Reserve Management	7,072.4	25	14.1	14.2
Chancellor Gov't Sec. Trust	187.6	37	12.9	13.0
Columbia Daily Income	908.8	25	13.2	13.3
Composite Cash Management	345.0	24	13.9	13.8
Current Interest	1,502.0	30	13.8	13.8
DBL Cash Fund M.M. Port	970.6	30	14.1	14.0
Daily Cash Accumulation	5,496.3	25	13.9	14.0
Daily Income	813.1	23	13.6	13.5
Dean Witter				
Active Assets Money Trust	528.3	32	14.0	14.0
InterCapital Liquid Asset	9,407.6	37	14.1	14.0
Delaware Cash Reserve	2,163.3	19	14.3	14.2
Dreyfus				
Instit. Gov't. Sec.	347.5	64	13.2	13.6
M.M. Instrmts Gov't.	555.0	67	12.9	12.6
Liquid Assets	9,604.0	40	14.1	13.9
ED Jones Daily Passport	783.2	35	13.9	13.8
EGT Money Market Trust	146.7	31	13.8	13.7
Eaton & Howard	256.6	28	13.8	13.7
Equitable Money Mkt Account	349.8	33	13.9	13.8
Fahnestock Daily Income	152.5	23	13.7	13.6
Fidelity Group				
Cash Reserves	3,666.1	30	14.0	14.0
Daily Income	3,733.0	27	13.9	13.9
U.S. Gov't Reserves	203.7	16	12.8	13.1
Financial Daily Income	281.6	17	14.3	14.3
First Investors Cash Management	614.3	27	13.8	13.7
First Variable Rate	1,312.8	*29	13.6	13.7
Franklin Federal M.F.	128.0	4	12.6	12.8
Franklin Money Fund	1,128.0	22	13.7	13.7
Fund/Government Investors	1,244.7	15	13.4	13.6
Government Investors Trust	635.7	20	13.6	13.7
Gradison Cash Reserves	694.0	28	13.7	13.7
Hilliard Lycons C.M. Inc.	189.4	13	13.1	13.4
I.D.S. Cash Management	1,243.5	33	14.0	14.0
INA Cash Fund	734.1	28	14.1	14.0
John Hancock Cash Mgt.	678.6	17	13.8	13.8
Kemper Money Market	3,320.1	40	14.4	14.4
Legg Mason Cash Reserve	319.0	33	13.7	13.8
Lehman				
Cash Management	497.9	24	14.2	14.1
Gov't Fund, Inc.	133.0	8	13.1	13.5
Lexington Money Market	300.3	24	14.5	14.5
Liquid Capital Income	2,125.3	17	13.9	14.0

*–average term to next rate adjustment date.

Table 31—Continued

Fund	Assets ($ million)	Average Maturity (Days)	7-day Average Yield(%)	30-day Average Yield(%)
Liquid Green Trust	120.4	23	13.8	13.8
Lord Abbett Cash Reserve	375.0	20	13.7	13.7
MIF/Nationwide M.M.	427.8	28	13.8	13.8
Mass. Cash Management	911.0	29	13.7	14.2
McDonald Money Market	204.5	25	13.2	13.3
Merrill Lynch				
CMA Gov't Securities	755.7	36	12.1	13.6
CMA Money Fund	13,603.8	37	13.1	13.9
Government	1,362.8	37	13.1	13.4
Institutional	1,152.6	24	13.9	13.8
Ready Assets	22,347.0	37	13.1	13.9
Midwest Income ST Income	254.7	14	13.0	13.2
Money Market Management	535.8	35	13.6	13.7
MoneyMart Assets	4,021.0	21	14.2	14.2
Morgan Keegan Daily Cash	100.3	37	13.8	13.7
Mutual of Omaha	470.0	23	13.7	13.7
National Liquid Reserves	1,976.3	25	14.0	14.0
N.E.L. Cash Management Trust	745.2	29	13.9	13.9
NRTA-AARP U.S. Gov't. M.M. Trust	4,187.0	34	12.6	12.8
Oppenheimer Money Market	1,577.1	31	14.2	14.2
Paine Webber Cash Fund	6,207.9	30	14.0	14.1
Putnam Daily Dividend	374.9	32	13.6	13.7
Reserve Fund—Gov't	312.2	10	13.0	13.4
Reserve Fund—Primary	2,980.9	16	14.1	13.8
Rothschild(LF.)Earnings & Liquidity	190.6	21	14.0	14.1
St. Paul Money Fund, Inc.	187.0	30	13.8	13.8
Scudder Cash Investment Trust	1,335.6	30	13.9	13.8
Sears US Gov't M.M.T.	183.3	9	13.0	13.4
Seligman Cash Mgt. Fund., Inc.	838.9	19	14.4	14.2
Shearson/American Express				
Daily Dividend	5,837.5	32	14.2	14.1
Fed Fund	1,152.5	30	13.5	13.6
Govenment & Agencies	700.2	32	12.9	13.1
T-Fund	478.5	31	13.1	13.4
Temp Fund	3,937.0	31	14.2	14.2
Short-Term Income	273.2	23	13.7	13.6
Standby Reserve Fund	201.3	23	14.0	13.9
SteinRoe Cash Reserves	823.0	27	13.9	13.9
T. Rowe Price Prime Reserve	3,264.2	29	14.0	14.0
Transamerica Cash Reserves	341.5	23	14.4	14.2
Trust/Cash Reserves	223.7	33	13.7	13.7
Tucker Anthony Cash Mgmt.	353.2	25	13.7	13.7
USAA M.M. Fund	148.6	24	13.6	13.5
United Cash Management	512.3	24	14.1	14.1
Value Line Cash	564.7	20	14.5	14.6
Vanguard Federal	419.0	26	13.3	13.4
Vanguard M.M.T. Prime	1,134.4	34	14.1	14.0
Webster Cash Reserve	1,345.1	27	14.0	14.0
Ziegler Money Market	125.5	37	13.8	13.7
Donoghue's Money Fund Average (All Funds)		31	13.6	13.7

(Average for all 173 funds reported by DMFR).

Yields represent annualized total return to shareholders for past 7- and 30-day period. Past returns not necessarily indicative of future yields.

Source: Donoghue's Money Fund Report of Holliston, Mass. 01746; from *The New York Times*, May 7, 1982, © 1982 by The New York Times Company; reprinted by permission.

Deep-Discount Bonds

Only a few years ago corporate bonds were a relatively ho-hum investment. Differences in yield, of course, existed for companies with higher or lower credit ratings, but bonds with the same credit rating looked as if they were all stamped out by the same cookie cutter. Nothing fancy—just plain chocolate chip.

Record levels of inflation and interest rates have turned a humdrum business into one where innovation has become the key to survival.

To entice buyers, deep discount securities have been developed. By the summer of 1981 over $2½ billion of such bonds have been sold by corporations, including such giants as Alcoa, General Motors Acceptance Corporation, and J. C. Penney.

Such bonds are priced at considerably less than their face value of $100 (often the discount is 40 to 55 percent or more). The discount bonds pay lower interest rates (usually 6 to 7 percent) but on the full face value. A discount bond price at 50 paying 7 percent provides a current yield of 14 percent and yields 15 percent to maturity, if it matures in twenty years.

1. The buyer is protected against lower interest rates in the future because he is paying only a fraction of the redemption price of 100. Thus, his bonds will not be redeemed before their maturity, which can run up to twenty or thirty years, unless interest rates drop below the coupon rate of 6 or 7 percent, a highly unlikely probability.

2. If interest rates drop, the buyer might receive substantial capital gains quickly as bond prices rise. In the above example, if interest rates declined and the bond rose from 50 to 60, the entire 10 increase is long-term capital gain if the bond is held for more than one year and taxed at only a 20 percent rate.*

---

*But watch out on the capital gain score because it is not always as large as it looks. The investor must declare interest on a new discount bond that the IRS considers the difference between the coupon rate and the yield to maturity that the bond has. Thus, if the bond has a yield to maturity of 15 percent and the coupon yield is 14 percent, the bondholder must declare the extra 1 percent of income. In the previous case, for example, the $50 bond paid a $7 coupon; the investor would declare this income (7 on 50 is 14%) and in addition another

For the seller, the advantage is the ability to pay a somewhat lower rate of interest than standard bonds (usually between ½ to ¾ percent less) for granting this privilege. For a major issuer of bonds, however, this can add up to a substantial savings.

Such bonds can be purchased through almost any major brokerage firm. Again, remember to get several quotes to make sure the price offered is reasonable.

Zero-Coupon Bonds

These were pioneered by Pepsico (parent company of Pepsi-Cola) and J. C. Penney several years ago and pay no interest at all, following the principle developed by the U.S. Treasury when it sold U.S. savings bonds at $37.50 and redeemed them at $50 some years later. The interest is implied—that is, it has already been figured into the deep discount that the buyer receives, a discount large enough to give him a return near the going rate of interest (currently 16 to 16½ percent).

The major advantage of such bonds is that when the interest is imputed in this fashion, it is reinvested at the same rates as the original principal, something that cannot be done with ordinary interest, if rates drop sharply. Thus, the buyer is assured that all income to maturity will be invested at the current high rates. With a regular bond that pays 17 percent, for example, if interest rates drop to 12 percent, the interest coupons would be invested at this lower figure as they come due.

Zero-interest bonds thus lock up high yields right to maturity no matter what happens to rates. And with compound interest over a fifteen- or twenty-year period, how it adds up!

Take a company issuing a zero coupon bond at 17½ percent today, redeemable in twenty years at 100. The price would be $23½. The bond has been structured so that each year it has an imputed yield of 17½ percent (at this rate the principal doubles every four and a quarter years through the magic of compound interest). Thus,

---

50 cents per $100 annually, which adds up to the 15 percent yield to maturity. With old discount bonds, however, this does not apply, and the full difference is allowed in capital gain —usually at the cost of a somewhat lower yield.

the $23½ initial price rises over fourfold to 100 at the end of ten years. Again, if interest rates came down in the interim, the price would move higher, perhaps sharply, and this would all be capital gain.* Zero-coupon bonds, because of the locked-in high rates, are the best bond play if you think rates are heading down, since they will provide the highest appreciation.

These are excellent vehicles for investors to use in Keogh, IRA, and other retirement and tax-free accounts to increase capital, as the appreciation in the above example demonstrated. Such bonds can be purchased for these accounts through any major brokerage firm. Once again the familiar caveat—shop around to ensure you get a reasonable price.

Variable Interest Bonds

Although I'm not one of them, there are large numbers of investors who believe interest rates can go still higher than the recent record 18 percent for AAA bonds—perhaps to 25 percent or more.

Corporate and municipal finance officers have devised some new adjustable-rate issues for the bond buyer who does not want to bet on the direction of future interest rates. There are a number of such issues that may be interesting to buyers with this belief.

A. Floating Rate Notes

The principle of all floating rate securities is the same—interest rates are recalculated at fixed intervals based on the current level of some widely known rate, such as that for six-month treasury bills. Recently, Manufacturers Hanover Corporation sold over $100 million of an issue maturing in seven years. Continental Illinois, Chase Manhattan, and other major banks all came up with similar notes, each of which had some individual "perks." These notes are issued in $1,000 denominations, so even the smallest investors can participate. The notes pay interest monthly on a rate tied to the average yield for AA commercial paper through to maturity.

---

*Although the buyer must again declare his income annually for taxes (17½ percent of the original $23½ price, or approximately $4.00 a year).

B. *Floating Rate Bonds.*

Like the shorter-term floating rate notes, these bonds are normally pegged against a rate such as that for twenty-year treasury bonds. Usually they pay a fixed rate for the first year or two, or sometimes longer, and then adjust to a fixed percentage above the U.S. government bonds. Other issues are also tied to treasury bonds, but the interest on them changes much more slowly, sometimes over a two- or three-year period. GMAC, for example, in late November 1980, sold a $250 million adjustable rate issue with a fixed rate for two years, which then fluctuated annually based on the ten-year treasury bond rate.

C. *Variable Rate Tax Exempts*

These are another recent development. Such issues are adjusted to maintain a return competitive with municipal bonds of similar credit ratings. Again, the variable rate results in the issuer paying a slightly lower overall yield.

The major advantage to buyers of floating rate issues is that, since the rate of interest is adjusted to the market, whether the bond has a short or long maturity your principal should stay pretty much intact.

The 1979–81 bond market break was worse than any stock market break in the postwar period. For millions of investors the experience was traumatic, resulting in their holdings often falling to 50 cents or less on the dollar (in constant dollars, their losses were far greater).

Small wonder, then, that many people who purchase bonds desire this new and safer alternative, which protects their capital from increasing volatility of the bond market while still providing them with current interest rates.

Some Other New "Perks"

1. *Bonds with Puts*

A put feature, like the put option, allows the seller to sell the bond in the future at a predetermined price—almost always at par, or

$100. Bonds with puts normally have long maturities—from twenty to thirty years, with the puts exercisable at a specific date in the future, usually five or ten years after the offering.

The option is designed to protect the bondholder against a sharp rise in interest rates, which would otherwise drive the price down sharply. Once again, there is a price to pay for this protection—some reduction in yield from that currently prevailing. Given the volatility of interest rates, it's good insurance for people who don't want to gamble with their capital.

2. Bonds That Play Interest Rate Futures

A number of recent new bond issues have warrants attached that allow the buyer to purchase an equal amount of the same bond for a specified time, usually a year, at the same price and yield as the original bonds. Recently such issues have been sold to the public by the Kingdom of Sweden and the Municipal Assistance Corporation of New York (the financial "Big Mac").

The advantage to a buyer is a free call on the additional bonds. If interest rates decline during the period, he can sell the warrant at a substantial profit. (If interest rates go up, of course, they become valueless.) The warrant is thus akin to a financial future contract, without the risk to the buyer if interest rates go against him. The cost to the buyer is a rate of interest on the issue somewhat below the rates currently prevailing.

The warrant can also be sold at the time of issue, giving the buyer a reduction in his purchase price. In the case of the Big Mac bonds, for example, the warrants were originally priced at $4 per hundred and shortly thereafter doubled.

3. Delayed-Payment Bonds

Another interesting development was recently introduced by General Motors—a delayed-payment bond. Such issues normally require the buyer to make a 25 percent down payment with the balance due in six months. If you think interest rates are heading south, you can make a big capital gain before paying for the bonds. In effect, you again have a free-interest-rate futures contract on a 4 for 1 basis (since your initial payment is only 25 percent). If interest rates move

down and the bonds appreciate 4 points, you would get total appreciation of $16 on a $100 investment, plus interest—not a particularly
bad return for six months by any standards.

A More Exotic Touch

One of the more exotic touches is the silver-index bonds. These bonds
at maturity are exchangeable for their face value of $1,000 or 50
ounces of silver. If silver at the maturity date exceeds the cash value
(over $20 an ounce), the investor would naturally trade for silver.
Two such bonds were issued in 1980, each with a fifteen-year life.
However, this option was not cheap; the bonds had an initial coupon
of 8½ percent, well below the current market at the time. Too, if the
silver does not move well over $20 fifteen years out, the investor will
receive a substantially lower return than he would by buying higher-
yielding bonds.

Undoubtedly, if interest rates stay up, there will be many more
innovations that can prove of benefit to the alert bond buyer.

Deferred Annuities

Popular in nineteenth-century England, where they paid the grand
return of 2½ to 3 percent, annuities in recent years have become
some of the quicker-selling items on the Street, with sales of between
$1 billion and $2 billion a year.

The advantage of the annuity is that it gives the higher-income
investors a tax break. Buying these instruments defers the tax on
income, which then compounds tax-free until the person retires or
otherwise falls into a lower tax bracket.

Just how much an annuity can save an individual in a high tax
bracket can be seen in the following example. Say you have $5,000
a year to save and are in a 50 percent bracket. If interest rates are
15 percent, after taxes, you would receive $750 of net income. In ten
years, if you continue to invest $5,000 each year, and interest rates
remain unchanged, your contributions of $50,000 would become
$75,870. By comparison, using a tax-deferred annuity and saving the
same amount, you would accumulate $118,00. The income would

be taxed at presumably much lower rates as you withdraw it.

The initial investment, known as the premium, and the interest earned on it are normally invested in long-term bonds. A purchaser of an annuity can decide over what time period (up to the remainder of his life) to receive payments. The deferred annuities also give the investor absolute assurance that he can get his principal back at any time he wants it—before or after the payments are scheduled to begin. Once a purchaser starts to get his monthly checks, he must pay income tax on the difference between what he receives and the original investment. The initial investment, which is nontaxable, is prorated over the life of the payout period.

Now for the caveats:

1. Be careful to buy an annuity that is no-load—one where the salesman gets no hefty front-end payoff from your capital. This must be discovered by you prior to the sale. (Brokerage house annuities and some of the smaller and medium-sized insurance companies usually do not have such charges.)

2. A major problem with fixed annuities is that, because they are invested in long-term bonds, they can at times have returns well below market. Those bought only a few years ago, for example, yield 7 or 8 percent, against prevailing long-term rates of 16 percent. Since interest is compounded during the accumulation period, this has a significant effect on the eventual payout. The buyer is thus at the mercy of prevailing rates (and, to a lesser extent, continues to be so through the distribution period).

Variable Annuities

Because of the increasing volatility of interest rates, many investors have opted for an innovative new product called the variable annuity. Some allow investors to put their money into a variety of mutual funds—stock funds, long-term bond funds, and money market funds. All of these funds are no-load. The investor is also allowed to switch from one fund to another with little or no charge.

One of the better solutions to the problem of purchasing an annuity with current volatile interest rates is to buy a variable annuity that concentrates heavily in money market funds. Yields thus will vary with the rate of inflation. Many money market funds offer such annuities. A number of these are found in table 32 (page 254).

In my opinion, it's probably smart to buy a fixed annuity when interest rates are near their current levels of 16 to 18 percent. However, if interest rates drop sharply, a variable annuity package heavily weighted toward money market funds would be the better vehicle. Thus, if interest rates move up again, the investor can switch to the higher-yielding bond funds.

Variable annuity funds also allow the investors to take either fixed payments or payments that fluctuate with the performance of the investment into which they are placed.

The caveats:

1. Watch for heavy front-end loads. Such charges are much more prevalent in variable than in fixed annuities. Table 32 presents a number of no-load variable annuity funds.

2. The annual charges are also heavier than in the money market funds themselves because of the added bookkeeping, and normally result in yields of about 1 percent or so under prevailing rates.

Municipals

Although an old investment instrument, municipals have taken on a new lease on life, with sky-high interest rates. If you need large investment income and are in a high tax bracket, there are few better investments at such times.

Recently (October 1981), for example, some AAA-rated (highest quality) municipals yielded 13.7 percent and one new-issue Washington Power (WHOP) provided an astounding 15 percent yield with an indirect guaranty by a U.S. government agency. This 15 percent tax-free yield is equivalent to 30 percent from a U.S. government bond for someone in a 50 percent tax bracket. Municipals can thus have tremendous attraction to upper-bracket investors.* The 15 percent rate increases your capital over eightfold in fifteen years and thirty-three times in twenty-five years.

Now for the usual check list:

---

*There may be state and perhaps city taxes on municipals if you buy them out of state.

Table 32

ANNUITY FUNDS

(A sampling of money market funds with the tax-deferred annuity feature)

FUND	MANAGER	MINIMUM INITIAL DEPOSIT	ANNUAL FEES	SALES CHARGE	WITH-DRAWAL CHARGE
Federated Flexible Plan	Federated Securities Corporation	$1,000	$30 + 1.4% of assets	No	No
Galaxy	Putnam Fund Distributors	$3,000	$25 + 0.95% of assets	No	Yes[a]
Rainbow	Dreyfus Corporation	$1,500	$35 + 1% of assets	No	No
Spectrum	Merrill Lynch	$1,500	$30 + 1.3% of assets	No	Yes[b]
Variable Annuity Contracts	Oppenheimer Management Corporation	$2,000	1% of assets	Yes	No

[a]In first six years.
[b]In first eight years.

1. Buy quality: normally no lower than an AA rating.*

2. Again, watch the spread your broker offers on the bonds by getting at least two bids for each issue—to avoid having 2 or 3 percent of your capital going into the salesman's pocket as an extra commission.

3. With the tremendous volatility of interest rates in recent years, it is a good idea to buy long-term municipals only when the yields are 12 percent or better. If yield declines drastically, keep your maturities short.

4. Make sure a new bond has at least a ten-year no-call protection feature (this means it cannot be called for new financing throughout this period), assuring you of this high rate of interest until then.

5. A second and better way is to buy either new or outstanding low coupon bonds, as they will sell at a major discount. If, for example, you purchase an AA-rated bond with a twenty-year maturity trading at 60 that had a 7 percent coupon, you would get a 12.5 percent current yield and a 12.9 percent yield to maturity.

These bonds will definitely not be called before maturity because of the low coupon. At that time you will get $100 for your original $60 investment.

Beating Your Life Insurance Company

In Appendix II, you will find a table (table 36, on page 312) that indicates why low-cost, no-frill term insurance is by far the best buy for almost every individual. The price of such insurance can be as little as 25 percent of that of the higher-priced whole-life policies that give you a variety of extra benefits.[2] However, all the perks cost— and cost heavily.

Many of us were not aware of such discrepancies at the time we bought whole-life policies. In the late fifties, for example, I bought a $25,000 policy that provided me with a phenomenal 6 percent rate of return on the invested portion over thirty years.

*See Appendix II for credit ratings.

Fortunately, there is a way out of such situations, or at least a partial escape route—borrowing against your policy. Most old policies allow the policyholder to borrow a specific amount each year against it. The longer you hold the policy, the greater the amount you can borrow.

The insurance companies believed the borrowing rates they charged to be almost prohibitive at the time the policies were issued. Sometimes they were 5 percent or maybe even 6 percent, to ensure that nobody would use the privilege except in dire emergencies. You can borrow indefinitely at these rates and reinvest the proceeds in long-term bonds at 17 percent or in money market funds. The yield spread, approaching 10 percent at the present time, is more than a little in your favor.

As an example, if you borrow $10,000 against a policy of $25,000 you can net $1,000 of interest a year on long-term bonds. Too, if interest rates move down sharply, the bonds might also give you a substantial capital gain. There is no limit on the length of time you can keep the loan outstanding; all you must do is make sure to repay the interest each year—it's tax-deductible. Further, your insurance is only reduced by the amount of the actual loan. Thus, if you have a $50,000 policy and borrow $10,000, you still have $40,000 of insurance in force.

Progressively larger numbers of policyholders have caught on to this act. By mid-1981 the policy loans of fifteen major insurance companies had increased 37 percent from a year earlier. Currently, there is about $45 billion in loans against such policies.

The insurance companies might not like it but, to quote the title of one of Robert Ringer's books, it's "looking out for number one."

Bank Certificates of Deposit—NOW Accounts et al.

Again, Appendix II provides the basic mechanics of these financial instruments. However, in the three years since the *Contrarian Investment Strategy* was published, there have been some dramatic changes in their structuring. One of the most important was the introduction of the NOW account. These are interest-bearing checking accounts that were authorized by the Federal Reserve at the beginning of 1981. A maximum ceiling of 5¼ percent was allowed by the regulators on such accounts, whether in banks or other thrift institutions.

What is important for you to know is that the NOW accounts vary enormously in their terms; the only common denominator is that they all pay 5¼ percent interest.[3]
The differences:

1. Some place charges on checks or other transactions and don't pay any interest at all if your balance is too low.

2. Many banks normally require minimum balances in NOW accounts of at least $1,000 and sometimes $2,000. Below these figures there is a monthly service charge. If you keep small balances in NOW accounts (for example, only a few hundred dollars) there is no advantage at all, because the monthly service fees of $3.50 or $5.00 will often wipe out your interest and also some of your capital.

Sometimes the fees are even higher. For example, Citibank (an outstanding innovator in finding new charges for its customers) imposes a $6 minimum monthly fee on depositors who do not have at least a minimum of $3,000 in a combination of NOW accounts, savings certificates, or savings accounts.

All in all, the money funds again stack up far better because of yields over twice as high and the absence of all such hidden charges.

The banks and thrift institutions, incidentally, are fully aware of the situation and are lobbying heavily with Congress to give them less-stifling controls under which to work or, at the very least, to stifle the competition with the same measures. Currently, for example, 12 percent of bank NOW accounts must be deposited in non-interest–bearing reserves with the Federal Reserve—while none must be posted by the money market funds.

Certificates of Deposit

These pay much higher interest rates than NOW accounts, but must be held for six months or more with maturities running up to thirty months. Normally, most require minimums of $5,000 to $10,000. Certificates of deposit are government-insured up to $100,000 and also provide the saver with rates much more competitive with those of money market funds.

Some banks offer checking privileges on the savings certificates —in effect, you can borrow as much as 90 percent and at times more of the face value from the bank by creating a loan against the certificate. The interest rates are reasonable, running only from 1½ percent to 3 percent above the certificate yield.

To promote such certificates, banks are offering cash bonuses to friends to bring you in—$250 for each $10,000—along with the usual bevy of cameras, food processors, television sets, and calculators.

The interest on six-month certificates is tied to the treasury bill rate and is ¼ percent less, with a minimum rate of 9½ percent at savings institutions (9¼ percent at banks).

The banks, particularly the commercial ones, have introduced a wide variety of other plans, mostly for larger amounts of money, so it will pay you to shop around, particularly if you have $25,000 or more to invest in such instruments.

In August 1981, thrift institution deposits with a maturity of four years or longer were completely deregulated. Bank and thrift institutions can now offer any rate of interest they want to pay.

But be careful! The following incident, related by *Forbes* editor William G. Flanagan, indicates why. "Republic National Bank of New York recently advertised 66 month certificates at 20% with a minimum deposit of $5,000 and up to a maximum of $100,000. At that rate, your money doubles over the life of the certificate, and the money is federally insured. Sounds like a great deal."[4]

But, as Flanagan continues, "The interest quoted on such long-term certificates is often simple interest. It is not compounded, as it is with passbook accounts or 30 month CD's. For example, the East New York Savings Bank advertises a 17.8% certificate with a term of 48 months, but if the interest were compounded every 6 months, the equivalent yield (and the proper one) would be only 13.9%. If Republic interest were compounded every 6 months a 66 month 20% CD would yield only the equivalent of 13.95%." A slight drop from 20 percent.

You must be cautious approaching such merchandise. While the SEC has curbed many of the traditional advertising abuses of brokerage firms, there is little similar legislation for the banks and thrifts.

Who said bankers were dumb? They have done an excellent job cultivating and nurturing their important legislative lobbies.

All-Savers Certificates

The accelerating public awareness of the safe and profitable alternatives available for the individual investor as high interest rates continue has been devastating for savings and loan associations as well as other thrift institutions because the outflow of funds to these other sources has reached hemorrhage proportions. As a result, many financial institutions have become very shaky. (If you deal with a smaller bank or savings and loan, make sure that everything you invest with them is government-insured).

To shore up these hard-pressed victims of higher rates, the 1981 tax allowed the creation of the all-savers certificate.

Beginning in October 1981, all-savers certificates were offered by financial institutions. These are one-year, federally-insured savings certificates that pay totally tax-free interest—$1,000 for an individual, $2,000 for couples (only married ones, unfortunately) who file jointly.

Denominations start at $500 and up, and have an interest rate equal to 70 percent of the yield on the fifty-two-week treasury bill rate previous to the week they are purchased. The yield will vary to the end of December 31, 1982, tied to this rate. At the end of that time, these certificates will no longer be offered. Thus, the investor will be given the opportunity to get this tax break.

If a married couple, for example, has $15,000 to invest and T-bills stayed at 14 percent, they would receive 70 percent of this rate, or 9.8 percent in interest, all of which would be government-insured and none of which is taxed.

Now for the customary caveats:

1. Don't buy more of the certificates than the amount you need for your maximum exemption—$1,000 if you're single, $2,000 if married—because you will be earning a lower rate of interest than you could get elsewhere and will be taxed at regular rates above the exemption.

2. There are sharp penalties for premature withdrawal—loss of the tax benefits and three months of interest.

Are all-savers a great deal? Not particularly, when you remember you can get a yield of 13 percent or more on high-grade municipal bonds and a tax deduction applying not to $1,000 or $2,000 but to any amount of interest you have.

To borrow a sixties' phrase, "tokenism." The all-savers are a step in the right direction, but of no great benefit as presently structured. If you are in a tax bracket of 35 percent or less, stay with your money market fund.

In this chapter we have reviewed a number of innovative financial instruments that should prove particularly useful in these times in building your portfolio. What I think comes out most strikingly from this overview is the rapidity of the development of new products and the equal rapidity of their change.

It's also important to note that there are more than a few catches with many of these instruments, so that thorough investigation is essential.

The next topic, and one that is extremely important to most investors, is how much they can rely on the professional advisor. Is he likely to be helpful to you in carrying out the strategies previously outlined?

CHAPTER TWELVE

The Problems
of the Investment
Advisor

If your broker is of limited help at best in guiding your investment decisions, is the investment advisor any better? Unlike a broker, the investment advisor, whether with a bank trust department, mutual fund, or independent investment advisory organization, is usually paid a flat fee for his services. He is thus under no pressure to trade your account or put you into the high-markup but dangerous games we have just seen. Quite the contrary, in fact: investment advisors like to point out that one of their chief functions is to make decisions solely in the client's best interest, an important result of which is to avoid precisely such pitfalls. Since their tenure depends on how well their accounts perform, their decisions must always be based on optimizing the client's results. At least this is how the matter is stated in theory.

However, from the statistics we saw earlier, investment advisors have also generally failed to provide clients with profit-making advice. Now we'll look at an important reason why. The professional investor often has a difficult psychological barrier to overcome, one that fortunately does not interfere with the judgment of the individual decision maker. The expert must cope with career pressures inside an organizational setting in addition to the cognitive biases each of us is subject to. Such pressures repeatedly result in groups of very bright people making poor decisions. In the investment setting, they normally lead many committees to follow the prevailing consensus and shun out-of-favor stocks.

Naturally, career pressures extend to decision making in many areas outside of the stock market. But in the investment scene, they are particularly striking because of the increasing dominance in the marketplace of the larger institutions. Because of this increasing domination, I believe the individual investor may very well maintain, if not increase, his "edge" over the institutions with time.

Further understanding of the forces that create institutional consensus should also prove helpful to investors who select and use investment advisors. Let's turn next to why these pressures exist and how strong they can be.

What Is Groupthink?

In *Victims of Groupthink,* Irving Janis, professor of psychology at Yale, analyzed the subtle pressures of career as they influenced the decision making of individuals in many areas, including the making of national policy. These pressures, according to Janis, caused people acting within committees to abandon time-tested standards and make extremely risky decisions, which often turned out badly.

In the committee situation, Janis indicates, the executive in charge may not intentionally try to influence the group; indeed, he may sincerely foster open discussion and encourage dissenting opinion. Too, its members are often anything but yes men; most firmly believe they can and should speak their minds. Still, members often do not fully assess the suggested course. Subtle restraints may prevent fully discussing all options or dwelling too long on dissenting views once most group members have made up their minds. By his stance, the leader may unintentionally reinforce the consensus. The subtle pressures of superiors and colleagues can make it easy for committees to follow what appear to outsiders at times to be inane courses of action.[1]

Janis defined groupthink as a "mode of thinking that people engage in when they are deeply involved in a cohesive in-group, when the members, striving for unanimity, override their motivation to realistically appraise alternative courses of action. . . . Groupthink refers to a deterioration of mental efficiency (and reality-testing) . . . that results from in-group pressures."[2]

The more cohesive the decision-making group and the more they respect and are attuned to each other's thinking, the greater the danger that independent assessment will be abandoned and will be replaced instead by concurrence-seeking tendencies. Poor decisions are frequently the result.

Victims of Groupthink describes in detail how such pressures affected some highly sophisticated groups: the Kennedy brain trust and the ill-fated Bay of Pigs invasion; the confidence of top advisors in the Truman administration that the Chinese would never enter the Korean war as MacArthur's troops fanned toward the Chinese border; the conviction of Admiral Husband E. Kimmel and his staff that the Japanese could not and would not launch an aerial attack on Pearl Harbor. In each case, a great deal of contradictory evidence was at hand but was ignored because of the pressures toward consensus.

Janis says that groups are not always affected by groupthink. However, when two conditions are present—an extremely cohesive group and consistently defective decision making—groupthink is often at work. In his words, "When the conditions specified by these two criteria are met, there is a better-than-chance likelihood that one of the causes of the defective decision-making was a strong concurrence-seeking tendency, which is the motivation that gives rise to all the symptoms of groupthink."[3]

Groupthink and Money Management

In the investment scene we have repeatedly seen the abandonment of past standards and the exceptional rate of error as a result. Career pressures subtle and not so subtle also serve to reinforce the prevailing consensus.*

Money managers in a bank trust department or an investment management firm are usually well qualified for their jobs. Clients turn money over to them because they believe the professionals are better equipped to deal with the problems of investing and because they are willing to delegate responsibility and pay for this expertise.

*Chapters 5 through 9 of my earlier book, *Psychology and the Stock Market,* provide considerably more detail of how this phenomenon affects institutional investors in the stock market.

But what happens next hardly follows the script. Many clients second-guess the money manager when the decisions he makes run counter to market fashions currently in vogue. If the manager holds firm, he may lose the account—a more than common occurrence. In 1973, for example, a money management firm, Capital Guardian, refused to play the soaring highfliers, favored by most, at P/E multiples of 40, 50, 60, and more. Instead, the firm invested primarily in low-multiple stocks faring poorly at the time. As a result, they lost a number of their clients. As one disgruntled client put it: "Capital Guardian was like an airline pilot in a power dive, hands frozen on the stick; the name of the game is to be where it's at.'"[4] Had the firm been "where it's at," the account would have been decimated in short order.

Money management is a business with a high break-even point, which, once passed, generates large and rapidly expanding profit margins. To be out of fashion for too long, even if the course eventually results in outstanding returns, may cause the firm to lose enough accounts in the meantime to force it to close shop or cut staff drastically. It is not surprising that few people have the conviction or resources to be proven "dead right" in this manner. Survival pressures in the committee, either with or without the decision makers' awareness, work in the direction of reinforcing the cognitive biases we've already seen. On the other hand, money management firms capturing trends early and staying with them can do remarkably well —some making incomes up to seven figures.

To complete the picture, it is not only the unsophisticated investor who puts pressure on the money manager. Executives representing billions of dollars of pension funds of many of the country's largest corporations do precisely the same thing!

Some estimates have indicated that a 1 percent improvement in the performance of corporate pension funds will result in a reduction of about 25 percent in the mandatory annual corporate contributions. Since pension fund contributions have been projected to be as large as 25 percent of corporate pretax profits, the urge to find money managers who will provide above-average performance is strong indeed.*

---

*Since the passage of ERISA (the Employee Retirement Investment Security Act of 1974), pension fund contributions have skyrocketed. Peter Drucker estimated that pension

Given such stakes, many corporations view pension funds as independent profit centers and expect their managers to outperform the market and other money managers consistently. And because corporations divide their operations neatly into yearly, semiannual, and quarterly periods, money managers are often expected to turn in above-average performance smoothly—and on schedule. Good results should be almost as systematic as the flow of products down an assembly line.

Consequently, many financial officers, through their pension fund consultants, monitor in minute detail the performance of the professionals they have hired (as well as those of promising replacements). Usually, detailed review of the account takes place every three months. The manager whose moves are out of step, resulting in returns below par for even a relatively short time, is under mounting pressure. The "twelve/twenty-four rule," as it is called, is followed by not a few corporations—fire the manager whose performance is 12 percent below the S&P 500 for twenty-four months.[5] In short, money managers have increasingly found themselves in an impossible position—one that demands results far too quickly, with its inevitable reliance on playing the popular trends.

Those who refuse can lose the account or a portion of it. One money manager, for example, was fired when his value-oriented philosophies did not work well. The corporate officer responsible for the dismissal justified it by saying: "I never asked him to change his approach, you know. . . . My attitude was 'fine, this is your philosophy, let's just wait and see what the figures show.' "[6] The figures, of course, were for a too brief time period. After the manager was dismissed, his philosophy proved to be dramatically correct in short order.

Similar pressures apply to institutional research firms specializing in in-depth research for the major money managers. With brokerage firms merging and going out of business on an accelerating basis, the job market for securities analysts has decreased sharply. Institu-

---

funds alone now account for over one-third of all stock ownership on the New York Stock Exchange, and by 1985 they will account for 60 percent. Thus, huge and ever-increasing amounts of money are flowing into increasingly fewer large institutional hands. (Edward Malca, *Proceedings, Hearings by the Benson Committee on S 2787 and S 2842*, Subcommittee on Financial Markets, U.S. Senate Committee on Finance, 93 Cong., 2 sess., 1976; Peter F. Drucker, "American Business' New Owners." *Wall Street Journal*, May 27, 1976.)

tions demand the "best" research from the survivors. Since what is considered to be the "best" research is determined by the money managers through their allocation of commission dollars, the result is not surprising—"good" research usually means recommending the current fashions the institutions themselves are backed into.

A final source of pressure on the professional is ERISA (the Employee Retirement Investment Security Act of 1974), which mandates that pension fund managers be "prudent." Not to be so considered can result in crippling lawsuits against the money manager. At the present time, the definition of what is prudent is extremely "iffy," which results in advisors acting as most other investment advisors do. Those who don't—and prove wrong—may be staring at bankruptcy.

But market professionals are not alone, of course, in succumbing to career pressures. Indeed, the same forces apply to the "best and the brightest" in most areas of organizational decision making, and the push to conform can be found in Detroit or Georgetown as easily as on Wall or Broad streets. For us as investors, I think it is important to consider how pervasive and universal the problem actually is.

In *Bureaucratic Politics and Foreign Policy,* Morton Halperin, a former member of the staff of the National Security Council, speaks of exactly the same problems of the careerist in many branches of the federal government and the military. The desire for promotion forces a career officer to support the "shared images" of the day. Halperin writes: "Participants seem to believe that their influence and even their continuation in office depends on their endorsement or seeming endorsement of shared images. Even men who appear invulnerable to opposition zealously guard their reputation for accepting shared images."[7] When Dean Acheson, for example, accused Eisenhower of being soft on communism, the then-President vehemently denied it, reading from *Crusade in Europe* to defend himself. Even Eisenhower thought it essential to protect himself on this shared image.

Both Richard Neustadt, in *Alliance Politics,*[8] which discusses government policy making, and Adam Smith, writing about money managers in *The Money Game,*[9] speak of "players" in almost identical terms. Both sets of players are normally trying to accumulate as many career chips as they can. The career officer's major source of motivation is his desire for promotion; the foreign officer wants to reach ambassadorial rank; the military officer, flag or general rank;

the money manager, a partnership. And each career officer believes that his promotion will further the national interest, just as the money manager or analyst feels his advancement will further the interests of the firm and its clients.

According to Halperin, bureaucratic players shape their arguments in terms of current shared images—because of their influence on others—even when they do not personally believe them: "If participants believe that taking a certain stand which they think wise will be interpreted as a deviation from shared images, they will take the opposite stand for fear of losing influence or indeed their position in government."[10]

Players quickly learn to avoid positions that mean abandoning shared images. Robert McNamara did not view Russian missiles in Cuba as particularly dangerous. "A missile is a missile," he argued in the opening deliberations of the Cuban missile crisis of 1962, and advanced the case that no military action was necessary. He quickly dropped opposition when he saw that such was definitely not the view of the other important policy makers.

The problem in the foreign service is almost identical. In *Anatomy of the State Department,* Smith Simpson, a former career officer, writes of the tremendous stress on careerism in the department. "The desire for the top led to an overdeveloped sense of status, and minimized the sober business of policymaking, research, planning, man-

"Wait a minute, you guys—I've decided to make it unanimous after all."

Drawing by Vietor; © 1978, The New Yorker Magazine, Inc.

agement, and diplomacy itself. It developed self-promotion to a finished art, forcing officers to pay more attention to their personal security than to the nation's."[11]

According to Simpson, the problem has been exaggerated by the department's "up or out" rule—the officer either gets promoted or is forced to retire. "The yes man spirit, already developed to a fine art, has been enhanced by this practice; particularly vicious because the officer's prospects depend entirely on an efficiency report by a superior wherever he is located."[12] The report is reviewed many thousands of miles away in Washington by a board usually entirely unfamiliar with the officer. The assessment is the only evidence the board has to work from. The State Department panel reviewing the situation concluded the policy was a powerful detriment to officers expressing opinions at variance with those of their superiors—at best, a diplomatic understatement.

All of this is little different from the career pressures in the investment world. A recent article describing the pressures on a corporate officer administering his firm's pension fund revealed the parallels. Although the pension fund officer is responsible to his board of directors, he may be far more sophisticated in his invest-ment understanding than its members. He thus often finds himself on a precarious perch, swinging between "professional conviction and career longevity. As an officer summed it up . . . 'you really don't have much choice . . . you either say what others wish to hear or the firm will hire someone else who will . . .' It is nonsense to blame someone in his thirties or forties with his corporate career ahead of him for judiciously ducking a confrontation with an opinionated director or senior officer who is perhaps fighting the equivalent of the Spanish-American War on the investment scene."[13] Or, as Sam Rayburn put it, "To get along, go along."

In the market the threat of outright dismissal or the downgrading of the Wall Streeter's role is always present if he does not go along. In the words of one manager of corporate pension funds: "If the committee doesn't approve of my recommendations, it's like a vote of No Confidence, and, like a Prime Minister of England, I'd have to think about resigning."[14] Pressure enough to share the investment image of the moment.

With the increasing job scarcity of recent years, deteriorating institutional performance, and the crumbling of the brokerage in-dustry, survival pressures have gotten worse. In 1977, for example, 25 percent of all money managers lost one or more accounts. The money managers in turn have been dealing with fewer and fewer research firms. One major New York City bank cut its list of brokers from 105 to 30 that same year. An out-of-towner observing the institutional research scene in New York City commented: "It's absurd, impossible to talk to any analyst. You can't get on with business . . . because these guys are worried about their jobs."

While it's impossible to say with any finality whether career pressures on Wall Street professionals are worse than elsewhere, it's obvious that they are not light and that they push many a player toward consensus opinion.

But of course there are still individuals who see through the prevailing images when they are wrong, and some of them adamantly refuse to be swept along, even by the influential organizations to which they belong.

Unfortunately, as any careerist knows, the ending is all too often the same. A long literature exists in psychology on deviancy—people who refuse to accept the opinion of the group. One experiment showed that dissenters were always chosen to perform unpleasant tasks. Another required a group to select someone from among them to receive electric shocks. Naturally, it always chose the deviant.[15]

And in sophisticated committees, the proceedings, while more subtle, are really little different. Historian James Thomson, Jr., a member of McGeorge Bundy's White House staff, illustrated the dangers for careerists who stand against current policy in what he called the "effectiveness trap": "The effectiveness trap [is] the trap that keeps men from speaking out as clearly or as often as they might in Government. . . . The most important asset that a man brings to bureaucratic life is his 'effectiveness,' a mysterious combination of training, style, and connections. The most ominous complaint that can be whispered about a bureaucrat is 'I'm afraid Charlie's beginning to lose his effectiveness.' "[16] The enigmatic quality of effectiveness is just as vital in the investment scene as it is in government.

David Halberstam captured the committee spirit well in *The Best and the Brightest* when he wrote of the "Harvard Business School approach played with loaded dice": speak out and present the situation and alternatives realistically; points are given for examining contrary arguments. But don't overstate, don't present opposing views too forcefully or you may wind up on the outside.[17]

The same game, of course, with the same loaded dice is an essential part of the current investment environment. Portfolio managers can speak out, but they had better take note of which way the wind is blowing. A lawyer from Boston once told me of a suit he was filing for a bank money manager who spoke out against the dangers of investing in the highfliers in 1972. He saved his clients large sums of money and found himself unemployed in the process. And a highly successful manager of a bank trust department in Denver was fired because the board of directors thought his investment strategies were out of line with those of the big city banks (all of which were doing poorly at the time). Effectiveness in career, then, is a compelling inducement to follow the prevailing images.

The Use of an Investment Advisor

The combination of the powerful individual cognitive biases that are reinforced by organizational consensus pressures provides a good explanation, I think, of why professional performance has been mediocre through the years. The problem is one not of the quality of people but of basic flaws in the individual's ability to make some types of decisions and in the institutional structures themselves. The group-decision problem can occur in many a sophisticated committee or organization.

Yes, there are numbers of talented advisors who can avoid the hurdles, but unless you search carefully, your odds of finding one are not great. If you try, it's important to discover how successful and independent a decision maker your investment advisor actually is, and, of course, to carefully measure his record over a significant period of time.*

It seems best to avoid committee decision making wherever possible. Naturally, there will be outstanding leaders heading first-rate committees, but usually the makeup changes with time, and you will probably end up having your money managed by a hardworking group that has the problems indicated in this chapter.

If you are lucky enough to find a money manager, whether in an organization or independent, who has a long-standing record of

*Ideally, three to five years.

success, remember the problems just outlined. Don't second-guess him. Give him enough time for his philosophy to work. I know I've said it before, but time is one of the crucial elements in investment success and also the single commodity in shortest supply.

But for most investors, judging from the professional record, it seems better to go it alone. It's obviously not the popular route, and very often you are going to be considered misguided for investing in out-of-favor stocks. But if the goal is market success, it certainly appears the best bet, for the methods eliminate most of the problems we have seen.

The institution's problems become the individual's edge. At least until the causes of consensus opinion in committee decisions are better understood, and "prudent" investments are more liberally defined by the regulators or the courts, the individual possesses an advantage that looks much like the elusive Holy Grail of the technical analyst: a system for beating the market that can't be universally adapted. And, as was indicated earlier, he is left in the out-of-favor ball park with fewer and fewer players as ever larger amounts of money are concentrated in institutional hands. All he needs to make the method work, it would appear, are faith in the efficacy of the low P/E method and the conviction to follow it up.

The last topic in this book, and one as important as any we have discussed thus far, is why common stocks represent good value in today's inflationary environment, where inflation may increase at much faster rates than through much of the postwar period.

CHAPTER THIRTEEN

Are Common Stocks
a Good Investment Today?

The persistent inflation the Western world has experienced since the advent of the Keynesian revolution has no precedent in history.* And, in the radically changed world economic environment of the last ten years, the rate of inflation has been accelerating. The roots of the new phenomenon often seem as baffling to the expert as to the average investor. Nevertheless, reasonable assumptions about future inflation are crucial to a successful investment strategy.

Inflation, deflation, and recession are problems of enormous economic complexity, involving not only many controversial monetary and fiscal inputs but also a web of political and sociological factors. In recent years, new forces appear to be at work which are far less susceptible, if at times seemingly immune, to the fiscal and monetary remedies that have been traditionally applied. We'll now look at recent inflation and some of the reasons why it may reignite at levels higher—perhaps substantially higher—than any prior to the last decade.

As investors, we have been accustomed to assume that rising inflation is bad for equity investments. But is this necessarily so? The evidence of the recent past indicates that corporations can survive

*With the exception of a few isolated cases, such as Germany's Weimar Republic in 1920–22.

Figure 15.
A seven-hundred-year consumer price index.

SOURCE: Reprinted by permission of *Forbes* Magazine from the November 15, 1976, issue.

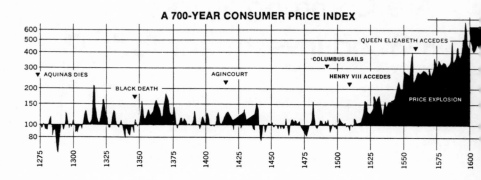

A 700-YEAR CONSUMER PRICE INDEX

and even flourish during periods of rapid price escalation. While the discussion that follows is intended to be anything but definitive, I believe it focuses on some of the major contributors to the accelerating rate of inflation of recent decades. If the analysis makes sense, it should prove useful to investors as they decide how to structure their portfolios and what role both common stocks and bonds should play within them.

The Contemporary Price Environment

Figure 15 shows the rate of inflation over a time span of seven hundred years.* As can be seen from the chart, prices exploded in the century following 1528, fueled by the plundered gold and silver of the Inca and Aztec empires. This was the classic type of inflation economists understand so well—too much money chasing too few goods. The primitive production capacity of the time could not keep up with the vast increase in money supply, and wild inflation re-

---

*The *Forbes* figures come from a variety of sources. English economist E.H. Phelps Brown carefully checked both the salaries of carpenters (three pennies a day in 1275) and what this "market basket" should buy (food, fuel, and clothing) to 1660. From 1661 on, *Forbes* used more sophisticated indices, which, they indicated, "nevertheless conformed neatly to those of the Professor."

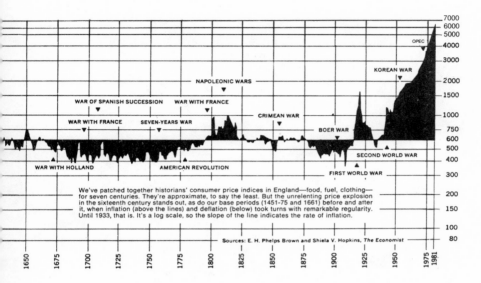

We've patched together historians' consumer price indices in England—food, fuel, clothing—for seven centuries. They're approximate, to say the least. But the unrelenting price explosion in the sixteenth century stands out, as do our base periods (1451-75 and 1661) before and after it, when inflation (above the lines) and deflation (below) took turns with remarkable regularity. Until 1933, that is. It's a log scale, so the slope of the line indicates the rate of inflation.

Sources: E. H. Phelps Brown and Shiela V. Hopkins, *The Economist*

sulted, first in Spain and not long thereafter in England. Price levels then remained stationary for almost three hundred years and were actually higher in 1650 than they were in 1932.

So, with the exception of odd and quickly corrected price surges (at least when looked at over the long historical time span), the world enjoyed relative price stability. For example, prices rose 75 percent between 1350 and 1370, but by 1380 they were lower than they had been in 1350. Similar price surges and corrections accompanied most major wars. In Victorian England, price levels were so stable that government bonds for the most part returned 2.5 percent, as we saw earlier.

If you examine the chart, you will see that there have been only two periods of sustained inflation—the one lasting a hundred years, beginning in the sixteenth century, and the one we are currently undergoing. The chart makes clear that the current inflationary period is by far the worse of the two. By the end of 1974, prices had appreciated over 480 percent in twenty-eight years, and by the end of 1977, 620 percent!

More alarming, however, is that the inflation rate has been accelerating in recent years, as figure 16 (page 276) indicates. Further, while other periods, even the 1500s, show sharp deflationary dips, the current inflation has moved continuously higher with virtually no respite.

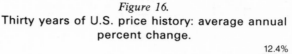

Figure 16.
Thirty years of U.S. price history: average annual
percent change.

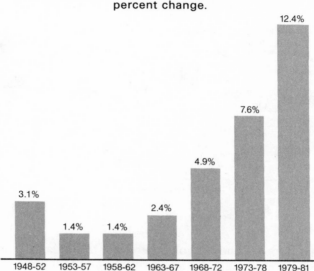

SOURCE: Department of Labor, Bureau of Labor Statistics, Consumer
Price Index.

What does one make of such figures? As chairman of the Federal Reserve Board, Arthur Burns warned repeatedly that inflation might mean the end of Western civilization, and Burns's own precipitous monetary policy, a major factor in two sharp recessions—one the worst of the postwar period—almost made him a self-fulfilling prophet.

Paul Volcker, Burns's successor at the Fed, has stalwartly continued the holy war against inflation. In the little over two years Volcker has been at the helm, his monetary policies have been largely responsible for two additional recessions—the current one likely to top the 1973–74 downturn under Burns's aegis for severity.

However, before drawing any doomsday conclusions either for the economy or for the investor, we should look carefully at some of the fundamentals of the new inflation and see why they appear so different from those we have traditionally viewed. What are the forces at work that move prices higher almost without relapse, a pattern unknown to any previous period in economic history? And why do the fine-tuned methods of contemporary economic theory seem unable to cope effectively with the phenomenon? A good place to start is the Phillips curve, one of the mainstays of current inflation theory.

The Phillips Curve

In 1958 Professor A.W. Phillips, a British economist, formulated an important hypothesis on inflation, one still at the forefront of a good part of economic planning. According to Phillips, there is a definite correlation between the rate of inflation and the level of unemployment. Higher levels of unemployment produce less pressure for wage increases, and dampened wages in turn keep down price increases* and result in lower levels of inflation. With higher levels of employment the reasoning is reversed.

The Phillips curve quickly became a chief support of Keynesian economics. If the government could hold the rate of wage gains equal to the level of productivity increases, profits would not be squeezed, and prices would not have to be increased—the business cycle would finally be tamed.

You can see why the Phillips curve appeals to government policy makers. For by using monetary and fiscal policy properly, the rate of inflation or unemployment could be precisely calibrated (or so it was thought) as surely as altering the rate of production on a complex assembly line by turning a number of knobs and dials. Figure 17 on page 278 shows a simple Phillips curve. If policy makers chose a low rate of unemployment (OB), it would come at the cost of a higher rate of inflation (OA). On the other hand, they may accept a Burns or Volcker crusade against inflation and demand zero inflation, in which case unemployment would rise sharply (OC). Or if they chose even more drastic measures and opted for deflation (which, it appears, Volcker is toying with), unemployment would expand sharply (OD)—perhaps a not entirely inappropriate pairing of letters.

As I said, an appealing hypothesis, and one that leaves the

*Productivity also increases with recessionary conditions, as business tightens up and eliminates marginal jobs, resulting in less need for rising prices, and perhaps even in falling ones.

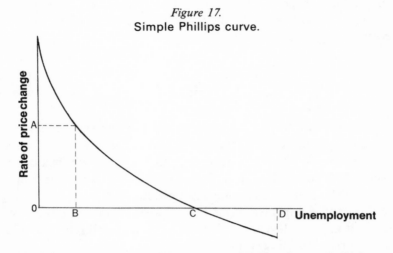

Figure 17.
Simple Phillips curve.

policy makers with an exciting sense of control over inflation and unemployment. And it's a game that has been played avidly by one group of policy makers after another, beginning with the Kennedy administration.

But again, we come to one of the problems of economic theory —its ofttimes stubborn refusal to explain or reflect conditions in the real world. For in this form, the Phillips curve does not work and never has worked.

If we look at the five recessions previous to the mid-seventies,* we see that prices during these periods have actually increased. The average rate of inflation measured by the GNP deflator was 4.5 percent compared with 2.9 percent for periods of expansion and 4.4 percent in the latter stages of expansion,† when price increases are theoretically skyrocketing, supposedly because of increasing wage demands, shortages, and capacity bottlenecks.[1] Figure 18 shows other corroborating evidence. According to contemporary theory, low capacity utilization (indicating low material and labor demand) should be accompanied by a moderation in price rises at the very least. But the figure paints a very different picture. Capacity utilization falls to abnormally low levels, yet is accompanied by continuing price increases.

*1953–54, 1957–58, 1960–61, 1969–70, 1974–75.
†The four quarters prior to the cyclical peak.

Figure 18.
Inflation and capacity utilization.

Abnormally High Inflation...

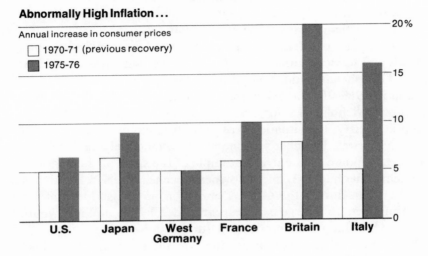

Annual increase in consumer prices
☐ 1970-71 (previous recovery)
▨ 1975-76

U.S.   Japan   West   France   Britain   Italy
                Germany

And Capacity Utilization is Abnormally Low

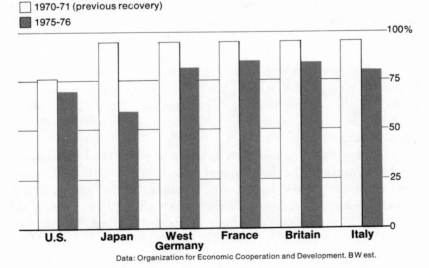

Capacity utilization rate
☐ 1970-71 (previous recovery)
▨ 1975-76

U.S.   Japan   West   France   Britain   Italy
                Germany

Data: Organization for Economic Cooperation and Development. BW est.

SOURCE: Reprinted from the March 21, 1977, issue of *Business Week* by special permission. © 1977 by McGraw-Hill, Inc., New York, NY 10020. All rights reserved.

The pattern has repeated again. Although domestic capacity usage has dropped to 70 percent from an optimum of 90 percent, in the worst domestic slump since the thirties, prices are still moving up (7 percent for the twelve months ended April 30, 1982) and at a higher rate than in any previous postwar recession.

Adequate plant and labor exists to produce significantly more goods and services without pushing up prices in the traditional manner. This phenomenon, first noted in the recession of 1953–54 and again in 1969–70, was far more dramatic in 1974–75. In the words of Lord Nicholas Kaldor, then president of Britain's Royal Economic Society, the situation was "totally unpredecented."[2]

Margaret Thatcher's economic medicine, relying heavily on monetary policy, is a current example of the same phenomenon. As indicated in chapter 1, unemployment reached levels in Britain even higher than during the Great Depression, in the summer of 1981 causing riots to a large extent spearheaded by unemployed youths. Meanwhile industrial production turned down resoundingly. The British have called the decay produced by these policies "de-industrialization." Still, inflation has continued at double-digit rates to the present time.[3]

Increasing concern was expressed about the value of high U.S. interest rates and tight money to cure inflation. Identical warnings came from the heads of states with political views as diverse as France's President François Mitterand and West Germany's Helmut Schmidt. According to Mitterand, dire consequences would develop if these policies didn't change. He continued, "Unemployment in France as well as in Germany and other countries in Europe was getting to a flash point where it might cause social upheaval." Mitterand indicated that West Europeans had to avoid such dangerous consequences.[4]

More recently, as this book is going to press, the United States is echoing much of the same type of dissatisfaction with tight money and high interest rates. Jack Kemp, co-author of the famous Kemp-Stockman Report on our "Economic Dunkirk," and one of the mainstays of supply-side economics, repeatedly asked for the resignation of Paul Volcker in early 1982. Senate Majority Leader Howard Baker also indicated that monetary policy is destroying the economy and should be eased or Congress may take steps to cut away some of the Federal Reserve's autonomy.

We have thus gone through the "stagflation" (a stagnating economy with inflation) of a decade ago and the "slumpflation" of the present day with no new approaches—even on the drawing board—that attempt to cope with this formidable problem.

Some New Causes

Let's next turn to some of the new developments that may be responsible for the "totally unprecedented" situation Lord Kaldor observed. First, a look at a wild card—the rise in prices in the 1970s of commodities in general and of oil in particular.

The moderate rise in inflation in the 1950s and 1960s was much more wage- than commodity-induced (food and industrial commodity prices increased at barely 1 percent annually from 1953 to 1970). But this was also a time of major social and economic change. Rapid industrial expansion in Japan, Germany, France, and other Western and Third World countries, together with the desire for rising standards of living, progressively expanded the demand for commodities, while rising pay scales often increased the cost base. Both the demand and the supply curves were shifting sharply—the new equilibrium would be at much higher prices. As figure 19 indicates, beginning in 1971, industrial commodity prices took off. By 1976, the price of thirteen key raw industrial commodities had doubled, and by the end of 1978, they were up almost another 25 percent. All this before food and oil.

Back in 1973 it seemed the price of oil at least would be held in check, probably not increasing much faster than the rate of inflation. True, world demand was growing quickly, and the major exporters were taking control of some of their own production. But OPEC, the Organization of Petroleum Exporting Countries, a cartel formed over a decade earlier with the sole purpose of getting higher oil prices, had up to that time improved its bargaining leverage precious little against the industrial countries.

The Arab embargo after the Yom Kippur war changed the path of economic history. Although a political act, it produced staggering economic consequences beyond the expectations of even the most optimistic OPEC policy maker. The embargo was initiated at a time when an altered political structure meant that Western military

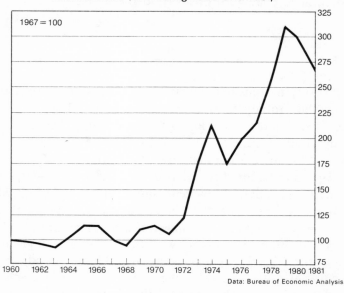

Figure 19.
Average of spot prices for thirteen raw industrial
commodities (excluding food and fuel).

Data: Bureau of Economic Analysis.

power could not be used to procure the most vital of industrial commodities. Frantic nations with limited reserves of oil were willing to pay almost any price to keep their economies from grinding to a halt. At the height of the embargo, oil was auctioned off at six to seven times the price of only weeks before. Oil prices rose fourfold between late 1973 and the end of 1974, and were boosted further in both 1975 and 1977. By the end of 1977 they had almost quintupled, and by early 1981—with the turmoil in Iran, followed by the Irani-Iraqui war—had reached $40 a barrel on the spot market, or some fifteenfold higher than in mid-1973, before trending down to the officially posted price of $32.

Even now, in the midst of a major glut caused by oversupply, substantial inventory reduction, and reduced usage, prices are still twelve times the mid-1973 level. While the major surge in oil hikes is probably behind us, many experts believe that these prices will again go up over time, at least at the rate of inflation.

The rise in oil prices has played a significant role in the acceleration of inflation around the world in the recent past. Although the oil surplus continues, it may not be as large or persistent as we might like to think. Saudi Arabia, for example, can cut its output by 2 to 3 million barrels a day from the current 8 million level and still have adequate resources to cover all of its balance of payments requirements. Indeed, factions within the country have been urging the government to reduce oil production now to gain higher prices in the future. Thus, given any disruption in Mideastern supplies, where literally dozens of unpredictable flash points can develop almost instantaneously, major shortages could again occur overnight, pushing prices higher.

All the same, as table 33 indicates, the price of fuel in the United States has been skyrocketing. In the period between 1972 and 1981, fuel costs increased at a 15.3 percent compound rate well above the general rise in the consumer price index. Some estimates have put oil-related inputs as high as 20 percent of agricultural costs, which may have made oil one of the major factors contributing to rising food prices. Oil pricing, then, is a wild card that filters into our domestic inflation rate—one that we can do very little to control by conventional fiscal and monetary mechanisms.

Aside from OPEC itself, there have been numerous attempts to set up "little OPECs" for a variety of products ranging from copper

Table 33
DOMESTIC INCREASES IN FUEL AND FOOD PRICES, 1972–81

YEAR	FUEL	FUEL PERCENTAGE INCREASE OVER PRECEDING YEAR	FOOD	FOOD PERCENTAGE INCREASE OVER PRECEDING YEAR
1972	114.3	8.0%	123.5	14.5%
1973	123.5	8.0	141.4	14.3
1974	159.7	29.3	161.7	8.4
1975	176.6	10.6	175.4	7.2
1976	189.3	17.2	180.8	3.1
1977	207.3	9.5	192.2	6.0
1978	220.4	6.3	211.4	10.0
1979	275.9	25.2	234.5	10.9
1980	361.1	30.9	248.0	5.9
1981	410.0	13.5	267.3	7.8
1972–81 increase		259%		116%

INDEX: 1967 = 100.

SOURCE: Bureau of Labor Statistics, National Energy Index. Components: gasoline, fuel oil and coal, motor oil, gas, and electricity.

to coffee by nations facing large trade deficits created by higher oil costs. Some have been successful. The fledgling uranium cartel (the Uranium Institute), organized in 1974, is made up of the producers, and at times government agencies, in France, South Africa, Australia, Great Britain, and Canada. Together they produce some 60 percent of the noncommunist world's uranium (40 percent comes from the United States). Since 1974, for example, the price of uranium has quadrupled.

The new policy toward oligopolistic pricing appears to be taking hold wherever the opportunity allows. Although well down from their highs, diamond prices were still sharply ahead in the past decade. Any pickup in demand would again send them higher. The same is true for dozens of industrial and agricultural commodities as well as precious metals. Copper, for example, down from $1.40 a pound to 70 cents, must rise substantially in price, according to the chairman of Phelps Dodge, one of the largest producers, to reach a level where the mines can work profitably. More recently, it closed all of its domestic mines, stating it was uneconomic to produce at current prices. Any expansion in industrial production or construction would likely see a major move in the price of this metal.

We have moved from a period of low commodities price increase into one where both industrial and agricultural prices have risen rapidly and oil has gone through the roof. The cost of basic commodities, then, has been an important contributor to worldwide inflation.

The problem that we face with traditional fiscal and monetary cures is that they are most effective on inflationary pressures within our domestic control, and indeed for decades such internal forces were the prime influences upon rising prices. High interest rates and tighter money, along with reduced government spending and higher taxes, for example, can certainly cut back production and demand, cooling off price pressures that stem from an overheated economy. However, when price increases are transmitted to our economy from abroad, through skyrocketing oil, diamond, bauxite, and other industrial and agricultural commodity costs, traditional fiscal and monetary policies become far less effective as a counter to inflation experienced domestically. Because the United States plays only a part in the supply and demand schedules of many of these major commodities, it naturally finds itself having a less than definitive role in setting prices, which are determined in the world market. In effect, many commodity prices are increasingly shielded from our domestic inflation-fighting techniques.

It's probable that OPEC, and even the diamond and uranium cartels, could be broken permanently by actions taken solely by the United States. But the cost would be prohibitive. To succeed, actions of this sort would require massive cutbacks in our industrial output, employment, and demand, through the use of even more extreme fiscal and monetary measures than anything seen to date.

Interest rates might have to be pushed higher than the highs of 1981 and sustained at these levels indefinitely. The result would be calamity for savings and loan associations (many already near bankruptcy in early 1982) and for many other financial institutions and industrial companies. This would very likely cause a depression accompanied by 1930s-style unemployment. I sincerely hope such an outcome is politically and socially unacceptable to current policy makers.

But it is by no means commodity pricing alone that is responsible for the new inflation. Next, let's see how it interacts with wage demands and business expectations.

Another Wild Card

After World War II a crucial new socioeconomic variable was introduced to the inflation picture in the United States—a variable that has become increasingly important ever since. In traditional microeconomic theory, labor is treated as a commodity, and its cost, like those of all other commodities, might rise or fall according to changing market conditions. In 1946 Congress passed the Full Employment Act, making labor something quite different. In the parlance of some economists labor is an administered market—or a market in which the flexibility of price movement is significantly restrained on the part of the buyer or the seller.[5]

In the labor market, wages are expected to be renegotiated upward regardless of prosperity or recession. And to the end of the last decade at least, to move up in real terms or faster than the rate of inflation. Moreover, the rigidity of the labor price structure is strengthened by high unemployment benefits, welfare, and the increasing number of women who work. So unions can afford long walkouts to achieve their goals. If strike funds run out, a wife or another member of the family working or welfare payments could ease the strain.

By 1981 the U.S. labor market had been an administered one for more than thirty years. During that time average weekly earnings increased from $45.58 to $255.10, or at a 5.2 percent annual rate. During the same period the cost of living increased at a 4.3 percent rate. Over the period wages increased 35 percent in real terms. Once again, we have a commodity whose cost is for the most part fixed and outside the reach of traditional economic remedies.

The Stress on Income Growth in Real Terms

How does the political principle of increasing or at least maintaining real wage income, predominant in all Western and Third World nations, relate to the secular change in commodity pricing? Unless the principle changes drastically, it means that wages must now be increased to cover the higher costs of food, fuel, service, housing, and consumer goods, and sometimes at a rate great enough to provide increased "real buying power" as well. On the whole, wages have more than kept pace with inflation in the United States. Wage rates increased 2.0 percent per year from 1962 to 1967, 4.6 percent annually from 1967 to 1972, and 7.7 percent per year from 1972 to 1977. As figure 20 shows, with the exception of the inflationary bulge in 1973–74, and the even sharper explosion of 1978–80, wage rates have outpaced one of the most rapid inflationary spirals in history, thus providing the wage earner with increased purchasing power in real terms.

With prices temporarily abating, and current wage settlements approximating 6–8 percent, it's likely that inflation-adjusted wages will move somewhat higher again.It is important to note the growing use of cost-of-living adjustment contracts (COLAs). Such contracts provide adjustments to offset inflation, along with the basic wage increase, which, as noted, labor almost invariably receives even during a recession. Unions have been in the forefront of negotiating such cost-of-living adjustment contracts, but it is likely their use will become increasingly more widespread among nonunionized workers.

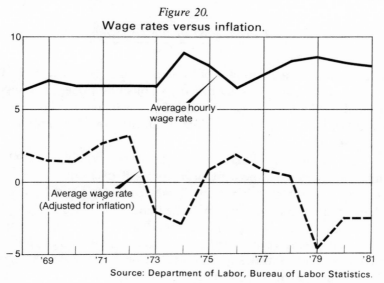

Figure 20.
Wage rates versus inflation.

Source: Department of Labor, Bureau of Labor Statistics.

Many administratons have attempted to attack the wage-price spiral by urging people to decrease their wage or salary demands voluntarily.* This has proven impossible for the three-and-a-half decades since the World War II. It is only when a union is in severe difficulty, because a company or industry it represents is facing near-demise, that members show any willingness to cut demands, and even then grudgingly—giving up only minimum ground. The UAW, whose ranks have dropped almost 40 percent, is such an example. Though the future of the U.S. auto industry is troubled, negotiations—to date, at least—have resulted in relatively minor changes.

No evidence exists in the postwar period that workers, or lawyers, or doctors, or anyone else will voluntarily curtail their earnings power. Put in its simplest form, each economic group says: "Why me?" It appears, then, that increases in wage rates, the major push behind previous inflation, will continue and contribute to the very inflation they attempt to overcome. It might be called a rat race, or the American Dream, or perhaps both.

*President Carter, on May 1978, admonished lawyers for increasing their fees "even faster than oil prices."

A Final Part of the Equation

The method of calculating profit margins on sales constitutes a third factor behind current inflation. In establishing prices, businessmen normally calculate projected rates of labor, material, and other cost increases into their selling prices in an attempt to maintain profit margins.

As a result, profit margins have been remarkably stable whether inflation averaged 2 percent or 10 percent over the past years, as column 1 in table 34 indicates. Some economists have labeled this phenomenon "anticipatory price hedging."

Such conditions explain the combination of both excess capacity and rising prices we saw earlier. Thus, once inflationary expectations have been built into the system, as they obviously have through the decade, businessmen will often attempt to increase or at least hold prices, knowing the cost squeeze they face if they don't.

In summary, then, I believe there are at least three major inputs to contemporary inflation, all interacting, none of which were nearly as persistent in the past:

1a. The ability of OPEC and of several junior international commodity cartels to hike prices sharply in line with or often ahead of the rate of world inflation.

1b. Strong upward pressure on other important agricultural and industrial commodity prices beginning in the early 1970s in line with expanding world consumption after almost two decades of minimal commodity inflation. Although prices have receded temporarily because of the current severe recession, a resurgence in demand will almost undoubtedly be accompanied by price hikes.

Table 34
PROFIT MARGINS, EARNINGS GROWTH, AND RETURN ON EQUITY OF THE S&P 400 INDUSTRIALS, 1952–81

	AVERAGE ANNUAL PROFIT MARGIN ON SALE	AVERAGE ANNUAL EARNINGS PER-SHARE GROWTH	AVERAGE ANNUAL RETURN ON BOOK VALUE
1952–61	14.8%	4.1%	11.6%
1962–71	15.5	5.0	11.6
1972–81	14.9	11.0	14.1

Because prices are frequently set to a significant extent in world, not U.S., markets, domestic policies have far less influence and effect upon them.

2. The sociopolitical belief that real income of the workingman must increase (or at the very least hold at current levels), and the effective economic power to back it up—regardless of the implications to the general rate of inflation. Commodity inflation, then, serves to accelerate the rate of wage hikes.

3. The ability of large numbers of corporations to maintain their profit margins during periods of rising prices. This results in fueling the price spiral because of the percentage of profit management tacks onto increasing labor, material, and other costs. In recessionary periods, because these costs often do not decline, it provides a strong incentive to hold the price line, even during periods of far less than optimal production.

As noted, a rise in one of these forces triggers a rise in the other two. For example, an increase in the price of oil affects hundreds of manufactured products—from tires, synthetic fibers, and clothing to plastics—as well as gasoline and fuel oil. The manufacturer passes on not only the increased price of oil but also an additional percentage of the increase in order to maintain his profit margins on sales (see table 34). The same markup is applied to increases in the dozens or even hundreds of items that make up his cost schedule.

Finding higher prices for clothing, tires, gasoline, and numerous other petroleum-based products, along with price rises in other goods and services, the consumer naturally escalates his wage demands. These wage hikes in turn can touch off another round of commodity boosts. The spiral moves along.

To me, this combination of factors could sustain future rates of inflation well above those we considered tolerable in the past. No offsetting domestic action short of severe recession- or even depression-creating fiscal and monetary policies can really cope with the puissant forces.

"Too much gold chasing too few goods," while applying perfectly to the Spanish and English economies of the sixteenth century, does not appear to fit what we have seen recently.

Investing Under Conditions of Accelerating Inflation

Assuming there will be no depression, through reckless monetary policy, what investment guidelines should one follow to withstand the inflation of our times?

Real estate and housing may continue to be good investments if they can be bought on reasonable terms, because of the major tax write-offs an individual gets of interest, property taxes, et cetera, when he buys rather than rents.

However, I agree with my *Forbes* colleague Ashby Bladen, senior vice-president for investments of the Phoenix Mutual Life Insurance Company, that the bloom is more than a little off the rose. High mortgage rates today put a cap on the gains of 15 to 20 percent annually that used to be built into the housing market. For the most part, such appreciation is behind us.

The case for bonds is far more troublesome than in the past. In the first contrarian book I wrote of what happens to investors buying bonds in periods of high inflation as follows: "We have already seen that at an 8 percent rate of inflation an investor in a 50 percent tax bracket buying a 9 percent ten-year bond finds himself losing 34 percent of his capital (after including interest) in real purchasing power at maturity. If inflation went up to 10 percent, he would lose 45 percent of his purchasing power, again after including both interest and principal."

Since then, of course, interest rates, as the preface noted, have moved sky-high, and bond values have crashed. Tax-free municipals currently yield 13 percent. Municipals are yielding a return almost 8 percent above the rate of inflation. With very high yields, it is definitely wise for an investor to own some bonds, particularly if the rate of inflation is temporarily declining.

In a high tax bracket, buy municipals. In a 50 percent bracket, for example, a municipal yielding 13½ percent is equivalent to a return of 27 percent after federal tax. The longer the term you can get this yield, the better.

But again, as I noted in chapter 11, be careful. If interest rates begin to decline, keep the maturity dates of your bonds short. The larger the decline in long-term interest rates, the shorter the maturity your bonds should be. Today, with widely swinging interest rates, bonds are every bit as volatile as stocks, if not more so, and must be watched extremely closely.

A case can be made to place a portion of your savings in gold, precious stones, and good artwork. But once again, you must be very careful.

1. Do not pay ridiculous prices. In buying gold, for example, the unwary investor can sometimes pay 50 percent or more above the going market. There are also all sorts of other ways for the investor to get bagged (chapter 10 only skimmed the surface). When people began collecting coins in droves in 1973–74, some Westchester dealers came up with the idea of selling coins with some silver content in sixty-pound bags on margin.[6] But naturally, there was a catch: the buyers were not allowed to open the bags. Since the silver content of different coinage varies enormously, it's not hard to figure whom the count favored in this case. Still, there were many takers.

And beware of the valuable "first edition" sets of gold and silver commemorative coins put out by a number of sophisticated marketers at three or four times the value of the specie. Parke-Bernet absolutely refuses to handle the merchandise, which, in the words of its first vice-president, Canton Kabe, is "limited edition trash."[7]

Curious about the value of one "limited edition set of 25 unique sterling silver gambling coins, one from each of the world's most glamorous casinos," Andrew Tobias, author of the best-selling *The Only Investment Guide You'll Ever Need,* phoned the Franklin Mint to check the silver content. As Tobias relates: "After a little hesitation—the collector service representative knew everything about the offer but this—I was told that the entire set of coins would weigh about 16 troy ounces, $86 worth at current prices. Yours for only $875 plus tax."[8]

Supposed inflation hedges have also taken investors in many other ingenious ways. John Train, author of *The Money Masters* (New York: Harper & Row, 1980) and a respected money manager himself, relates in *Forbes* how Scottish whisky brokers canvass gullible U.S. residents with direct mail advertisements proclaiming that 20 to 25 percent annual gains can be made by owning aging Scottish whisky.[9] The investor buys certificates presumably indicating the whisky is stored in bonded warehouses. In fact, the price of aged whisky has dropped very steeply over the last two decades. Moreover, the customers are sold the whisky at several times the going rate and often do not get the grades they've contracted for or sometimes even real title. Some inflation hedge!

2. Do not enter near the top of a period of excessive speculation (see chapter 4 for the symptoms).

3. Have some expertise if you are going into out-of-the-ordinary ventures. This is absolutely crucial in any form of collecting, from antiques to art. In art, for example, be wary of high prices of many contemporary artists—some have been known to rig their markets by bogus transactions very much like stock rigging by unscrupulous dealers. Further, what is considered "outstanding" at the moment can be almost valueless a decade later. The gallery also tacks on a 40 percent markup to the price the artist receives, so you need a bit of appreciation to break even, even if you are proven right on the particular piece of artwork.

One final illustration indicating the hazards of collecting art: two fine figurines of the T'ang dynasty, a camel and a horse, were put up for auction at the same time. One was sold for $92,000 and the other fetched $7,000. The reason, according to the auctioneer, was, "The rich love horses, but they have no romance with camels."[10]

Collecting, then, seems a game best left up to the experts.

Since this book is primarily concerned with investing in common stocks, how might they perform under the inflationary conditions anticipated?

Stocks, a Good Investment Today

For the sixteen years prior to 1982, stocks were most assuredly not a good investment. After all, the market in the summer of 1982 was some 22 percent below where it had been in 1966, and in constant dollars was lower than it had been in 1951, or for that matter, at the end of 1929. The anything-but-sterling record of equities in recent years has been accompanied by a forceful argument accepted by a good part of informed opinion that corporate earnings are significantly overstated in periods of rapidly rising prices. The rate of return, so the reasoning goes, was near 12 percent through most of the postwar period. But when capital assets had to be replaced, they would cost much more in "real dollars," thanks to inflation; therefore, the rate of return in constant dollars must necessarily have been dropping.

Take the example of a company that has been earning 12 percent, or $120,000, on its assets of $1 million. Assume when the assets have to be replaced, their cost has doubled to $2 million because of inflation. The company's rate of return on the new assets, adjusting for rising replacement costs, drops to 6 percent—if it continues to earn the same $120,000. The question, then, is raised, quite legitimately, about the quality of a company's earnings. Does rapid inflation mean that replacement costs are understated, thereby resulting in an overstatement of a company's income?

Some recent work makes the answer appear to be no. Burton Malkiel, former head of the economics department at Princeton, points out that the return on corporate assets was fairly stationary, even with rising inflation. In other words, the companies earned these returns on the replacement value, not on the original cost, of the assets, thus offsetting inflationary penalties.[11] Malkiel cited a study made by Martin Feldstein and Lawrence Summers of the Brookings Institution showing that there was no long-term decline in corporate profitability after correcting for inflation.[12]

Feldstein and Summers presented statistics to indicate that the major squeeze on corporate profits in recent years has been low rates of capacity utilization. In figure 21 (based on their numbers), on page 294, Malkiel shows what the return on capital *at replacement value* would have been with full employment (defined as 5 percent unemployment) and an optimum utilization rate of capacity of 86 percent.* As the figure shows, the cyclically adjusted rate of return of just over 10 percent in 1976 (after the abnormal 1971–74 period of price controls and the quintupling of oil prices) was not far from the more normal level of profitability of the late 1950s.

Too, return on equity of the Dow-Jones Industrial Average has not varied substantially over the thirty years their statistics were based upon. In the 1945–55 period, it was 12.8 percent; in the 1955–65 period, 10.1 percent; and in the 1965–75 period, 10.9 percent. Thus, even using these calculations, we see that profitability

---

*Return on capital was calculated by adding corporate profits (excluding inventory gains), along with interest payments, and dividing the sum by the replacement value of the assets.

Figure 21.
Returns on total corporate capital.

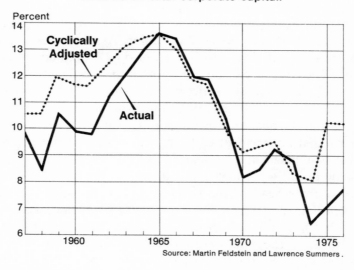

Source: Martin Feldstein and Lawrence Summers.

held up over a thirty-year period, although inflation supposedly ate into plant and equipment at a rate of better than 3 percent annually (or, for the twenty years between 1945 and 1965, 2.97).

Further, as Warren Buffett noted in *Forbes,* this argument would not be applicable to a large segment of the market—banks, insurance and finance companies, publishing houses, service companies, and the like—where buildings, plant, and equipment are a relatively small percentage of earning assets.[13] It would appear, then, if earnings of such companies were increasing at a rate faster than inflation, and in many cases they are (Aetna's, for example, grew at a cyclical but nevertheless 20 percent annual rate over the last decade), these stocks would continue to provide good value.

A recent paper by Franco Modigliani, the current president of the American Finance Association, also produced evidence against the widely accepted belief that corporate profits decline sharply during periods of high inflation. Modigliani, along with Richard Cohn, concluded that the poor performance of equity markets in recent years could be largely attributed to the inability of both institutional investors and brokerage houses to understand the effect of inflation on corporate profits.[14]

According to Modigliani and Cohn, investors repeat two mistakes in valuing common stocks during inflationary periods. First, they place too low a valuation on stock earnings relative to the interest rates on high-grade bonds. There is a relationship between the rate of return earned on common stocks and that on long-term bonds. Since stocks are riskier, they traditionally return somewhat more. This return on common stocks, called the earnings yield, is simply the earnings per share divided by the market price. Thus, if a stock earns $1 and the market price is $10, it would have an earnings yield of 10 percent.*

An error investors make during inflationary times is to calculate bond interest at nominal rates (the rate in effect was about 9 percent when the study was done) rather than at the real rate (the present rate minus the current rate of inflation). If the nominal rate is 9 percent and inflation is running at 7 percent, the real rate of interest is 2 percent. However, because investors ignore the real rate of interest and focus solely on the nominal rate, they consistently demand returns from stocks that are far too high.

As an example, take the Dow-Jones Industrial Average today. The average is presently trading at a P/E ratio of about 7, or provides an "earnings yield" of 14.2 percent. With inflation several years back running at 10 percent or more, and bonds yielding 9 to 10 percent, the "real interest rate" for bonds is zero at best. We are, then, comparing a return of 14.2 percent on the Dow with a "real interest rate" on bonds of zero. Thus, while stocks may have traditionally provided returns 3, 4, or 5 percentage points higher in terms of earnings yield than those of real interest rates, because of this investor misunderstanding, the spread between earnings yield and "real interest rates" has been substantially higher through the seventies and continues to be so today.†

The second Modigliani-Cohn argument is that although investment professionals continually adjust earnings downward to take account of "swollen inventory profits" and "inadequate depreciation of buildings, plant, and equipment," at the same time they ignore the fact that a good part of corporate assets are provided from borrowings, which in inflationary times will be repaid in much cheaper

*To get the earnings yield from a P/E ratio, simply apply the numerator 1 over the P/E ratio. If the P/E ratio is 8, the earnings yield is 1/8, or 12.5 percent.

†Although it has declined. With corporate bonds now paying 16 percent and inflation running at a 6 percent rate, the real rate of interest is 10 percent as against a 15 percent earnings yield for stocks.

dollars. The assets purchased with borrowed funds will appreciate relative to the shrinking dollars required to repay the debt. The burden of the "real debt" relative to the cost of the assets, then, continually diminishes. The greater the rate of inflation, the more "real debt" is reduced. The two sets of accounting adjustments—the overstating of inventory profits along with the understatement of depreciation reserves, and the appreciation of assets purchased with borrowed dollars—will about offset one another. However, investors concentrate only on the first adjustment, which reduces profitability, and ignore the second, which improves it. The result is to consistently undervalue the earnings of stocks.

Modigliani and Cohn conclude: "Rationally valued, the level of the S&P 500 at the end of 1977 should have been 200. Its actual value at the time was 100. Because of inflation-induced errors, investors have systematically undervalued the stock market by 50 percent." By the end of 1981 these errors were substantially compounded.

Inflation and Corporate Earnings and Dividends

If the above arguments are valid, and they appear well supported, we should consider one final important question: how able are corporations to pass on costs of wages, materials, and services in inflationary times? If corporations can maintain their profit margins on sales (the rate of sales before taxes in this case) and prices increase in line with inflation rates, as they have to date, then earnings should at the very least keep pace with higher inflation rates. Table 34 (on page 288), using the S&P 400 Industrials (where plant and equipment are weighted relatively heavier than in the S&P 500), shows how profit margins have fared. In the 1972–81 period they were 14.9 percent of sales, compared with 15.5 percent for the 1962–71 span and 14.8 percent for the previous ten years. Thus, profit margins in the last decade held up exceptionally well through accelerating inflation, two credit crunches, the wage-price freeze, and two sharp recessions. And, as the table shows, with the increasing rate of price rise, annual earnings growth has more than doubled in the 1972–81 period from 1962–71 and almost tripled the 1952–61 period.

More impressive is that in the last ten years of accelerating inflation ending in 1981, corporate earnings still outdistanced the rise in prices. This has occurred although profits have been flat since 1979 because of the recent sharp business downturn. Earnings of the S&P 400 were up 10.6 percent annually through this period, versus 8.7 percent for inflation, as table 35 demonstrates. While earnings fell back in the lingering recession of 1980–81, their ten-year growth rate is well above the rise in inflation. Corporate earnings, then, rather than being crippled, have fared remarkably well through some particularly heavy sailing. If the previous arguments stand, common stocks have provided not just a relative but an absolute hedge in terms of real purchasing power, despite what many market doomsayers have said.

As important to the investor is that dividends of the S&P 400 in the 1971–81 period have increased almost as fast as the rise in prices. (For the past five years, dividend increases matched the accelerating rise in prices.) Hardly an argument that common stock earnings and dividends are crippled under conditions of rapidly rising prices! Common stocks, then, by the most crucial yardsticks of worth—earnings and dividends—have proved to be a very good inflation hedge indeed. By comparison, the bondholder, as we have seen, would have had his capital severely reduced.

Other valuation yardsticks also indicate that the market appears very cheap. The Dow-Jones Industrial Average was recently trading 15 percent below book value (the value of all assets less all liabilities). Even in 1932, the year the market reached an all-time low in the Great Depression, the Dow did not trade below book value for more than a few months. Stock prices by this measure were only below "book" on two other occasions in the century: in 1949–50, just prior to the Great Bull Market (stocks then rose 500 percent in the next decade and a half); and in late 1974—the bottom of the worst market

Table 35
S&P ANNUAL EARNINGS AND DIVIDEND GROWTH RELATIVE TO INFLATION

| | AVERAGE ANNUAL INCREASE IN | | |
	S&P 400 EARNINGS	S&P 400 DIVIDENDS	CONSUMER PRICE INDEX
1961–71	5.3%	4.0%	3.2%
1971–81	10.6	8.3	8.7
1976–81	9.0	10.7	10.7

break of the postwar period. Moreover, because of inflation, the real value, of plant equipment, land, and other assets, today is at least 50 percent more than the value it was "put on the books at" years ago. In other words, the Dow presents better value by this widely followed measurement than it has for any prolonged period in the past.

The present situation has resulted in a rash of takeovers by foreign and domestic companies alike. (It is much cheaper to buy a company with a going business than to invest anew.) While the premiums vary, some analysts have estimated they average about 75 percent above book value.

Although the market multiple is near the bottom of its postwar range, there are still exceptional opportunities available for the low P/E investor. Today, large companies such as Aetna, Texaco, Standard of Ohio, and Travelers are trading at only three or four times earnings (about half of the market multiple) and yield 7 to 11 percent or more. When a company trades at three times earnings, you are buying it in effect at a 33 percent aftertax return and about a 66 percent pretax return. Not many investments—other than the odd lucky hit at the gaming tables—even remotely provide rewards like these.

Finally, bull markets are few and far between. In the past sixty years, there have only been two of any extended duration, one in the twenties and the other in the 1949–65 period. With large numbers of investors wrung out in speculations ranging from commodities and collectibles to precious metals and real estate, more and more are looking for the solid value found in good equities. Stocks, then, shouldn't stay undiscovered for long, a fact smart money already is well aware of. Two of the brightest money managers of our day, John Templeton and Warren Buffett, have both predicted a major new bull market that, within the next few years, could see present prices double or even triple.

To me, the stock market, then, appears cheap by nearly every historical standard. Since the 1930s, with the exception of the bottom of the 1974 market, stocks have never been as totally washed out as they have been recently. Though higher rates of inflation are a phenomenon I am convinced investors will have to live with from here on in, they are not devastating. Companies have proven they can not only survive but also prosper in this environment. The psychology of markets being what it is, it is probable that when this awareness becomes widespread, it will be anything but gradual. The end result might well be one of the great bull markets of the century—if not the greatest.

Doomsday Prophecies Are Premature

Our economic system does face new, increasingly difficult problems: record interest rates, high unemployment, the reduced competitive ability of many basic industries and government policies that tax business profits and capital gains too heavily.

I remain an optimist for the reasons I hope I have made clear to you. Industrial economies in the recent past have survived and even increased their productivity under far more severe conditions of economic disequilibrium than those we are now experiencing. We need only go back to 1941 to recall how the entire Russian industrial base was shifted east beyond the Urals in a matter of six weeks in order to avoid being captured by the swiftly moving Nazi Panzers; or how German industrial production was higher in 1944 than in 1941, in spite of the millions of tons of bombs dropped with precision on the most crucial segments of their industry—railroads, ball-bearing plants, and oil refineries.

As to destroying the profit system itself by government regulation, if ownership of stock is made valueless, it is not probable that other major classes of property will be unaffected. Real estate, bonds, and numerous other assets can maintain their value only within a flourishing economic system. Many investors lose sight of the fact that values are interrelated. If corporations falter, it is hardly likely that many other assets will be left untouched.

When I was a student reading the newspapers of the 1930s, 1940s, and 1950s, I was amazed by the value so abundant in the stock markets of those days and felt a little cheated because I thought the great days of investment coups all lay in the past.

Today, nothing seems further from the truth. Institutional concentration, conformity pressures on professionals, and overreactions to the current economic problems seem to me to present the investor with some of the greatest stock market opportunities in decades.

APPENDIXES
REFERENCES
INDEX

The Performance of the Favorite Stocks of Groups of Professional Investors

Surveys: Industrial Favorites

NAME OF SURVEY	NUMBER	YEAR(S)	NUMBER OF PARTICIPANTS	FAVORITE STOCK OR INDUSTRY	PERFORMANCE IN NEXT 12 MONTHS	S&P 500 PERFORMANCE IN NEXT 12 MONTHS
Trusts and Estates[a]	21	1953–56	75–175			
California *Business*	5	1967	100–150	Litton Industries	− 15.3	+20.0
		1968	100+	Occidental Petroleum	+ 51.0	+ 7.7
		1969	100+	Collins Food	− 50.0	−11.5
		1970	100+	GRT	− 78.6	0.0
		1971	100+	Diagnostic Data	+103.8	+10.8
Callan Associates[b]	2		36			
Business Week[c]	2	9/15/73	1	(ten favorite stocks)	− 48.6	−37.6
Institutional Investor	3	Feb. 1972	2000+	National Student Marketing	− 93.00	+ 12.8
		Mar. 1972	1,500+	Airlines	− 50.00	+ 4.0
		Mar. 1972	1,500+	Pan American and IBM	− 10.0	+ 4.0

		Market Direction		
Edson Gould				
Market Forecast[d]	1		—	35.0	—27.0
Total number of surveys	34			
Percentage under performing market	71			

[a]See table 6, page 111.
[b]See table 8, page 112.
[c]Survey of the ten favorite stocks for capital appreciation of two of the most prominent institutional brokerage research houses.
[d]As reported in the *Wall Street Letter*, December 17, 1973. The survey consisted of 75 portfolio managers representing "well over 100 billion dollars." The manager predicted the market as represented by the Dow-Jones Industrial Average, then at 840, would rise to between 900 and 1,000 by the end of the next year. In fact, it declined to 616.

Favorites, Five Stocks or More

NAME OF SURVEY	NUMBER CONDUCTED	YEAR(S)	NUMBER OF PARTI- CIPANTS	SIZE OF PORT- FOLIO	PERFOR- MANCE IN NEXT 12 MONTHS	S&P 500 PERFOR- MANCE IN NEXT 12 MONTHS
Cowles	1	1927–32	16a	469		
Cowles	1	1928–31	20b	—		
Cowles	1	Jan. 1928– June 1932	29c	113.7		
Institutional Investor	4	Jan. 1972	150	10	+ 1.3	+ 15.6
		1972	150	50	− 4.7	+ 15.6
		Jan. 1973	160	10	− 40.4	− 17.4
		1973	160	27	− 25.6	− 17.4
California Business	2	Jan. 1971	134	10	− 9.7	+ 12.4
		Aug. 1976	125	25	− 1.6	− 6.3
Edson Gould Seminar	1	1974	75	8	− 35.0	− 28.1
Callan Associates	2	12/31/74	36	6d		
Diefenbach		11/17/66–				
Buy & Sell	1	5/23/69	30e	42		
Mueller	4	Jan. 1974	275	9	− 31.7	− 28.1
		Jan. 1975	304f	7	+ 58.0	+ 29.4
		Jan. 1976	312g	13	− 4.6	+ 17.7
		Jan. 1977	264h	10	− 10.2	− 2.9
Financial World	1	Sept. 1980	20	8	+ 9.3	+ 14.1

Total number of
surveys conducted   18

NOTE: 88.3 percent underperformed market. All participants are from different investment firms.

aCowles measured the results of sixteen leading financial services firms. Overall, 7,500 recommendations were made; on average, they lagged the market by 1.43 percent annually.
bThe actual purchases and sales of twenty leading fire insurance companies were compared with the market in the 1928–31 time period.
cAll recommendations of twenty-four leading financial services publications, including four financial weeklies, one bank letter, and one investment advisory letter. On average they lagged the market by 4.0 percent annually.
dSee table 8, page 112.
eDiefenbach survey of twenty-four brokerage firms that in total made 1,209 buy recommendations between November 17, 1966, and May 23, 1969. The number per firm varied from 8 to 288, and averaged 50. He also measured the results of 46 sell decisions by 8 firms. The results were compared against the S&P 425. Of all recommendations, 53.2 percent subsequently underperformed this average.
fRepresenting assets of $86 billion.
gRepresenting assets of $102.9 billion.
hRepresenting assets of $98 billion.

Steps in Your Financial Planning

If you are something less than a seasoned investor, you may want to look at a number of important steps that should be considered in financial planning, along with some of the more common investment vehicles other than equities available.

The Starting Point: Liquid Assets and Insurance

Savings Banks

Everyone needs some liquid reserves, either for emergencies or to take advantage of unforeseen opportunities. The amount might vary anywhere from a few months' living expenses to a full year's, depending on both your personal temperament and how secure you believe your regular income is. Three months of living expenses kept in a savings account might allow some of you to sleep comfortably, while it may give others nightmares.

The investor can choose a number of places to place liquid reserves. He might put the funds into a savings bank, converting them to a checking account as funds are required. The current yield on savings accounts is 5.75 percent annually. It's foolish to keep money in a non-interest-bearing checking account without good reason.*

Money market funds (discussed on pages 242–245) are another and in most cases a far better alternative for these funds. Yields are normally much higher, but they will change more frequently than savings bank rates.

Savings Certificates

You can invest a portion of your liquid assets in savings certificates (from one to eight years). The rates are higher than in the day-to-day savings deposit and withdrawal accounts.† (At the present time, yields range as high as 14 percent for eight-year notes.)‡

Naturally, there is a catch. If you cash these certificates in before they mature, as their commercials advertise, the banks penalize you some of the interest. (The ads make it sound as though they are woeful about being forced to do this by law, although undoubtedly it was their lobbying skill that pushed the legislation through in the first place.) Such penalties may not be inconsequential. Should you withdraw early, you will receive the same amount of interest as you would have on the regular day-to-day rate and forfeit three months of interest. Thus, if you purchased a $5,000 seven-year note and cashed it several months before it was due, you would lose over $1,000 in interest. Before putting money in longer savings certificates, you should look at the additional choices available in bonds, unless the amounts are small or you are absolutely sure you will not cash them prematurely.

Treasury Notes

Another alternative to savings bank certificates for cash reserves likely to be held for a year or two is U.S. government notes. The minimum denomination is $1,000. Treasury notes react much more quickly to changes in monetary policy than do savings bank certificates. So when interest rates are moving up, you may be able to enhance your yield by investing in them.

*Recently, some commercial banks have instituted free check writing on savings accounts, but minimum balances are normally high—$2,500 to $3,000—or monthly fees are instituted.

†However, the minimum investment varies between $500 and $1,000.

‡But see chapter 11 for the various ways it can be calculated. Actual rates can be much lower than those advertised.

Accident and Health Insurance

For years, many pundits have considered the American Medical Association one of the best-run unions in the country. There were about the same number of doctors in the country per capita in 1970 as in 1880.* Naturally, the union says this ratio has improved the quality of the graduates. An obviously unanticipated result of such quality control is a major shortage of doctors and skyrocketing medical costs, which have been rising at about twice the rate of inflation for the past decade. Other medical expenses have risen almost as sharply.

It seems absolutely essential, then, to have adequate medical coverage. We've all heard stories of how unexpected serious illnesses have wiped out the savings of fairly affluent families. If you are employed by a corporation, you can probably get good low-cost group insurance, which you should take advantage of. If you are self-employed, it is well worth the cost to have Blue Cross, Blue Shield, and Major Medical.

A few years back, I ran into the tower of a chair lift on a ski slope, had to have a cartilage operation, and was hospitalized for six days. The hospital bill, tests, and drugs alone came to $2,800, all of which Blue Cross, Blue Shield paid. The surgeon and anesthesiologist's fees were another $1,200, half of which was paid by my Major Medical. This minor operation, then, cost $4,000, of which I paid only $600, thanks to my insurance.

Without medical coverage, there is simply no way of establishing what an adequate cash reserve is for you. A serious operation and recuperation might dock you two or three years' income or more. Such coverage is thus an essential aspect of proper investment planning.

Life Insurance

There are two kinds of insurance you can buy: whole (or ordinary) life, and term. But, as an investor, there is only one kind to consider—term.

Term provides you with no frills. It is bare-bones life coverage that can be bought on a renewable basis for twenty years or more. A decreasing renewable policy (decreasing coverage in later years

*163 per 100,000 in 1880; 166 per 100,000 in 1970.

Table 36
LIFE INSURANCE SHOPPING: COMPARATIVE RATES

	COST PER $10,000	
TERM: FIVE-YEAR RENEWABLE	MALE, AGE 35	AGE 45
Best special policy	48.8	114.0
Best generally available policy	63.6	131.6
Median policy	73.2	111.6
Worst policy	87.2	181.6
Savings bank life insurance (SBLI)	24.5	69.4
WHOLE LIFE: NON-PARTICIPATORY POLICIES		
Best special policy	150.0	231.60
Best generally available policy	150.0	231.60
Median policy	166.0	261.80
Worst policy	194.0	294.42

NOTE: All policies are $25,000, with the exception of SBLI, which is for $30,000. Cost figures make assumptions for dividends received.
SOURCES: Consumers Union Report on Life Insurance (which surveyed 125 companies) and New York SBLI rates (1981).

when your family has matured and your needs probably diminish) will allow you to renew over a number of fixed periods, usually every five years, normally to age sixty-five, when it terminates.* Renewal can be made without having to take a new physical, which is important if your health begins to deteriorate.

The cheapest term insurance offered is usually through a group plan where you are employed. In some states, insurance almost as cheap can also be purchased through savings banks. However, SBLI (savings bank life insurance) does have maximums on the amounts an individual can purchase.†

Whole, or ordinary, life, rather than providing just life insurance, has a myriad of other benefits, such as policyholder dividends, borrowing features, and cash payments upon maturity. But this is no free lunch. You pay far more for these perks than you would if you bought each feature on an item-by-item basis.

Whole life and endowment is by far the most profitable line of business for the insurance company and the salesman. In fact, one of the standard operating ratios in measuring an insurance com-

*Each renewal is at a somewhat higher price.
†At present, it can be bought only in New York, Connecticut, California, and Massachusetts, and the maximum amount is around $30,000.

pany's success is the amount of premium per thousand dollars of insurance the company gets. The premium on term, as table 36 shows, is often a very small fraction of what it is on whole life. For example, a male at age forty-five pays almost five times as much for the highest-priced whole-life policy as he would for SBLI insurance.

Whole life is actually so lucrative to the companies that about half of the first year's premium and a smaller but not inconsequential portion of the premiums for the next several years go directly into the salesman's pockets. By contrast, term yields very little in commissions. These policies are probably buried deep in the salesman's briefcase, not to be brought out until he knows there is no hope of selling anything else.

The whole-life policyholder is affected by more than just the initial commission. Insurance companies usually have very high administrative charges on the money they invest for you, far higher than for stock or bond mutual funds. So you are better advised to do your investing yourself. The difference saved in a ten- or twenty-year period will prove substantial.

As I've indicated, there are hundreds of ordinary- and whole-life plans available, each with its own unique characteristics and salient marketing features. The important point to remember is that the basics are the same.

Table 36 gave you some idea of just how much life insurance premiums per thousand dollars of coverage can vary. It will pay you to shop around if you need additional coverage, and *specify term, demanding no frills.* For guidance, you might look at the Consumers Union survey on life insurance, which is updated periodically and lists numbers of companies providing low-cost term coverage.

Investing in Bonds

Stockholders are the owners of the corporation and participate in its fortunes, either good or bad. The price of the stock and the company's dividends will vary with the corporation's success or failure. By contrast, in buying a bond, you are merely one of the company's creditors. You do not share in its rewards (and theoretically at least, in its risks). A bond, whether corporate, federal, state, or municipal, is simply an obligation to repay a loan at a specific time, promising a contractual rate of interest. It is, then, a far safer investment from the viewpoint of financial risk than a common stock. (Bondholders and other creditors must be paid in full before the common gets anything.) Nevertheless, bonds, too, have distinct risks.

An investor who is fairly certain he will not have to cash his savings certificates might ask why he should bother at all with government bonds, when he can get over 12 percent in the certificates (federally insured up to $100,000 individually and $200,000 for a joint account).

For one thing, the maximum savings certificate length is normally eight years. After this time, if interest rates go down, your 12 percent may become 10 percent or even 8 percent—although the latter seems pretty unlikely. The bond, on the other hand, can have a very long maturity (time outstanding before it is due)—twenty and twenty-five years or more are quite common. Thus, you may be assured of your income for a much longer period (but see "Call Features" on page 318).

Then, too, there are many excellent corporate bonds available that provide not only very long life spans but also higher rates of interest than you can get on savings certificates. Finally, some types of bonds provide distinct tax advantages to high-income investors that are not available in savings banks.

Tax-Exempt Bonds

If you buy a government or corporate bond, full tax rates apply. But bonds issued by state and municipal governments (and various state and local authorities, such as port authorities, toll roads, and so forth) are exempt from federal taxes. Too, if you buy a state or municipal bond where you reside, you are exempt from state and municipal taxes. New York City residents buying Big Mac bonds would be exempt from all taxes—federal, state, and city. However, if they bought Dallas bonds, they would only be exempt from federal taxes.

Naturally, tax-exempt bonds trade at lower yields than other bonds (a twenty-year AA-rated state bond would yield 12 percent against about 16 percent for a corporate bond with the same credit rating and maturity). So they are not useful to everybody, as table 37 indicates.

Table 37
CORPORATE VERSUS TAX-EXEMPT BONDS

TAX BRACKET	12% TAX-EXEMPT BOND[a]	AFTERTAX YIELD ON 16% AA CORPORATE
30 percent	12%	11.2%
35 percent	12	10.4
40 percent	12	9.6
45 percent	12	8.8
50 percent	12	8.0

NOTE: All bonds have AA rating and mature in twenty-five years.
[a]Assuming no state or local taxes in each case.

The person in the 25 percent tax bracket is still better off in corporate bonds at current rates. However, at the 40 percent level and above, he progressively loses ground by not buying tax-exempts.* If, for example, the bond buyer decided to invest $50,000 in long-term bonds and was in the 50 percent tax bracket, he would save $900 a year through the purchase of tax-exempts. Thus, under conditions of accelerating inflation and higher interest rates, tax-exempts are increasingly valuable investment vehicles for high-tax-bracket investors who desire fixed-income securities.

The spread between tax-exempts and fully taxable bonds will change periodically according to conditions of supply and demand and risk assessment in the corporate and municipal sectors. The potential for default, for example, of New York City bonds in late 1976 drove many tax-exempts down fairly sharply for a time.

State and local guaranteed bonds usually provide somewhat better yields, although less marketability than the issues of the state or municipality themselves. So these may be worth shopping for if liquidity is not a prime consideration.

Discount Bonds

If you are in a high tax bracket, you might also consider discount bonds. These are bonds that were issued years ago when interest rates were considerably lower. As interest rates have risen, these bonds have dropped in price to provide yields more attuned to other bonds

*If he is buying out-of-state tax-exempts, the state and local taxes will reduce the disparity to some extent.

of similar credit ratings and maturities. For example, suppose the General Motors Acceptance 7⅛ of 1992 trades at 56. The investor not only gets a 12.7 percent current yield, but on maturity in 1992 will be paid a premium of 44 over the current price. This premium is treated as a capital gain and will be taxed at a lower rate than regular income.

The discount bond, then, provides less ordinary income, important to taxpayers in higher tax brackets, because of its lower coupon, and a capital gain at maturity. Normally, these advantages cause some yield differential, but it can be worth it in a higher tax bracket.

Two Don'ts

1. Avoid U.S. savings bonds. These yield far less than you can get in either treasury bonds or savings bank certificates. This form of investing is only a step more sophisticated than stuffing money in a mattress.

2. There are also savings certificates (not government-guaranteed) that are sold in some rural parts of the country by fast-talking salesmen, usually with the aid of large stocks of booze in the trunks of their cars. These certificates give you returns of about 60 to 70 percent of going interest rates. And as you can guess, commissions on these certificates are not exactly low. If one of these fellows calls on you, drink his booze if you're in the mood, but avoid his wares.

Risk Features

FINANCIAL RISK. Before you buy a corporate, state, or municipal bond, a number of their features should be scrutinized closely.

Financial risk is the risk that the principal and interest will not be paid when due. Fortunately, since the Great Depression, default has been relatively rare. If you are not a credit analyst, there are two major credit-rating services that provide good information on the safety of individual bond issues: Standard & Poor's and Moody's.

Table 38 gives the rating categories of the two services. Usually the ratings by the two organizations are identical for most major corporate, state, and municipal bonds. If not, they normally don't vary more than one rank.

As the table shows, the very highest credit rating is AAA for

Standard & Poor's and Aaa for Moody's; the lowest is D for S&P,
C for Moody's. The higher the credit rating, naturally, the lower the
interest. There are only about a dozen AAA-rated corporations in
the country: Ma Bell, DuPont, General Motors, and the like. In the
AA's one would find excellent companies such as Xerox, Mobil Oil,
and Monsanto, and in the A's Honeywell, Tenneco, and Philip
Morris.

My own feeling is that even for very conservative investors, a
rating of AA or A is high enough. The yields are significantly better
and defaults are extremely rare. It seems that if we suddenly started
to get large-scale defaults in these categories, a chain reaction would
begin that would make everything else kaput anyway.

Bonds of the same credit rating may trade at slightly different
yields. The industry may be somewhat out of favor at the time, or
there may be an overabundance of financing in one industry that
results in lower yields (institutional investors like well-diversified
portfolios, and too many bonds issued by one industry may require
extra "sweeteners" to sell). This is something the bargain hunter can
take advantage of, as is the fact that new issues normally provide
slightly higher returns than those currently outstanding in order to
make them sell smoothly.

Table 38
BOND-RATING CATEGORIES

STANDARD & POOR'S	RATING	MOODY'S	RATING
AAA	Highest quality	Aaa	Highest quality
AA	Very high	Aa	Very high
A	High	A	High
BBB	Adequate	Baa	Medium
BB	Low degree of speculation	Ba	Speculative element
B	Higher degree of speculation	B	Speculative
CCC	Still higher degree of speculation	Caa	Poor standing
CC	Highest degree of speculation	Ca	Highly speculative
C	Income bonds on which no interest is being paid		
D	In default	C	Lowest rating

CALL FEATURES.   A second important factor in assessing bond risk is known as the call feature—the length of time an issue must remain outstanding before it can be recalled. Suppose you chose an A-rated industrial bond that is paying you 9 percent and is due in twenty-five years, but it has a five-year refunding call (it can be called away from you in five years' time if interest rates are lower, and the company can issue new bonds at the cheaper rates). You then have the chance of losing your investment in five years. Before selecting a long-term bond, you should therefore make sure it has a call feature of fairly extensive duration—aim for ten years or more. Most new issues have such call provisions. Your broker or investment advisor can readily provide you with the information on individual issues.

CHANGING INTEREST RATES.   This is the third and most important risk in bonds, given the current volatility of interest rates (see preface and chapter 11). All bond prices fluctuate with changes in market interest rates. Thus, if you do not hold your bonds to maturity, you have the chance of gain or loss depending on current interest rates. The longer the maturity, the more the movement of interest rates will affect the price. And as I mentioned earlier, the drop in long-term bond prices in the last few years was greater than any decline in stock prices in the entire postwar period. Table 39 shows you the effect of changes in the interest rate on the price of bonds with varying maturities from one to twenty-five years. For simplicity, it is assumed that all bonds have 12 percent coupons and cannot be called before maturity.

If interest rates drop to 8 percent, a twenty-five-year bondholder would be the greatest beneficiary, with his bond appreciating 43 percent versus 4 percent for the one-year issue. But this is a two-way street, and if yields went to 16 percent, his bond would drop to 75.5, while the one-year bond would decline only to 96.4.

As we have seen, then, the longer the maturity, the greater the market risk. Thus, before buying long-term bonds, you must decide how much market risk you can afford. If you intend to hold the issues for a fairly long time, you can probably place a portion of your bond portfolio in such issues, but look at table 39 to estimate your risk if you are forced to liquidate sooner than you had intended.

INFLATION.   A fourth risk, and as I've previously indicated the most serious one for the investor today, is inflation. In the past, bonds with little financial risk have tended to yield 2½ percent or

Table 39
THE EFFECT OF INTEREST-RATE CHANGES ON BOND PRICES

TERM OF BOND[a]	8 PERCENT[b]	10 PERCENT	12 PERCENT	14 PERCENT	16 PERCENT
1 year	$103.77	$101.86	$100.00	$98.19	$96.40
5 years	116.22	107.72	100.00	92.98	86.50
10 years	127.18	112.46	100.00	89.41	80.40
15 years	134.58	115.37	100.00	87.59	77.50
20 years	139.59	117.16	100.00	86.67	76.20
25 years	142.96	118.26	100.00	86.20	75.50

SOURCE: Expanded Bond Values Tables Coupons 1 Percent to 12 Percent (showing yields and values of bonds paying interest semiannually).

[a]For simplicity, it is assumed that all bonds have 12 percent coupons and cannot be called before maturity.

[b]The yield to maturity was calculated in all cases. This is the most accurate way of calculating yield, since it takes into account the principal to be received as well as the interest.

so above the rate of inflation. However, with inflation recently running as high as 13 percent, this is no longer the case. As table 1 (page 6) showed quite clearly, investors, whether in bonds or savings banks, were losing a portion of their capital each year in terms of real purchasing power. Inflation, then, is a factor to pay particularly close attention to in portfolio composition. At recent rates inflation destroys much of the traditional conservativism inherent in buying bonds or putting your money in the bank.

Convertible Debentures

Convertible debentures can be turned in for a fixed number of shares in a company. You thus have a part of both worlds: the lesser financial risk of debt, with the appreciation potential of equity if the company prospers. Sometimes the gains can be spectacular. Investment columnist Vartanig G. Vartan wrote about a Wainoco convertible issued at $100 in September 1977 which traded at 187½ less than eight months later as the stock moved sharply higher.*

However, as Vartan indicated, there is naturally a price to pay. Such debentures normally give you less interest because of the conversion privilege, and the conversion price is usually fixed 10 to 12 percent or more above the current market price of the stock. Con-

*New York Times, June 4, 1978.

vertible debentures are often overpriced in relation to the features offered in a bull market. In a bear market, or periods of tight money, the situation is frequently quite different. In this case, the conversion privilege is offered at a very limited premium, and the interest rates may not be too far off going rates for the particular credit rating.

Bond Funds

Selected by experts, these provide wide diversification. Many types are available, some specializing in tax-exempts, some in diversified funds, and others in lower- or medium-grade corporations. Some charge buying commissions and all charge management fees, usually between one-half and one percent a year, which is a good slice of your income.

The funds provide greater diversification, but that's about all. If you can select a number of bonds with good credit ratings, it is questionable whether the extra costs are worthwhile. (The extra diversification necessary with junk bonds would be an exception.)

Preferred Shares

These are a hybrid. Like a bond, they pay a fixed return,* which is almost invariably cumulative, which means that if it is omitted for any reason, it must be paid in the future. However, although preferred shares are considered to be stock, the holder has no participation in the fortunes of the business.† Preferred shareholders' rights to dividends and principal are subordinated to those of bondholders and other creditors, who must be paid in full before the preferred gets a penny.

When you buy a preferred, the most important thing to note is the credit worthiness of the issue, because of its lesser protection. However, once again, the rating agencies provide you with this information, and there are many excellent preferreds providing good yields with strong credit ratings.

---

*But it is called dividend rather than interest. Preferreds have no maturity date (although usually the company has the right to recall them on prestated terms).

†Unless the preferred is a convertible, when it would be in most ways very similar to a convertible debenture.

References

Chapter One

1. *Wall Street Journal,* September 11, 1978.
2. Ibid., June 26, 1981.
3. James Grant, "Don't Be a Gambler," *Barron's,* June 11, 1978.
4. "The Superstar Analysts," *Financial World,* November 1980, p. 16.
5. Ibid., p. 19
6. *Business Week,* March 31, 1980, p. 7.
7. *Barron's,* December 15, 1980.

Chapter Two

1. Robert D. Edwards and John Magee, *Technical Analysis of Stock Trends,* 7th ed. (Springfield, Mass.: J. Magee, 1967).
2. Joseph Granville, *Granville's New Strategy of Daily Stock Market Timing for Maximum Profit* (Englewood Cliffs, N.J.: Prentice-Hall, 1976), p. 5.
3. *Financial World,* July 15, 1980, p. 19.
4. Nikolai Kondratieff, "The Long Cycles," *Review of Economic Statistics* (November 1935).
5. R. N. Elliot, *The Bank Credit Analyst* (Toronto: Boulton, Trombley Report).
6. Granville, *Granville's New Strategy,* p. 103.
7. Louis Bachelier, "Théorie de la Spéculation," trans. A. James Boness, in *The Random Character of Stock Market Prices,* ed. Paul H. Cootner (Cambridge, Mass.: MIT Press, 1964), pp. 17–78.
8. Harry V. Roberts, "Stock Market Patterns and Financial Analysis: Methodological Suggestions," *Journal of Finance* 14 (March 1959): 1–10.

9. M.F.M. Osborne, "Brownian Motion in the Stock Market," *Operations Research* 7 (March–April 1959): 145–173.

10. Arnold B. Moore, "Some Characteristics of Changes in Common Stock Prices," in *The Random Character of Stock Market Prices,* pp. 139–161.

11. Clive W. J. Granger and Oskar Morgenstern, "Spectral Analysis of New York Stock Market Prices," *Kyklos* 16 (1963): 1–27.

12. Eugene F. Fama, "The Behavior of Stock Market Prices," *Journal of Business* 38 (January 1965): 34–105.

13. Eugene F. Fama and Marshall E. Blume, "Filter Rules and Stock Market Trading," *Journal of Business—Security Prices: A Supplement* 39 (No. 1, January 1966): 226–241.

14. Eugene F. Fama, "Efficient Capital Markets: A Review of the Theory and Empirical Work," *Journal of Finance* 25 (May 1970): 383–423.

15. Burton G. Malkiel, *A Random Walk Down Wall Street* (New York: Norton, 1973), p. 127.

Chapter Three

1. John Burr Williams, *The Theory of Investment Value* (Cambridge, Mass.: Harvard University Press, 1938).

2. J. Peter Williamson, *Investments: New Analytic Techniques* (New York: Praeger, 1974), pp. 152ff.

3. Benjamin Graham, David Dodd, Sidney Cottle, and Charles Tatham, *Security Analysis,* 4th ed. (New York: McGraw-Hill, 1962).

4. Irving Kahn and Robert D. Milne, *Benjamin Graham—The Father of Financial Analysis,* Occasional Paper No. 5, Financial Analysts Research Foundation, 1977.

5. Benjamin Graham, *The Intelligent Investor,* 2nd ed. (New York: Harper & Row, 1955).

6. Williamson, *Investments: New Analytic Techniques.*

7. *Financial World,* May 1, 1977, p. 27.

8. Robert Cirino, "Timing: Can Money Managers Deliver on Their Promises?" *Institutional Investor* 11 (March 1976): 277–279.

9. Ibid.

10. William F. Sharpe, "Likely Gains from Market Timing," *Financial Analysts Journal* 31 (March–April 1975): 60–69.

11. Michael C. Jensen, "The Performance of Mutual Funds in the Period 1945–1964," *Journal of Finance* 23 (May 1968): 389–416.

12. Irwin Friend, Marshall Blume, and Jean Crockett, *Mutual Funds and Other Institutional Investors: A New Perspective,* Twentieth Century Fund Study (New York: McGraw-Hill, 1971).

13. James Lorie and Richard Brealey, eds., *Modern Developments in Investment Management* (New York: Praeger, 1972).

14. Charles H. Dow, *Wall Street Journal,* July 20, 1901.

15. William Peter Hamilton, *Wall Street Journal,* October 4, 1921.

16. Eugene F. Fama, Lawrence Fisher, Michael Jensen, and Richard Roll, "The Adjustment of Stock Prices to New Information," *International Economic*

Review 10 (February 1969): 1–21; James H. Lorie and Mary T. Hamilton, *The Stock Market: Theories and Evidence* (Homewood, Ill.: Dow Jones–Irwin, 1973), pp. 171ff.

17. Roy Ball and Phillip Brown, "An Empirical Evaluation of Accounting Income Numbers," *Journal of Accounting Research* 6 (Fall 1968): 159–178.

18. James H. Lorie and Victor Niederhoffer, "Predictive and Statistical Properties of Insider Trading," *Journal of Law and Economics* 11 (April 1968): 35–53.

19. Eugene F. Fama, "Efficient Capital Markets: A Review of the Theory and Empirical Work," *Journal of Finance* 25 (No. 2, May 1970): 383–417.

GENERAL REFERENCES, CHAPTER THREE

Cohen, Jerome B., Edward D. Zenbar, and Arthur Zeikel, *Investment Analysis and Portfolio Management,* rev. ed. (Homewood, Ill.: Richard Irwin, 1973).

Crane, Burton, *The Sophisticated Investor,* 9th ed. (New York: Simon & Schuster, 1963).

Crowell, Richard, *Stock Market Strategy* (New York: McGraw-Hill, 1977).

Dougall, Herbert, *Investments,* 9th ed. (Englewood Cliffs, N.J.: Prentice-Hall, 1973).

Ellis, John, *Self-Reliant Investing* (Chicago: H. Regnery, 1971).

Engel, Louis, and Peter Wyckoff, *How to Buy Stocks,* 6th ed. rev. (Boston: Little, Brown, 1976).

Hazard, John W., *Choosing Tomorrow's Growth Stocks Today* (New York: Doubleday, 1968).

Knowlton, Winthrop, and John Furth, *Shaking the Money Tree* (New York: Harper & Row, 1965).

Levine, Sumner L., ed., *Financial Analyst's Handbook* (Homewood, Ill.: Dow Jones–Irwin, 1975).

Loeb, Gerald M., *The Battle for Investment Survival* (New York: Simon & Schuster, 1957).

———, *The Battle for Stock Market Profits* (New York: Simon & Schuster, 1971).

McWilliams, James D., "The Benefits and Costs of Timing Equity Investments," *Journal of Bank Research* 7 (Spring 1976): 22–29.

Phelon, Richard, "Time to Shun Stocks?" *New York Times,* August 20, 1977.

Rolo, Charles, *Gaining on the Market* (Boston: Little, Brown, 1982). A thoughtful new investment guide for the serious investor discussing the prevalent techniques and investments in the 1980s.

Chapter Four

1. Charles Mackay, *Extraordinary Popular Delusions and the Madness of Crowds* (New York: Noonday Press, 1974), p. 421. Originally published in London in 1841 by Richard Bently.

2. Gustave LeBon, *The Crowd* (New York: Viking, 1960), pp. 23–24.

3. Ibid., pp. 41, 61.

4. Ibid., p. 70.

5. John Kenneth Galbraith, *The Great Crash* (Boston: Houghton Mifflin, 1961), p. 9.

6. LeBon, *The Crowd,* p. 62.
7. Carl Sandburg, *Abraham Lincoln: Volume 2, 1861–1864* (New York: Dell, 1970), p. 410.
8. Leon Festinger, "A Theory of Social Comparison Processes," *Human Relations* 7 (1954): 117–140.
9. S. Schacter and J. E. Singer, "Cognitive, Social, and Psychological Determinants of Emotional States," *Psychological Review* 69 (1962): 379–399.
10. J. C. Flugel, *The Psychology of Clothes* (New York: International Universities Press, 1969).
11. "Over the Counter: Frantic, Frenetic, Frazzled," *Dun's Review* 92 (August 1968): 32–37.
12. Muzafer Sherif and Carolyn W. Sherif, *Social Psychology* (New York: Harper & Row, 1969), pp. 208–209.
13. William Samuels, *Contemporary Social Psychology* (Englewood Cliffs, N.J.: Prentice-Hall, 1973), p. 10.
14. Gilbert Kaplan and Chris Welles, *The Money Managers* (New York: Random House, 1969).
15. "Performance in Reverse?" *Forbes,* March 15, 1969.
16. *Forbes,* October 15, 1968.
17. GiGi Mahon, "Landing on Boardwalk," *Barron's,* November 20, 1978.
18. Charles Elia, "Here's a Short Story of a Short Gamble That Didn't Pay Off," *Wall Street Journal,* October 4, 1978, p. 1.
19. "Losses Blunt Hope of Big Payoffs for Atlantic City Casino Owners," *New York Times,* June 23, 1981.
20. "Gambling Stocks: A Return to Sanity," *Financial World,* March 15, 1981.
21. "How Silly Can You Get?" *Forbes,* November 10, 1980, p. 34.
22. Phyllis Feinberg, "The New Issue War of Nerves," *Institutional Investor,* December 1980.
23. "Tenuous Play in Synthetic Fuels," *Business Week,* July 23, 1979.
24. "Market Place," *New York Times,* June 30, 1981.
25. Douglas Martin, "Investing," *New York Times,* March 29, 1981.
26. "Investing," *New York Times,* March 19, 1981.
27. "Investing: Penny Stocks after Hours in Denver," *New York Times,* January 18, 1981.
28. *Institutional Investor,* December 1981.
29. *New York Times,* January 18, 1981.
30. Virginia Cowles, *South Sea: The Greatest Swindle* (London: Crowley Feature, 1960).
31. *Dun's Review,* August 1968, p. 36.

GENERAL REFERENCES, CHAPTER FOUR

Allport, Gordon W., and Leo Postman, *The Psychology of Rumor* (New York: Russell & Russell, 1965).
Asch, S. E., *Social Psychology* (Englewood Cliffs, N.J.: Prentice-Hall, 1952).
Brooks, John, *The Go-Go Years* (New York: Weybright and Talley, 1973).
———, *Seven Fat Years* (New York: Harper & Row, 1958).

Clough, Shepard B., *European Economic History: The Economic Development of Western Civilization,* 2nd ed. (New York: McGraw-Hill, 1968).

Durant, Will, and Ariel Durant, *The Age of Voltaire* (New York: Simon & Schuster, 1965).

Freedman, J. L., J. M. Carlsmith, and D. O. Sears, *Social Psychology* (Englewood Cliffs, N.J.: Prentice-Hall, 1970).

Gerard, H. B., and J. M. Rabbie, "Fear and Social Comparison," *Journal of Abnormal and Social Psychology* 62 (1961): 586–592.

Gerard, H. B., R. A. Wilhelmy, and Edward S. Conolley, "Conformity and Group Size," *Journal of Personality and Social Psychology* 8 (1968): 79–82.

Hollander, E. P., "Confidence and Conformity in the Acceptance of Influence," *Journal of Abnormal and Social Psychology* 61 (1960): 365–369.

Kaplan, Gilbert, and Chris Welles, *The Money Managers* (New York: Random House, 1969).

Katona, George, *Psychological Economics* (New York: American Elsevier, 1976).

Kiesler, C. A., and S. B. Kiesler, *Conformity* (Reading, Mass.: Addison-Wesley, 1969).

Melville, Louis, *The South Sea Bubble* (London: Burt Franklin, 1968).

Posthumus, N. W., "The Tulipmania in Holland in 1636 and 1637," in *The Sixteenth and Seventeenth Centuries,* ed. Warren C. Scoville, J. Claybouch, and T. LaForce (Lexington, Mass.: D.C. Heath, 1969).

Regan, Donald T., *A View from the Street* (New York: New American Library, 1972).

Robbins, Paul R., "Immediate and Delayed Effects of Social Influence upon Individual Opinion," *Journal of Social Psychology* 53 (1961): 159–169.

Smith, Adam, *The Money Game* (New York: Dell, 1969).

———, *Supermoney* (New York: Popular Library, 1973).

The Wall Street Reader (New York: World Publishing, 1972).

Zimbardo, P. G., "Involvement in Communication Discrepancies as Determinants of Opinion Conformity," *Journal of Abnormal and Social Psychology* 61 (1960): 86–94.

Chapter Five

1. Warren Buffett, partnership letter, January 1966.

2. Herbert Simon, "Theories of Decision Making in Economics and Behavioral Sciences," *American Economic Review* 69 (No. 2, June 1959): 273.

3. Ibid.

4. Herbert Simon, *Models of Man: Social and Rational* (New York: Wiley, 1970).

5. P. E. Meehl, *Clinical Versus Statistical Predictions: A Theoretical Analysis and Review of the Literature* (Minneapolis: University of Minnesota Press, 1954); Robyn M. Dawes and Bernard Corrigan, "Linear Models in Decision Making," *Psychological Bulletin* 81 (No. 2, 1974): 95–106.

6. Stewart Oskamp, "Overconfidence in Case Study Judgments," *Journal of Consulting Psychology* 29 (1965): 261, 265.

7. L. H. Garland, "The Problem of Observer Error," *Bulletin of the New York Academy of Medicine* 36 (1960); Hans Elias, "Three-Dimensional Structure

Identified from Single Sections," *Science* 174 (December 1971): 993–1000.

8. Harry Bakwin, "Pseudodoxia Pediatricia," *New England Journal of Medicine* 232 (1945): 691–697.

9. P. J. Hoffman, P. Slovic, and L. G. Rorer, "An Analysis of Variance Models for the Assessment of Configural Cue Utilization in Clinical Judgment," *Psychological Bulletin* 69 (1968): 338–349.

10. L. G. Rorer, P. J. Hoffman, B. D. Dickman, and P. Slovic, "Configural Judgments Revealed," *Proceedings of the 75th Annual Convention of the American Psychological Association* 2 (Washington, D.C.: American Psychological Association, 1967): 195–196.

11. Lewis R. Goldberg, "Simple Models or Simple Processes? Some Research on Clinical Judgments," *American Psychologist* 23 (1968): 483–496.

12. Paul Slovic, "Analyzing the Expert Judge: A Descriptive Study of a Stockbroker's Decision Processes," *Journal of Applied Psychology* 53 (No. 4, August 1969): 225–263; P. Slovic, D. Fleissner, and W. S. Bauman, "Analyzing the Use of Information in Investment Decision Making: A Methodological Proposal," *Journal of Business* 45 (No. 2, 1972): 283–301.

13. Goldberg, "Simple Models."

14. Paul Slovic, "Behavioral Problems of Adhering to a Decision Policy," IGRF speech, May 1973.

15. Reba F. White, "The Dangers of Falling in Love with a Company," *Institutional Investor,* November 1975.

16. *Wall Street Transcript,* September 23, 1974.

17. Garfield A. Drew, *New Methods of Profit in the Stock Market* (Boston: Metcalf Press, 1941).

18. L. Chapman and J. P. Chapman, "Genesis of Popular but Erroneous Psychodiagnostic Observations," *Journal of Abnormal Psychology* (1967): 193–204; Chapman and Chapman, "Illusory Correlations As an Obstacle to the Use of Valid Psychodiagnostic Signs," *Journal of Abnormal Psychology* (1974): 271–280.

19. "What's in the Cards for 1972?" *Institutional Investor* 6 (January 1972): 25–36.

20. The favorites are listed in *Institutional Investor,* January 1973.

GENERAL REFERENCES, CHAPTER FIVE

Anderson, N. H., "Looking for Configurality in Clinical Judgments," *Psychological Bulletin* 78 (1972): 93–102.

Dawes, R. M., "The Mind, the Model, and the Task," in *Cognitive Theory,* vol. 1, ed. F. Restle, R. M. Shiffron, N. J. Castellan, H. R. Lindman, and D. B. Pisone (Hillsdale, N.J.: Lawrence Erlbaum Associates, 1975).

———, and B. Corrigan, "Linear Models in Decision Making," *Psychological Bulletin* 81 (No. 2, 1974): 95–106.

Goldberg, L. R., "Five Models of Clinical Judgment: An Empirical Comparison Between Linear and Nonlinear Representations of the Human Inference Process," *Organizational Behavior and Human Performance* 6 (1971): 458–479.

———, "Man Versus Model of Man: Just How Conflicting Is That Evidence?" *Organizational Behavior and Human Performance* 16 (1976): 13–22.

March, James G., and Herbert A. Simon, *Organizations* (New York: Wiley, 1967).
Simon, Herbert A., *Administrative Behavior* (New York: Free Press, 1976).

Chapter Six

1. Amos Tversky and Daniel Kahneman, "Judgments Under Uncertainty: Heuristics and Biases," *Science* 185 (September 27, 1974): 1124–1131; Paul Slovic, Baruch Fischhoff, and Sarah Lichtenstein, "Cognitive Processes and Societal Risk Taking," in *Cognition and Social Behavior,* ed. J. W. Payne and J. S. Carroll (Hillsdale, N.J.: Lawrence Erlbaum Associates, 1976).
2. Amos Tversky and Daniel Kahneman, "Belief in the Law of Small Numbers," *Psychological Bulletin* 76 (No. 2, 1971): 105–110.
3. Tversky and Kahneman, "Judgments Under Uncertainty: Heuristics and Biases"; Amos Tversky and Daniel Kahneman, "Intuitive Predictions: Biases and Corrective Procedures," *Management Science,* Spring 1981.
4. Amos Tversky and Daniel Kahneman, "Causal Schemata in Judgments Under Uncertainty," in *Progress in Social Psychology,* ed. M. Fishbein (Hillsdale, N.J.: Lawrence Erlbaum Associates, 1973); Amos Tversky and Daniel Kahneman, "On the Psychology of Prediction," *Psychological Review* 80 (1973): 237–251.
5. Tversky and Kahneman, "Judgments Under Uncertainty: Heuristics and Biases"; Tversky and Kahneman, "Intuitive Predictions: Biases and Corrective Procedures."
6. Roger G. Ibbotson and Rex A. Sinquefield, *Stocks, Bonds, Bills, and Inflation: The Past (1926–1976) and the Future (1977–2000)* (Charlottesville, Va.: Financial Analysts Research Foundation, 1977).
7. Tversky and Kahneman, "Intuitive Predictions: Biases and Corrective Procedures."
8. Kahneman and Tversky, "On the Psychology of Prediction."
9. Benjamin Graham, David Dodd, Sidney Cottle, and Charles Tatham, *Security Analysis,* 4th ed. (New York: McGraw-Hill, 1962), p. 424.
10. Amos Tversky and Daniel Kahneman, "Availability: A Heuristic for Judging Frequency and Probability," *Cognitive Psychology* 5 (1973): 207–232.
11. Tversky and Kahneman, "Intuitive Predictions: Biases and Corrective Procedures"; Tversky and Kahneman, "Causal Schemata in Judgments Under Uncertainty"; Don Lyon and Paul Slovic, "Dominance of Accuracy Information and Neglect of Base Rates in Probability Estimation," *Acta Psychologica* 40 (No. 4, August 1976): 287–298.
12. R. W. Kates, *Hazard and Choice Perception in Flood Plain Management,* Research Paper No. 78, University of Chicago Department of Geology, 1962.
13. S. C. Lichtenstein and Paul Slovic, "Reversals of Preference Between Bids and Choices in Gambling Decisions," *Journal of Experimental Psychology* 89 (1971): 46–55; S. C. Lichtenstein, B. Fischhoff, and L. Phillips, "Calibration of Probabilities: The State of the Art," in *Decision Making and Change in Human Affairs,* ed. H. Jungermann and G. de Zeeuw (Amsterdam: D. Reidel, 1977).
14. Baruch Fischhoff, "Hindsight Does Not Equal Foresight: The Effect of Outcome Knowledge on Judgment Under Uncertainty," *Journal of Experimental Psychology: Human Perception and Performance* 1 (August 1975): 288–299;

Fischhoff, "Hindsight: Thinking Backward?" *Psychology Today,* April 1975, p. 8; Fischhoff, "Perceived Informativeness of Facts," *Journal of Experimental Psychology: Human Perception and Performance* 3 (1977): 349–358; Baruch Fischhoff and Ruth Beyth, "I Knew It Would Happen: Remembered Probabilities of Once-Future Things," *Organizational Behavior and Human Performance* 13 (No. 1, 1975): 1–16; Paul Slovic and Baruch Fischhoff, "On the Psychology of Experimental Surprises," *Journal of Experimental Psychology: Human Perception and Performance* 3 (1977): 544–551.

15. Paul Slovic, Baruch Fischhoff, and Sarah Lichtenstein, "Behavioral Decision Theory," *Annual Review of Psychology* 28 (1977): 1–39.

GENERAL REFERENCES, CHAPTER SIX

Bar-Hillel, Maya, "The Base-Rate Fallacy in Probability Judgments," *Acta Psychologica* 44 (No. 3, 1980): 211–233.

Dawes, Robyn M., and Bernard Corrigan, "Linear Models in Decision Making," *Psychological Bulletin* 81 (No. 2, 1974): 95–106.

Fischhoff, Baruch, Paul Slovic, and Sarah Lichtenstein, "Knowing with Certainty: The Appropriateness of Extreme Confidence," *Journal of Experimental Psychology: Human Perception and Performance* 3 (1977): 552–564.

Kahneman, Daniel, and Amos Tversky, "Subjective Probability: A Judgment of Representativeness," *Cognitive Psychology* 3 (No. 3, July 1972): 430–454.

Payne, J. W., "Alternative Approaches to Decision Making Under Risk: Moments Versus Risk Dimensions," *Psychological Bulletin* 80 (1973): 439–453.

Shaklee, Harriet, "Limited Minds and Multiple Causes: Discounting in Multicausal Attribution," Ph.D. dissertation, University of Oregon.

Slovic, Paul, "Choice Between Equally Valued Alternatives," *Journal of Experimental Psychology: Human Perception and Performance* 1 (No. 3, 1975): 280–287.

———, "Psychological Study of Human Judgment: Implications for Investment Decision Making," *Journal of Finance* 27 (September 1972): 779–799. I think this is a particularly interesting article and one easily understood by the lay financial reader.

———, "From Shakespeare to Simon: Speculations—and Some Evidence—About Man's Ability to Process Information," Oregon Research Institute Research Monograph 12 (No. 2, April 1972).

———, and Baruch Fischhoff, "On the Psychology of Experimental Surprises," *Journal of Experimental Psychology: Human Perception and Performance* 3 (1977): 544–551.

———, and Sarah Lichtenstein, "Behavioral Decision Theory," *Annual Review of Psychology* 28 (1977): 1–39. A thorough review of the literature in the field.

———, Bernard Corrigan, and Barbara Combs, "Preference for Insuring Against Probable Small Losses: Implications for the Theory and Practice of Insurance," *Journal of Risk and Insurance* 44 (No. 2, June 1977): 237–258.

Slovic, Paul, Howard Kunreuther, and Gilbert F. White, "Decision Processes, Rationality, and Adjustment to Natural Hazards," in *Natural Hazards, Local, National and Global,* ed. Gilbert F. White (New York: Oxford University Press, 1974).

Tversky, Amos, and Daniel Kahneman, "Availability: A Heuristic for Judging Frequency and Probability," *Cognitive Psychology* 5 (1973): 207–232.
———, "On the Psychology of Prediction," *Psychological Review* 80 (No. 4, 1973): 237–251.
von Holstein, C. S., "Probabilistic Forecasting in Experiments Relating to the Stock Market," *Organizational Behavior and Human Performance* 8 (1972): 139–158.

Chapter Seven

1. Most analysts arrive at prices by estimating future earnings. For example, see Ralph A. Bing, "Survey of Practitioner's Stock Evaluation Methods," *Financial Analysts Journal* 27 (May–June 1971): 55–60.
2. William Breen, "Low Price/Earnings Ratios and Industry Relatives," *Financial Analysts Journal* 24 (July–August 1968): 125–127.
3. Sanjoy Basu, "The Information Content of Price/Earnings Ratios," *Financial Management* 4 (No. 2, Summer 1975): 53–60; Sanjoy Basu, "Investment Performance of Common Stocks in Relation to Their Price/Earnings Ratios: A Test of the Efficient Market Hypothesis," *Journal of Finance* 32 (No. 3, June 1977): 663–682.

Chapter Eight

1. Victor Niederhoffer and Patrick J. Regan, "Earnings Changes, Analysts' Forecasts, and Stock Prices," *Financial Analysts Journal* 28 (May–June 1972): 65–71.
2. "Analysts Find Ways to Improve Forecasts of Economy's Course," *Wall Street Journal,* December 30, 1977, p. 1.
3. "Here Comes 1970," *Wall Street Journal,* September 30, 1969, p. 1.
4. James Ramsey, "Economic Forecasts—Models or Markets?" Hobart Paper No. 74 (London: The Institute of Economic Affairs, 1978).
5. Lester Thurow, "Economics 1977," *Daedalus* 2 (October 1977): 79–94.
6. Ronald M. Copeland and Robert J. Marioni, "Executives' Forecasts of Earnings per Share Versus Forecasts of Naive Models," *Journal of Business* 45 (October 1972): 497–512.
7. David Green, Jr., and Joel Segall, "The Predictive Power of First Quarter Earnings Reports," *Journal of Business* 40 (January 1967): 44–55.
8. Bart A. Basi, Kenneth J. Carey, and Richard D. Twark, "Comparison of the Accuracy of Corporate and Security Analysts' Forecasts of Earnings," *Accounting Review* 51 (1976): 244–254.
9. R. Malcolm Richards and Donald R. Frazer, "Further Evidence on the Accuracy of Analysts' Earnings Forecasts: A Comparison Among Analysts," *Journal of Economics and Business* 29 (No. 3, Spring–Summer 1977): 193–197.
10. R. Malcolm Richards, James J. Benjamin, and Robert W. Strawser, "An Examination of the Accuracy of Earnings Forecasts," *Financial Management* (Fall 1977).
11. J. G. Cragg and Burton Malkiel, "The Consensus and Accuracy of Some

Predictions of the Growth of Corporate Earnings," *Journal of Finance* 23 (March 1968): 67–84.

12. Ibid.

13. Edwin J. Elton and Martin J. Gruber, "Earnings Estimates and the Accuracy of Expectational Data," *Management Science* 18 (April 1972): 409–424.

14. I.M.D. Little, "Higgledy Piggledy Growth," *Bulletin of the Oxford University Institute of Economics and Statistics* (November 1962).

15. I.M.D. Little and A. C. Rayner, *Higgledy Piggledy Growth Again* (Oxford, Eng.: Basil Blackwell, 1966).

16. See, for example, Joseph E. Murphy, Jr., "Relative Growth in Earnings per Share—Past and Future," *Financial Analysts Journal* 22 (November–December 1966): 73–76.

17. Richard A. Brealey, *An Introduction to Risk and Return from Common Stocks* (Cambridge, Mass.: MIT Press, 1968).

18. Benjamin Graham, David Dodd, Sidney Cottle, and Charles Tatham, *Security Analysis,* 4th ed. (New York: McGraw-Hill, 1962), p. 179.

19. "Speculative Bonds," *Barron's*, October 10, 1977.

20. "Personal Investing," *Fortune,* June 30, 1980.

21. *Pensions and Investment Age,* February 2, 1981.

GENERAL REFERENCES, CHAPTER EIGHT

Hammel, J. E., and D. A. Hodes, "Factors Influencing Price-Earnings Multiples," *Financial Analysts Journal* 23 (No. 1, January–February 1967): 90–93.

Chapter Ten

1. "Up and Down Wall Street," *Barron's,* September 4, 1978.

2. "Plain Pie-Racks on Wall Street," *Forbes,* September 17, 1979.

3. Newton Lamson, "A New Way to Ride the Commodity Roller Coaster," *Money,* September 1975, p. 39.

4. "Let the Buyer Beware," *Barron's,* November 7, 1977.

5. *Wall Street Journal,* June 17, 1981.

6. "Commodity Scams Move into Gear," *Business Week,* May 11, 1981.

7. Dana L. Thomas, "Gimme Shelter," *Barron's,* October 21, 1974, p. 3.

8. "How a Prudent Investor Can Stay That Way," *Business Week,* December 29, 1980, p. 161.

9. Deborah Rankin,"Personal Finance: There's a Sting to the Tax Bill," *New York Times,* September 6, 1981.

10. "Municipal Bond Swaps," *New York Times,* August 18, 1981.

GENERAL REFERENCES, CHAPTER TEN

Hershman, Arlene, "Born-Again Tax Shelters," *Dun's Review* 109 (April 1977): 55–66.

The Only Investment Guide You'll Ever Need, by Andrew Tobias (New York: Harcourt Brace Jovanovich, 1978), covers a lot of the material that has been outlined in this chapter in an amusing, clever, and far more detailed manner.

White, Shelby, "Reaping the Rewards of Junk Bonds," *Institutional Investor,* March 1976, pp. 51–52.

Readers interested in up-to-date articles on many of the subjects discussed in this chapter will often find them in such periodicals as *Barron's, Business Week, Dun's Review, Esquire, Forbes, Financial World, Money, New York,* and the *New York Times.*

Chapter Eleven

1. "The Creative New Look at Finance," *Dun's Review,* July 1981, p. 28.
2. Isador Barmash,"Cashing in on Your Insurance," *New York Times,* September 5, 1981.
3. Deborah Rankin, "NOW Accounts Are Not All Alike," *New York Times,* February 22, 1981.
4. William G. Flanagan,"Walk, Don't Run, to Your S&L," *Forbes,* September 14, 1981.

Chapter Twelve

1. Irving L. Janis, *Victims of Groupthink* (Boston: Houghton Mifflin, 1972).
2. Ibid., p. 9.
3. Ibid., pp. 11, 13.
4. Nancy Belliveau, "Why Pension Funds Are Firing Their Money Managers," *Institutional Investor,* February 1974.
5. John Quirt, "Confessions of an Underperformer," *Institutional Investor,* July 1973.
6. Robert J. Cirino, "The Pension Fund Officer Versus the Board," *Institutional Investor,* July 1973.
7. Morton H. Halperin, *Bureaucratic Politics and Foreign Policy* (Washington, D.C.: Brookings Institution, 1974), p. 152.
8. Richard Neustadt, *Alliance Politics* (New York: Columbia University Press, 1970).
9. Adam Smith, *The Money Game* (New York: Dell, 1969).
10. Halperin, *Bureaucratic Politics and Foreign Policy,* p. 155.
11. Smith Simpson, *The Anatomy of the State Department* (Boston: Houghton Mifflin, 1967), p. 28.
12. Ibid., p. 17.
13. Cirino, "The Pension Fund Officer Versus the Board."
14. Ibid.
15. J. L. Freedman, J. M. Carlsmith, and D. O. Sears, *Social Psychology* (Englewood Cliffs, N.J.: Prentice-Hall, 1970), p. 122.
16. James Thomson, Jr., "How Could Vietnam Happen?" in *Who We Are: Chronicle of the United States and Vietnam,* ed. Manning and Janeway (Boston: Little, Brown, 1965).

17. David Halberstam, *The Best and the Brightest* (Greenwich, Conn.: Fawcett Publications, 1973).

GENERAL REFERENCES, CHAPTER TWELVE

Bower, Joseph L., "The Role of Conflict in Economic Decision-Making Groups: Some Empirical Results," *Quarterly Journal of Economics* 79 (May 1965): 263–277.

Dudar, Helen, "The Price of Blowing the Whistle," *New York Times Magazine,* October 30, 1977.

Green, D., and E. Conolley, "Groupthink and Watergate," Paper presented at the annual meeting of the American Psychological Association, 1974.

Janis, Irving, *Decision Making* (New York: Free Press, 1977).

Katona, George, *Psychological Economics* (New York: Elsevier Publishing, 1976).

Katz, Daniel, and Robert L. Kahn, *The Social Psychology of Organizations* (New York: Wiley, 1967).

Kiesler, C. A., and S. A. Kiesler, *Conformity* (Reading, Mass.: Addison-Wesley, 1969).

Lindblom, Charles E., *The Intelligence of Democracy* (New York: Free Press, 1965).

McGarvey, Patrick J., *CIA: The Myth and the Madness* (New York: Penguin, 1973).

Mills, C. Wright, *White Collar* (Oxford, Eng.: Oxford University Press, 1951).

Stagner, Ross, "Corporate Decision Making: An Empirical Study," *Journal of Applied Psychology* 3 (February 1969): 1–13.

Chapter Thirteen

1. Harold L. Shapiro, "Inflation in the United States," in *World Inflation,* ed. L. Krause and W. Salant (Washington, D.C.: Brookings Institution, 1977).
2. *Business Week,* March 21, 1977.
3. *New York Times,* December 31, 1980.
4. "Interest Rates, Inflation and Tight Money," *New York Times,* July 21, 1981.
5. William D. Nordhaus, "The Flexibility of Wages and Prices," *Inflation Theory and Policy* issue, *American Economic Review* 66 (May 1976): 59–64.
6. "Inflation: You Are Losing Your Assets," *Forbes,* April 1, 1974.
7. Ibid.
8. *Esquire,* November 21, 1978.
9. *Forbes,* May 29, 1978.
10. "Inflation: You Are Losing Your Assets."
11. Burton Malkiel, "Reports of the Death of Common Stocks Are Greatly Exaggerated," *Fortune,* November 1977.
12. Martin Feldstein and Lawrence Summers, *Brookings Paper on Economic Activity, 1977–I* (Washington, D.C.: Brookings Institution, 1977).
13. Warren Buffett, *Forbes,* August 6, 1979, pp. 25–26.
14. Franco Modigliani and Richard Cohn, "Inflation and the Stock Market," *Financial Analysts Journal* 35 (March–April 1979): 24–44.

GENERAL REFERENCES, CHAPTER THIRTEEN

Beaman, Louis, "Capacity: The New Questions About the American Economy," *Fortune,* May 1974.

Brinner, Roger, "The Death of the Phillips Curve Reconsidered," *Quarterly Journal of Economics* 91 (August 1977): 389–407.

Brunner, Karl, and Allan H. Meltzer, "The Explanations of Inflation: Some International Evidence," *American Economic Review* 67 (February 1977): 148–154.

Foster, John, and Mary Gregory, "Inflation Expectations: The Use of Qualitative Survey Data," *University of Glasgow Applied Economics* 9 (1977): 19–29.

Friedman, Milton, "Nobel Lecture: Inflation and Unemployment," *Journal of Political Economy* 85 (No. 3, 1977): 451–471.

Kravis, Irving B., and Robert E. Lipsey, "Export Prices and the Transmission of Inflation," *American Economic Review* 67 (February 1977): 155–163.

Laidler, David, "The 1974 Report of the President's Council of Economic Advisors: The Control of Inflation and the Future of the International Monetary System," *American Economic Review* 64 (No. 4, September 1974).

Nadler, Paul S., "Inflation, Unemployment, Why Both at Once?" *Banker's Monthly,* November 15, 1977.

Nordhaus, William D., "The 1974 Report of the President's Council of Economic Advisors: Energy in the Economic Report," *American Economic Review* 64 (No. 4, September 1974).

Rose, Sanford, "Far-Reaching Consequences of Higher-Priced Oil," *Fortune,* March 1974.

Shepard, David, "Unemployment and the Current Inflation," *The Banker,* January 1978, p. 41.

"South Land Values Rise 60 Percent in Three Years," *Los Angeles Times,* November 14, 1976.

Wachter, Michael, "Some Problems in Wage Stabilization," *American Economic Review* 66 (May 1976): 65–71.

INDEX

334